BECOMING
A SELF

Purdue University Press Series in the History of Philosophy

General Editors

Arion Kelkel

Joseph J. Kockelmans

Adriaan Peperzak

Calvin O. Schrag

Thomas Seebohm

BECOMING A SELF

A Reading of Kierkegaard's
*Concluding Unscientific
Postscript*

Merold Westphal

Purdue University Press
West Lafayette, Indiana

00   99   98   97   96   5   4   3   2   1

∞ The paper used in this book meets the minimum requirements of
American National Standard for Information Sciences—Permanence
of Paper Printed Library Materials, ANSI Z39.48-1992.

Printed in the United States of America

Interior design by Anita Noble

Library of Congress Cataloging-in-Publication Data

Westphal, Merold.
    Becoming a self : a reading of Kierkegaard's Concluding
unscientific postscript / Merold Westphal.
        p.   cm. — (Purdue University Press series in the history of
philosophy)
    Includes bibliographical references and index.
    ISBN 1-55753-089-0 (cloth : alk. paper). — ISBN 1-55753-090-4
(pbk. : alk. paper)
        1. Kierkegaard, Søren, 1813–1855. Afsluttende uvidenskabelig
efterskrift. 2. Christianity—Philosophy. 3. Apologetics. 4. Self
(Philosophy) 5. Postmodernism. I. Title. II. Series.
B4373.A4723W47 1996
201—dc20   96-8604
                                                    CIP

C O N T E N T S

vii PREFACE

xi NOTES ON TEXT, TRANSLATION,
AND ABBREVIATIONS

1 PART ONE: Introduction

   3 CHAPTER ONE
   Placing *Postscript* in Kierkegaard's Life

   8 CHAPTER TWO
   Placing *Postscript* as a Pseudonymous Text

  20 CHAPTER THREE
   Placing *Postscript* in the Theory of the Stages

33 PART TWO: Commentary

  35 CHAPTER FOUR
   Preface and Introduction

  49 CHAPTER FIVE
   The Objective Issue of the Truth of Christianity

  59 CHAPTER SIX
   The Subjective Issue—Something about Lessing

 100 CHAPTER SEVEN
   The Subjective Issue—Becoming Subjective

 114 CHAPTER EIGHT
   The Subjective Issue—Truth Is Subjectivity

 134 CHAPTER NINE
   The Subjective Issue—The Subjective Thinker

 144 CHAPTER TEN
   The Subjective Issue—
   For Orientation in the Plan of *Fragments*

 150 CHAPTER ELEVEN
   The Subjective Issue—Pathos

 180 CHAPTER TWELVE
   The Subjective Issue—The Dialectical

 190 CHAPTER THIRTEEN
   The Subjective Issue—
   Conclusion Together with Appendix

 194 CHAPTER FOURTEEN
   Beyond *Postscript:*
   The Teleological Suspension of Hidden
   Inwardness in Religiousness C

201 PART THREE: **Text**

   203 TEXT
       Part 2, Section 2, Chapter 2
       Subjective Truth, Inwardness; Truth Is Subjectivity

255 SELECT BIBLIOGRAPHY

257 INDEX

PREFACE

The reader will find here a commentary on the whole of *Conclud-ing Unscientific Postscript,* along with that famous portion of the text that deals with truth as subjectivity. My hope and expecta-tion is that some readers will be interested in this interpretation of the entire work and that others, especially in classroom situa-tions, will want to focus on such smaller themes as truth as sub-jectivity, both in the text and in the commentary, or the distinction between Religiousness A and Religiousness B. Which other portions of the commentary will be most helpful to these latter groups will probably vary from case to case. Some might want to situate their discussion in the theory of the stages (chap-ters 3 and 14), while others might find the discussion of Lessing (chapter 6) most helpful.

Because *Postscript* is rightly seen as an anti-Hegelian text, I have tried to focus on its confrontation with Hegel. In doing so I have not concerned myself with questions about what Hegelian texts Kierkegaard read and which Hegelian themes he knew only secondhand. Where there is a relation to Hegelian texts that we should notice today, regardless of whether and in what form Kierkegaard may have noticed it, I have pointed to it.

I have also sought to trace some of the interesting relations between Kierkegaard and contemporary postmodern philoso-phies. Those interested in this way of reading Kierkegaard will want to pay special attention to the notes, where much of this theme is developed. Just as the existentialist appropriation of Kierkegaard often involved filtering out or watering down his deepest religious concerns, so those who today allow Kierkegaard to be party to postmodern discussions *usually* require him to check his faith at the door. My own view is that he is a much more interesting participant when he is allowed to be himself and to introduce a little alterity into otherwise overwhelmingly secular conversations. If Climacus, the pseudonymous author of *Concluding Unscientific Postscript*, is a kind of postmodernist, he is not just another pea in the po-mo pod. Today's postmodern authors *usually* presuppose a world without God and without immortality. Climacus shatters the widespread assumption that there is any conceptual, as distinct from biographical, link between postmodern insights and atheism.

The emphasis on "usually" in the previous paragraph is meant to signify that neither postmodernism nor postmodern readings of Kierkegaard are monolithic and without variety. The tendency to see postmodernism as a new Nietzscheanism is not without foundation, especially for thinkers like Michel Foucault and Gilles Deleuze. But Jacques Derrida is surely more than his Nietzschean dimension (especially as he becomes more and more Levinasian); and if one speaks of a postmodern ethical reflection in Emmanuel Levinas or a postmodern theology in Jean-Luc Marion, the image of peas in a po-mo pod signifies little more than the wish of *some* postmodernists for a world free of moral obligation and divine grace.

The title, *Becoming a Self*, touches on both of these linkages. Hegelian speculation is presented as a variation on the Platonic flight from temporality to eternity, a flight to be fled just because it involves the loss of one's self. And what shall it profit me to gain the whole world in a presuppositionless Logos or an all-encompassing world history and lose my own self? In this text we are confronted with the claim that the only way to be a self is to be in the process of becoming a self. This translates into the surprising charge that Hegelian speculation is insufficiently dialectical, since it flees the tensions of temporal existence for the relaxation of premature resolution. Conceptual repose gives rise to the illusion that ethical tasks have been fulfilled.

Postmodern philosophies today are as little enamored with onto-theo-logical speculation as are Kierkegaard and his pseudonyms. They operate in a world that does not welcome either Platonic souls or Cartesian egos. Even the transcendental grandchildren of the latter in Immanuel Kant, Johann Gottlieb Fichte, and Edmund Husserl are dismissed as dogmatic. Postmodernists have learned from Friedrich Nietzsche and Martin Heidegger that even Kant's affirmation of human temporality is insufficiently radical.

Here, too, there is the danger of a loss of self. Does the death of long-honored philosophical paradigms of the self entail the death of the self itself? In a world where "it gives" and "language speaks," is it possible that the self once again disappears in impersonal systems and structures that differ from the Hegelian system epistemologically, by resisting full intelligibility, but not ethically, since the self becomes primarily the passive function of something else?

For those postmodernists who do not wish to follow this path to its bitter conclusion, the notion of becoming a self presented in *Postscript* can be useful. It assumes that "self" is a task word and not an achievement word; that selfhood is the goal rather than the presupposition of my existence; and that I am enough of a self to undertake the tasks of becoming a self in fear and trembling but not enough of a self to think that I have completed those tasks. Epistemologically such a self remains *fallible*, unable to see the world *sub specie aeterni*. In postmodern vocabulary this means that it is not seduced by the metaphysics of sheer presence or by totalizing logocentrism. Ethically such a self remains *responsible*. It does not have to leave the driving to an It that gives or a Language that speaks, even while it realizes that it is as little a pure origin in action as it is in thought.

Since the best of postmodern thought has wrestled with the problem of how to retain a responsible but fallible self, Kierkegaard might be as good a partner for the next round of thought as Nietzsche and Heidegger have been for the first round.

For a long time I have been interpreting Kierkegaard's so-called individualism and irrationalism in a postmodern light. By this I mean simply that I see them as reactions to excesses perceived to be all too typical of modernity. Thus Kierkegaard's "individualism" is to be understood as both remedy and resistance to the false collectivism of modernity. This allows us to see that he (and his pseudonyms) view the self as essentially relational, first to God and then to neighbor, and that isolation from the crowd is not an end (as if human nature were atomic) but a means to the self's proper relationships, once again first to God and then to other human selves. This "to other human selves" means that chapter 14 below is utterly essential to my reading of Kierkegaard's writings.

Just as important, I think, is the realization that the critique of reason that we find in those writings is not an invitation to sloppy thinking. This "irrationalism" is rather a protest against exorbitant claims made on behalf of *human* thought that wishes to deify itself, without really seeming to, by calling itself reason. This interpretation of *Postscript* continues the attempt to understand Kierkegaard's "individualism" and "irrationalism" in these ways.

I want to express my warmest thanks to John D. Caputo and to C. Stephen Evans for reading the penultimate draft of this essay and making helpful suggestions for improvement. I am also grateful to Cathy Jack for her help in preparing the index.

References to works of Kierkegaard in the text and the notes will employ the abbreviations in the following list, which also serves as a guide to Kierkegaard in English. The entire text of *Postscript* is found in the first volume of the Hongs' edition (the second volume contains introductory and supplementary materials). References in the text that give only page numbers are to this first volume. Works that are included in the select bibliography will be cited only by author or editor and title even in their first appearance in the notes.

AN   *Armed Neutrality* and *An Open Letter*. Trans. Howard V. Hong and Edna H. Hong. Bloomington: Indiana University Press, 1968.

C   *The Crisis [and a Crisis] in the Life of an Actress*. Trans. Stephen Crites. New York: Harper and Row, 1967.

CA   *The Concept of Anxiety*. Trans. Reidar Thomte in collaboration with Albert B. Anderson. Princeton, N.J.: Princeton University Press, 1980.

CD   *Christian Discourses,* including *The Lilies of the Field and the Birds of the Air* and *Three Discourses at the Communion on Fridays*. Trans. Walter Lowrie. London and New York: Oxford University Press, 1940.

CI   *The Concept of Irony* together with "Notes on Schelling's Berlin Lectures." Trans. Howard V. Hong and Edna H. Hong. Princeton, N.J.: Princeton University Press, 1989.

COR   *The Corsair Affair*. Trans. Howard V. Hong and Edna H. Hong. Princeton, N.J.: Princeton University Press, 1982.

CUP   *Concluding Unscientific Postscript*. Two vols. Trans. Howard V. Hong and Edna H. Hong. Princeton, N.J.: Princeton University Press, 1992.

| xi

EO *Either / Or.* Two vols. Trans. Howard V. Hong and Edna H. Hong. Princeton, N.J.: Princeton University Press, 1987.
EPW *Early Polemical Writings.* Trans. Julia Watkin. Princeton, N.J.: Princeton University Press, 1990.
EUD *Eighteen Upbuilding Discourses.* Trans. Howard V. Hong and Edna H. Hong. Princeton, N.J.: Princeton University Press, 1990.
FSE *For Self-examination* and *Judge for Yourselves.* Trans. Howard V. Hong and Edna H. Hong. Princeton, N.J.: Princeton University Press, 1990.
FT *Fear and Trembling* and *Repetition.* Trans. Howard V. Hong and Edna H. Hong. Princeton, N.J.: Princeton University Press, 1983.
JC *Philosophical Fragments* and *Johannes Climacus.* Trans. Howard V. Hong and Edna H. Hong. Princeton, N.J.: Princeton University Press, 1985.
JFY *Judge for Yourselves;* see FSE.
JK *The Journals of Kierkegaard.* Trans. Alexander Dru. New York: Harper & Row, 1959.
JP *Søren Kierkegaard's Journal and Papers.* Ed. and trans. Howard V. Hong and Edna H. Hong, assisted by Gregor Malantschuk. Bloomington: Indiana University Press; vol. 1, 1967; vol. 2, 1970; vols. 3–4, 1975; vols. 5–7, 1978. Arabic numbers are paragraph and not page numbers.
KAUC *Kierkegaard's Attack upon "Christendom,"* 1854–1855. Trans. Walter Lowrie. Princeton, N.J.: Princeton University Press, 1944.
LD *Letters and Documents.* Trans. Hendrik Rosenmeier. Princeton, N.J.: Princeton University Press, 1978.
LY *The Last Years.* Trans. Ronald C. Smith. New York: Harper & Row, 1965.
NSBL "Notes on Schelling's Berlin Lectures"; see CI.
OAR *On Authority and Revelation, The Book on Adler.* Trans. Walter Lowrie. Princeton, N.J.: Princeton University Press, 1955.
P *Prefaces: Light Reading for Certain Classes as the Occasion May Require.* Trans. William McDonald. Tallahassee: The Florida State University Press, 1989.
PC *Practice in Christianity.* Trans. Howard V. Hong and Edna H. Hong. Princeton, N.J.: Princeton University Press, 1991.
PF *Philosophical Fragments;* see JC.
PV *The Point of View for My Work as an Author,* including the appendix "'The Single Individual': Two 'Notes' Concerning My Work as an Author" and *On My Work as an Author.* Trans. Walter Lowrie. London and New York: Oxford University Press, 1939.

R　　*Repetition;* see FT.

SLW　*Stages on Life's Way.* Trans. Howard V. Hong and Edna H. Hong. Princeton, N.J.: Princeton University Press, 1988.

SUD　*The Sickness unto Death.* Trans. Howard V. Hong and Edna H. Hong. Princeton, N.J.: Princeton University Press, 1980.

TA　　*Two Ages: The Age of Revolution and the Present Age. A Literary Review.* Trans. Howard V. Hong and Edna H. Hong. Princeton, N.J.: Princeton University Press, 1978.

TDIO　*Three Discourses on Imagined Occasions.* Trans. Howard V. Hong and Edna H. Hong. Princeton, N.J.: Princeton University Press, 1993.

UDVS　*Upbuilding Discourses in Various Spirits.* Trans. Howard V. Hong and Edna H. Hong. Princeton, N.J.: Princeton University Press, 1993.

WL　　*Works of Love.* Trans. Howard V. Hong and Edna H. Hong. Princeton, N.J.: Princeton University Press, 1995.

P A R T
O N E

Introduction

Placing *Postscript* in Kierkegaard's Life

Just about the time that Karl Marx and Friedrich Engels completed their collaboration on *The German Ideology,* Søren Kierkegaard pseudonymously published a big book with a wickedly anti-Hegelian title, *Concluding Unscientific Postscript to "Philosophical Fragments."* It, too, was an assault on the German ideology of Hegel and his followers, and that is part of its ongoing importance. It is a major player in the aftermath to Hegel, in which speculative idealism was subjected to devastating critique.

But there are at least four more reasons why it is an important text. (1) It is a central text as regards Kierkegaard's role as a founding father of existentialism, and its influence can be traced through the existential philosophies and theologies of the early twentieth century. (2) It has deep affinities with, as well as deep divergences from, major postmodern philosophies of the late twentieth century. As such it deserves to be a dialogue partner with them. (3) It is a central text in the pseudonymous authorship of Kierkegaard, and thus in Kierkegaard's authorship as a whole. Any attempt to understand the Kierkegaardian corpus—a major treasure trove by any account—must come to grips with it. (4) Finally, all by itself it is a rich and challenging text. Quite apart from assisting us in the effort to understand something else, whether it be existentialism, postmodernism, the Kierkegaardian corpus, or whatever, it rewards the most careful reading.

In many respects Kierkegaard is a biographer's dream. His personality was many-layered and complex, and his life was filled with dramatic conflicts. But, as we shall see, he felt it of utmost importance to distance himself from his writings so as not to distract the readers' attention from their subject matter. Pseudonymity and indirect communication are important aspects of this deliberate attempt to disappear. Accordingly, this biographical introduction can afford to be very brief.[1]

Søren was born the youngest of seven children on 5 May 1813. His father was the dominant influence in his childhood and subjected him to a very intense religious upbringing that was heavily colored by his own personal melancholy. This worldview was not, according to the adult Kierkegaard, any more appropriate for a child than the childish Christianity he found all around him was appropriate for adults.

In 1830 he matriculated at the University of Copenhagen in the faculty of theology, though it would be ten years before he took his final exams. Meanwhile he devoted himself largely to sowing wild oats and to reading literature and philosophy. It is not surprising that during this period he became alienated from his father and the Christianity in which his father had brought him up.

What Walter Lowrie calls "the prodigal's return"[2] occurred in 1838. Shortly after his twenty-fifth birthday, Kierkegaard had a profound religious experience, which he described as bringing him "an *indescribable joy*" (JP 5.5324). He wrote the following prayer in his journal a few weeks later: "How I thank you, Father in heaven, for having kept an earthly father present for a time here on earth, where I so greatly need him; with your help I hope that he will have greater joy in being my father the second time than he had the first time" (JP 5.5328). Lowrie writes, "The prayer of July 9 (the first inscribed in S. K.'s Journal) shows that he had returned to his 'earthly father,' with a devotion we cannot easily account for. But it appears no less evident that he had returned to the 'Father in heaven.'"[3] The next month, his father died.

This conversion, against the background of the long, intense process (beginning with his childhood religious instruction) that led to it, is the precondition and presupposition for Kierkegaard's authorship as a whole.[4] He always writes as a passionate believer. But the immediate occasion that triggered his career as a writer was his broken engagement to Regina Olsen. So far as the evidence available to us is concerned, he never told anyone, not even Regina, exactly why he became convinced that he could not go ahead with their marriage.

He became engaged to her in 1840, shortly after taking his theology examination. A year later his formal education and his engagement came to an end together. His dissertation, *The Concept of Irony,* was accepted in July 1841. In August he returned Regina's ring with a letter breaking off their relationship. In September he published and publicly defended his dissertation. And in October, after vain attempts by Regina and her father to change his mind, Kierkegaard made it clear that his decision was irrevocable and left for Berlin. The flow of Regina's tears was paltry compared with the flood of works that gushed from Søren's pen from that point on. *Either / Or,* a large work of two volumes, was published on 20 February 1843. Thus began Kierkegaard's pseudonymous authorship, which was regularly accompanied by edifying or upbuilding discourses published under his own name.[5] The former consists of the following (accompanied by the name of the pseudonymous author or editor):

1843   *Either / Or* (Victor Eremita)
          Fear and Trembling (Johannes de Silentio)
          Repetition (Constantin Constantius)
1844   *Philosophical Fragments* (Johannes Climacus)
          The Concept of Anxiety (Vigilius Haufniensis)
          Prefaces (Nicolaus Notabene)
1845   *Stages on Life's Way* (Hilarius Bookbinder)
1846   *Concluding Unscientific Postscript* (Johannes Climacus)

In "A First and Last Explanation," appended to *Postscript,* Kierkegaard acknowledged that he had written these works, along with three articles in *The Fatherland,* under the names of Victor Eremita and Frater Taciturnus (a contributor to *Stages*). He seemed to think of this as the conclusion of his authorship, but it was followed by a second authorship of even greater size. Most of it was published under his name (some only posthumously), but two volumes were published under the pseudonym Anti-Climacus: *Sickness unto Death* (1849) and *Practice in Christianity* (1850). Along with *Works of Love,* the Anti-Climacus writings are the heart of Kierkegaard's second authorship.

Just as the writing of *Postscript* represents the halfway point in his authorship (roughly speaking), so it stands between the tumultuous relationships with his father and with Regina and two equally tumultuous personal episodes, known as the *Corsair* affair and "the attack upon Christendom." Just after completing *Postscript,* but prior to its publication, a brawl broke out between Kierkegaard and *The Corsair,* a weekly paper usually referred to as a scandal sheet but of enormous impact on educated public opinion in Denmark. Through its satires and rumor-mongering, it was virtually a literary version of the Terror of the French Revolution (see COR, ix–x).

The affair began with a review of *Stages on Life's Way* by P. L. Møller, a powerful influence at *The Corsair* and the possible model of the seducer whose diary appears in *Either / Or I*. Although neither the review nor Kierkegaard's immediate response (in the name of Frater Taciturnus, one of the pseudonyms from *Stages*) appeared in *The Corsair,* the response shifted attention from *Stages* to *The Corsair,* Møller's relation to it, and "the loathesome *Corsair* attacks on peaceable, respectable men" (COR 46). Taciturnus writes, "Would that I might only get into *The Corsair* soon. It is really hard for a poor author to be so singled out in Danish literature that he (assuming that we pseudonyms are one) is the only one who is not abused there" (COR 46).

The Corsair responded with a series of satires that quickly moved from Taciturnus to Kierkegaard himself, focusing largely on his physical appearance. (There is some evidence that he was hunchbacked and had legs of unequal length). This public ridicule lasted from January 1846 until January 1848 and made Kierkegaard a laughingstock in Copenhagen during the time immediately following the publication of *Postscript* in February 1846. But long before it was over, it had two important consequences for Kierkegaard. First, it played a major role in reversing his decision to end his authorship with *Postscript.* Though one would scarcely guess it from reading them, we owe his later writings largely to this episode.

Second, it reinforced his view that "the crowd is untruth."[6] By giving him a very concrete experience of the depravity of the culture that called itself Christendom while feeding on *The Corsair,* it prepared the way for his final conflict.[7] The works now published as Kierkegaard's *Attack upon Christendom* come from the last year of his life, published between August 1854 and September 1855. They consist of twenty-one articles in *The Fatherland* and a dozen pamphlets, ten of which were a numbered series bearing the title *The Instant.*[8] Their import is well summarized by James Collins: "On the ground of simple human honesty, he asked the Church officials to make public admission of the discrepancy between the Christian ideal and their preaching. He called upon them to confess that they were no longer presenting New Testament Christianity in its full rigor, that they were no longer asking men to follow Christ in unconditional discipleship."[9]

The background for this demand had been laid a few years earlier. "The three hard-hitting books of this 1850–52 period— *Training in Christianity, For Self-examination* and *Judge for Yourselves!*—championed Kierkegaard's version of undiluted Christianity. They affirmed the substance of religion to be the following of Christ in His lowliness and heterogeneity with the world. In sharp, scandalous contrast to this Christian message stands the accepted position of Christendom. The latter does away with the need to choose Christ at a sacrifice to oneself, since it simply erases the distinction between the way of the world and the way of the Lord."[10] As we shall see in chapter 3, this means that Christendom represents the ethical rather than the religious stage on life's way and that the "attack upon Christendom" begins at least as early as *Fear and Trembling* in 1843.

In October, before number ten of *The Instant* was taken to the publisher, Kierkegaard was taken to the hospital suffering from a paralysis. He died on 11 November 1855.

| N O T E S

1. For a somewhat fuller account, see the first two chapters of James Collins, *The Mind of Kierkegaard*. For a rich and full-length biography, see Walter Lowrie, *Kierkegaard*.
2. Lowrie, *Kierkegaard*, 168–88.
3. Ibid., 168.
4. Especially in *Point of View*, Kierkegaard insists that we consider his writing as a whole.
5. In 1845 Kierkegaard published both *Three Discourses on Imagined Occasions* and *Eighteen Upbuilding Discourses,* a collection of discourses published in groups of two, three, and four, during 1843 and 1844.
6. This is a recurring theme of "The Individual," published in PV.
7. For detailed accounts of the *Corsair* affair, see the Hongs' historical introduction to COR and the editor's introduction to Robert L. Perkins, ed., *International Kierkegaard Commentary: The Corsair Affair.*
8. The last of these remained unpublished at the time of his death.
9. Collins, *The Mind of Kierkegaard*, 16.
10. Ibid., 16.

Placing *Postscript* as a Pseudonymous Text

> The concept of author in our day has been dis-
> torted in an extremely immoral way. (JP 5.5944)

In his biography of Mozart, Wolfgang Hildesheimer tells us that Kierkegaard "wanted to start a sect to revere Mozart, not above others, but exclusively."[1] In a footnote, Hildesheimer refers to *Either/Or*. The only problem is that *Either/Or* is written by five different authors, none of whom is Kierkegaard.[2]

The effusive encomium for Mozart is found in an essay on his operas written by A, the otherwise unidentified young aesthete of *Either/Or I*. This means that in the text in question it is not Kierkegaard who speaks. He is most emphatic about this: "Thus in the pseudonymous books there is not a single word by me . . . if it should occur to anyone to want to quote a particular passage from the books, it is my wish, my prayer, that he will do me the kindness of citing the respective pseudonymous author's name, not mine" (626–27; cf. JP 6.6786, 6566). Hildesheimer thus should have said that Kierkegaard created an author who "wanted to start a sect to revere Mozart."

Pseudonyms are sometimes a means whereby authors express their own views without getting into trouble with the censors or without embarrassing those whose names must be changed to protect the innocent. The point is to hide the true identity of the author. Because Kierkegaard denies that this is the point of his own pseudonymous writing (625), he can insist, precisely while acknowledging publicly that he is the producer of these works, that they remain pseudonymous. He wrote them, but he is not their author. If we are to understand this, we must recognize that the authors and editors to whom the pseudonymous works are attributed are personae rather than disguises.[3]

Such personae are familiar to us in the characters produced by novelists and playwrights. Kierkegaard notes that "all poetic creativity would *eo ipso* be made impossible or meaningless and intolerable if the lines [spoken by such characters] were supposed to be the producer's own words" (627). What is different in Kierkegaard's case is that he creates fictitious authors, who in turn create their own characters, tell their own stories, present their own theories. The creativity of his writing would become "impossible or meaningless and intolerable" if the words of his authors were supposed to be his own.

To attribute to Kierkegaard the enthusiasm for Mozart expressed by A is like confusing Fyodor Dostoyevski with Raskolnikov or Arthur Miller with Willy Loman. What is probably the most irresponsible book ever written on Kierkegaard is constructed on just such a confusion. Theodor Adorno's *Kierkegaard: Construction of the Aesthetic*[4] ranges through the pseudonymous writings and assigns to Kierkegaard the views of first this and then that pseudonym, giving us a construction, to be sure, but not so much of the aesthetic as of a thoroughly fictitious Kierkegaard.

We can avoid Adorno's arbitrariness by simply following the injunction to attribute the pseudonymous texts to their respective authors. But if we would go beyond blind obedience, we must try to understand the point of Kierkegaard's "polyonymity" (625). One strategy for doing that is to compare what Kierkegaard says about authorship with the "death of the author" motif in the French postmodernism of Roland Barthes, Michel Foucault, and Jacques Derrida.

They join Hans-Georg Gadamer in denying the claim that the intention of the author (*mens auctoris*) determines the meaning of a text.[5] According to this claim, a text is the outward expression of an inward meaning that is complete and fixed in the mind of the author prior to writing. The task of reading or interpretation is that of divination or deciphering, using the text as the basis for the recreation or reproduction in the mind of the reader of the author's inner state.[6]

According to this view, the meaning of a text (the author's experience and the intention to express it) is fixed before it is written, and the text itself has a fixed identity prior to its interpretation. In the movement from authorial experience to text to reader's recreated experience, the prior moment is externally related to the subsequent moment. Gadamer denies this relation of the text to both writer and reader. The text cannot be externally related to some prior meaning that underlies it because works "become detached from their origins and, just because of this, begin to speak—surprising even their creators . . . neither the word nor the sentence nor, as one would say today, the discourse refers back to the intention of the author." This is because "the intention has, so to speak, 'gone into' the work, and can no longer be sought behind it or before it."[7]

Nor can the text be externally related to its interpretation. "The mens auctoris is not admissible as a yardstick for the meaning of a work" because "the idea of a work-in-itself, divorced from its constantly renewed reality in being experienced, always has something abstract about it . . . in other words, *understanding belongs to the being of that which is understood*."[8]

For Gadamer, reading a text is like translating a text or performing a piece of music. Just as there is no single translation or performance that is *the* right one, so there can be no translation or performance that is *simply* the reduplication of the author's experience or intention. "Not occasionally but always, the meaning of a text goes beyond its author. That is why understanding is not merely a reproductive but always a productive activity as well."[9] It follows that for determinate meaning to occur, the author always needs the reader as coproducer of that meaning. Does this support the notion that the interpreter understands the text better than its author does? No. "It is enough to say that we understand in a *different* way, *if we understand at all*."[10]

Translated into French, this challenge to the author's unilateral control over the text does indeed come out differently, but nonetheless recognizably. The sustained attack on the expression theory of writing, and thus on the "prestige"[11] and "privilege"[12] of the author, is part of a larger assault on modernity's notions of self or subject as autonomous and self-transparent.[13] Since for Kierkegaard pseudonymity seems to be the voluntary renunciation of the perks of authorship, we will want to see as clearly as possible what this "prestige" and "privilege" amount to.

It is in theological terms that Barthes, Foucault, and Derrida interpret the perks of authorship as seen by the expression theory. Just as God the creator is the author of the world, so the human author is conceived as the creator of the work, a pure origin, prior to and outside of the product to which he or she imparts a fixed and final meaning. The author is the Alpha and Omega of the work. But, the postmodernists insist, language is prior to its "user," and far from being "equipped with a being preceding or exceeding the writing," the author is "born simultaneously with the text" and "can only imitate a gesture that is always anterior, never original."[14] Whether or not a creator is the author of the world, the human author cannot be creator of the text.

The three postmodernist writers before us do not call attention to this "whether or not" feature of their argument and therefore fail to notice that the death of the author neither entails the death of God, since the fact that human authors are not God does not entail that no one else is God nor does it require the death of God as a premise, since human authors could fail to be God even if there is a God. What the death of the author motif entails (and is entailed by) is not the death of God but the death of Man, where "Man" stands for modernity's conception of the human self as fully autonomous, both self-positing and self-transparent. If we notice these facts, we will notice that there is no reason why a religious writer like Kierkegaard, who also thinks that human beings lack divine powers, should not agree with atheistic postmodernism in denying divine "prestige" or "privilege" to human authors.

The crucial premise of the "death of the author" argument is not atheism but human temporality. It is Derrida who is most insistent on this point.[15] For the author as for every human self, "Being has always already begun." This means that the history of a text "is not only its *past,* the eve or the sleep in which it precedes itself in an author's intentions, but is also the impossibility of its ever being *present,* of its ever being summarized by some absolute simultaneity or instantaneousness [even in the author's intentions]."[16] No one can claim to be the author of books "whose unfinished movement assigns itself no absolute beginning."[17] Our books have neither Alpha nor Omega.

In giving this "theological" twist to authorial finitude, our three French writers agree with Gadamer in emphasizing the writer's dependence upon the reader. For all three, the death of the author is the birth of the reader.[18] But Foucault introduces a theme not present in Barthes when he writes, "Writing has become linked to sacrifice, even to the sacrifice of life: it is now a *voluntary effacement* . . . the effacement of the writing subject's individual characteristics . . . the writing subject cancels out the signs of his particular individuality."[19]

What is the meaning of this shift from viewing the death of the author as a necessity that cannot be avoided to seeing it as a possibility that might be voluntarily chosen? Foucault does not say. But Derrida provides one possible answer. In reality the author has no choice but "to emancipate [the work] or lose one's hold on it, to let it make its way alone and unarmed."[20] But just like parents in relation to children they once thought they owned, this release can be reluctant or willing.

Reluctant release takes the form of nostalgia, the sighing sadness for a past that never was. Derrida finds this nostalgia especially pronounced in Jean-Jacques Rousseau, Claude Lévi-Strauss, and Martin Heidegger.[21] But Friedrich Nietzsche signals for Derrida another possible response, an *amor fati,* "a joyous affirmation of the play of the world . . . the affirmation of a world of signs without fault, without truth, and without origin which is offered to an active interpretation. This *affirmation* then determines the noncenter otherwise than as loss of the center. *It plays without security.*"[22] This risky but joyous affirmation is the form that "voluntary effacement" takes in Derrida.

For Kierkegaard, as for Foucault and Derrida, the very limited ability of the author to control the process of communication is at once a structural necessity and a personal choice; it is a "voluntary effacement," a kind of self-denying ordinance in which the author, who in fact is not God, willingly agrees to play a role other than God vis-à-vis text and reader. For him, as for the French, the issue of authorship will be theologically loaded from start to finish.

Writing pseudonymously is one of the most dramatic ways in which Kierkegaard voluntarily forgoes the privileges of authorship. But the most inclusive expression of this posture is the constantly reiterated claim that he writes "without authority," for this claim applies in the first instance even to those writings published under his own name. During 1843–44, while producing the pseudonymous works, he published six small volumes of "upbuilding discourses," which in 1845 he published together as *Eighteen Upbuilding Discourses*. The six prefaces differ from one another, but each begins with these words: "Although this little book (which is called 'discourses,' not sermons, because its author does not have authority to *preach*, 'upbuilding discourses,' not discourses for upbuilding, because the speaker by no means claims to be a *teacher*. . ." (EUD 5, 53, 107, 179, 231, 295; cf. PV 143n).[23]

Sometimes authors derive their authority from being authorized by either the church or the university. Kierkegaard tells us that his writings are not authorized in either of these ways, and that our respect for such teaching institutions of human society will not dispose us to take him seriously (CUP 273; OAR 111). At the same time, he is disclaiming two other kinds of authorization, both of which occur outside the official institutions of society. While seeking to clarify the important difference between a genius and an apostle, he insists that he is neither (OAR 103–20). What distinguishes him from both the apostle, who is authorized directly by God, and the genius, who writes "without authority" from God or church or state and is authorized only by his unmistakable talent (PV 142n), is the fact that he is not epistemologically above or ahead of his readers but is, just like them, a learner

(PV 75, 160; cf. 29, 73). This motif of the writer as fellow learner with the reader occurs frequently in the journals (see JP 1.649 [p. 273], 1038; 6.6533, 6700, for example), and Kierkegaard puts the same idea in the mouth of Climacus (CUP 622–23).

Kierkegaard's fourfold forfeiture of authorial authority, his voluntary refusal to claim the privileges of pastor, professor, genius, or apostle, has theological presuppositions. With regard to finite truth, hierarchical teaching relations based on human differences have their temporary place, though consensus is the ultimate criterion. Here a democratic theory of truth like that of C. S. Peirce or of Jürgen Habermas holds. But with reference to ethical-religious matters, or what Kierkegaard calls eternal truth, "the crowd is untruth," that is, human consensus is not the final standard. Moreover, here a more radical democracy obtains, for here there are no experts and all are equally learners. This is why "it is only religion that can, with the help of eternity, carry human equality to the utmost limit . . . [and why] religion is the true humanity" (PV 107–18). The only teachers here are God and the apostle, who, by a miracle that can be believed but not guaranteed by either proof or social institution, speaks as the direct representative of God (OAR 109, 112, 117). In matters of the spirit, short of apostolic authority, the pastor, the professor, and yes, even the genius, are every bit as much learners as those they would instruct. Under the rubric "without authority" Kierkegaard voluntarily adopts this posture as an essentially religious act.

There is a similar humility in our three French writers, but it is also very different. In both cases the author refuses to play God. But there is all the difference in the world between saying, "There is no God, so I am not God," and saying "There is a God, so I am not God." We shall have to ask whether this theological difference plays a role when Kierkegaard, as emphatically as either Gadamer or the French, denies that the intention of the author governs the meaning of the text. For him this is in the first instance an autobiographical discovery. In *The Point of View*, which was written after *Postscript* (between 1846 and 1849) but published only posthumously, Kierkegaard argues that his authorship as a whole, not just this book or that one, has the character of being written by *an* author. In spite of its obvious diversity, it is a religious authorship from start to finish, and it has a coherent, unified meaning. But he is not its origin. He insists repeatedly that he did not have the full meaning of his authorship in view at the outset but only came to see it in retrospect, and he attributes the coherence of his writings to governance or providence (PV 13, 72–73, 150, 160; cf. JP 5.5991; 6.6346, 6523, 6700).[24]

Out of this experience he anticipates twentieth-century critiques of making the *mens auctoris* the meaning of a text. He vigorously stresses the importance of keeping his own inner life separate from the reading of his texts (PV 9; TA 99), and he ridicules the idea that the religious character of his authorship could be established simply on his own say-so (PV 15). Most importantly, he recognizes that "in spiritual things all receptivity is productivity" (JP 1.878).

Moreover, he has Climacus present us not only with this hypothesis that "all receiving is a producing" (78) but also with the thesis "that the reception intrinsic to inwardness is not a direct reproduction of what was communicated, since that is an echo" (260). To equate understanding with reproduction is to reduce it to "learning by rote" (263–64, 623). In keeping with this, Climacus praises the pseudonyms for not misusing their prefaces "to take an official position on the production, as if in a purely legal sense an author were the best interpreter of his own words, as if it could help a reader that an author 'intended this and that'" (252).

Kierkegaard presents two corollaries to this refusal to let the writer's intention be equated with the meaning of the text. First, the writer is but a reader of his or her own texts. In "A First and Last Explanation," in which Kierkegaard publicly acknowledges that he is the author of the pseudonymous writings—that is, the creator of the pseudonyms—he says, "I have no opinion about them except as a third party, no knowledge of their meaning except as a reader" (625–26). In other words, for him pseudonymity is a device to distance the writer from his texts and to accentuate his role as *an* interpreter rather than *the* origin of their meaning. In *The Point of View,* when he repeats this claim to being only a reader of these texts, he explicitly links it not only with his rejection of the *mens auctoris* theory of hermeneutics but also with two closely related themes presented above: his personal claim to write "without authority" and his understanding of his authorship as constituting "my own upbringing" (PV 15, 151). In linking the notion that he is just one of his own readers with the notion that he is a fellow learner with his readers, he introduces us to his understanding of the egalitarianism of the spirit.

To the corollary that he is but a (co)reader of his own writings Kierkegaard adds the corollary that the reader is a (co)writer of these texts. As with Gadamer and the French, the reader comes to share in producing their meaning. It turns out that distancing the author from the text is a means toward distancing the author from the reader and leaving the reader alone with the text. Howard and Edna Hong have written that "no thinker and writer ever tried as Kierkegaard did to leave the reader alone with the work. The dialectic of thought and existence is properly that of the reader with the work, not of the reader's curious interest in the writer."[25]

A week after the publication of *Either / Or,* Kierkegaard published a letter under the pseudonym A. F. that claims that its readers are fortunate not to know who the author is, "for then they have only the book to deal with, without being bothered or distracted by his personality" (COR 16). His pseudonymous editor, Victor Eremita, applies this to the other pseudonymous authors: "The point of view ought to speak for itself. . . . Thus, when the book is read, A and B are forgotten; only the points of view confront each other" (EO 1:14).

It is Johannes Climacus, however, who develops this theme most fully. He praises his own *Philosophical Fragments* for not solving the problem it poses; he praises *Either / Or* for not choosing between the aesthetic and the ethical; and he praises *Stages on Life's Way* for reaching no conclusion and leaving its question unanswered because—and this is the central point—instead of making the reader "safe and secure" vis-à-vis the dialectic of existence, "it is left to the reader to put it all together by himself, if he so pleases, but nothing is done for the reader's comfort" (CUP 15, 254, 289, 298). So when Climacus constantly tells his readers that he has no opinion about the issues he raises (CUP 224, 226, 231, 271n, 273, 369, 379, 619), his purpose is clear even without the benefit of Kierkegaard's remark that Climacus "dialectically formulated the issue so sharply that no one could directly see whether it was an attack on Christianity or a defense, but it depended on the state of the reader and what he got out of the book" (JP 6.6690). In *Point of View* Kierkegaard calls attention to the epigram of *Stages,* "Such works are mirrors: when an ape looks in, no apostle can look out" (PV 95; cf. SLW 8).

Climacus takes it to be his task "first and last to watch himself lest he become important in relation to others" (CUP 278), and he spells out two dangers in this regard. A writer's "renown," "celebrity," or "fame" on the one hand (CUP 13, 14, 63, 65, 72) or the rhetorical skill that the writer employs on the other hand (CUP 12–14, 260, 278) can all too easily dispose the reader to accept what is written as true without examination or personal appropriation. To complete this thought by his pseudonym, Kierkegaard notes that the author's "personal actuality" might just as easily dispose the reader against the text, and he does not wish to be a "constraint" (or "embarrassment," as the older translation has it) to the ideas in his books (CUP 627). The distance he seeks from his readers is precisely to leave them alone with the text.

And yet this way of putting it is not quite right. Just as Kierkegaard is always trying to separate the individual from the "crowd," from the "public," from the "present age," so here he seeks to separate the reader from the writer. But in neither case is his purpose to leave the individual simply alone; and if we add "with the text," we have still left out the essential point. He wants to help the individual get *alone before God,* and to that end he both assaults the apotheosis of the age and deliberately forgoes the privileges of authorship. His whole theory of indirect communication, in which pseudonymity plays such a prominent part, is necessary "because ethically the task is precisely this— that every man comes to stand alone in the God-relationship" (JP 1.649, p. 273). In this mode the author "shyly withdraws (for love is always shy), so as not to witness the admission which [the reader] makes to himself alone before God" (PV 25–26; cf. 111, 135, 150).

Strangely, Kierkegaard thinks that the author who in this way declines to play God in relation to the text and the reader is nevertheless acting in a truly godlike manner. Our twentieth-century critics can only wonder how this could be, since the Kierkegaardian writer, like their own, does not try to be the Alpha and Omega of the text or the teacher of the reader. The answer is that Kierkegaard has a different conception of God from theirs. Because he sees creation in the light of incarnation, he views it as *kenosis* rather than as *imperium*. Climacus hints at this view when he writes that God "communicates creatively in such a way that in creating he gives independence vis-à-vis himself" (CUP 260). But it is Kierkegaard himself who spells this out more fully:

> The greatest good, after all, which can be done for a being . . . is to make it free. In order to do just that, omnipotence is required. This seems strange, since it is precisely omnipotence that supposedly would make [a being] dependent. But if one will reflect on omnipotence, he will see that it also must contain the unique qualification of being able to withdraw itself again in a manifestation of omnipotence in such a way that precisely for this reason that which has been originated through omnipotence can be independent. That is why one human being cannot make another person wholly free. . . . Only omnipotence can withdraw itself at the same time it gives itself away, and this relationship is the very independence of the receiver. (JP 2.1251)

Human withdrawal does not have the same effect as divine withdrawal, but it has the same goal, and the author who withdraws to leave the reader alone with God is imitating, but not replacing, the Creator.

So, as promised, the understanding of authorship is as intensely theological an issue for Kierkegaard as for Barthes, Foucault, and Derrida, but in such a different direction that his important and impressive agreements with them take on a very different meaning. Authorship and anxiety are linked for him as for them, but as we might now expect, in a different way. They see a Cartesian anxiety about certainty and control as the underlying source of the idea of the author as Alpha and Omega, and they seek to overcome this anxiety in the courage to be merely human, even when there is no other origin or center. They are Nietzscheans. For Kierkegaard, the anxiety of authorship is the "fear and trembling lest one do anyone harm" (JP 6.6230). This anxiety is not to be overcome but nourished as a constant warning against the danger of coming between the reader and the text or, even worse, failing to withdraw so as to leave the reader alone before God.

❙ N O T E S

This chapter is a shorter version of "Kierkegaard and the Anxiety of Authorship," *International Philosophical Quarterly* 34(1994), 5–22. Used by permission of Fordham University Press. The longer version explores in greater detail the kinship and conflict that characterize the relationship between Kierkegaard and contemporary French postmodernism.

   1.   Wolfgang Hildesheimer, *Mozart,* trans. Marion Faber (London: J. M. Dent & Sons, 1983), 6.

   2.   There is Victor Eremita, the editor of the whole text but author only of the preface. There is the aesthete, identified only as A, whose papers comprise volume 1 except for the diary of the seducer, who is known only as Johannes. Finally, there is Judge William, whose letters comprise volume 2 except for the homily written by an unnamed pastor.

   3.   "A Kierkegaardian pseudonym is a *persona,* an imaginary person created by the author for artistic purposes, not a *nom de plume,* a fictitious name used to protect his personal identity from the threats and embarrassments of publicity . . . his purpose was not mystification but distance" (Louis Mackey, *Kierkegaard: A Kind of Poet,* 247).

   4.   Adorno, *Kierkegaard: Construction of the Aesthetic,* trans. Robert Hullot-Kentor (Minneapolis: University of Minnesota Press, 1989).

   5.   Gadamer's philosophical hermeneutics is usually seen in its difference from French postmodernism. See, for example, *Dialogue and Deconstruction: The Gadamer-Derrida Encounter,* ed. Diane P. Michelfelder and Richard E. Palmer (Albany: SUNY Press, 1989). The agreement between the two traditions deserves more attention that it has received.

6. For a clear statement of the view that Gadamer rejects, see Emilio Betti, "Hermeneutics as the General Methodology of the *Geisteswissenschaften*," in *Contemporary Hermeneutics: Hermeneutics as Method, Philosophy, and Critique,* ed. Josef Bleicher (London: Routledge & Kegan Paul, 1990), 51–94.

7. Gadamer, "Hermeneutics and Logocentrism," in *Dialogue and Deconstruction,* 123.

8. Gadamer, *Truth and Method,* trans. Joel Weinsheimer and Donald G. Marshall (New York: Crossroad, 1991), xxxi. Emphasis added.

9. Ibid., 296.

10. Ibid., 297; cf. 373.

11. Roland Barthes, "The Death of the Author," in *Image – Music – Text,* trans. Stephen Heath (New York: Noon Day Press, 1977), 143.

12. Michel Foucault, "What Is an Author?" in *The Foucault Reader,* ed. Paul Rabinow (New York: Pantheon Books, 1984), 103, 105, 117.

13. Derrida uses a postal metaphor to interpret the expression theory, which "in effect implies a *transmission charged with making pass, from one subject to another, the identity of a signified* object, of a *meaning* or of a *concept* rightfully separable from the process of passage and from the signifying operation" (*Positions,* trans. Alan Bass [Chicago, Ill.: University of Chicago Press, 1981], 23). The commonsense idea here is that it does not matter whether I sent this manuscript to the publisher by Federal Express or United Parcel Service, since its meaning is unconditioned by, and indifferent to, the system that conveys it from one place to another. The philosophically loaded move is to identify language with a series of such postal systems for conveying meanings from one mind to another, meanings that in their "pure" state exist "outside," "before," or "beneath" the texts of their linguistic incarnation (*Positions,* 30–32, 63). *The Post Card: From Socrates to Freud and Beyond* (trans. Alan Bass [Chicago, Ill.: University of Chicago Press, 1987]) is, among other things, an attempt to show that writing does not work that way. Derrida's critique of Edmund Husserl in *Speech and Phenomena: And Other Essays on Husserl's Theory of Signs* (trans. David B. Allison [Evanston, Ill.: Northwestern University Press, 1973]) is a sustained critique of the notion that meaning is exterior and prior to language.

14. Barthes, "The Death of the Author," 144–46. Cf. the argument of Harold Bloom in *The Anxiety of Influence* (New York: Oxford University Press, 1973).

15. One could argue that Kierkegaard, Heidegger, and Derrida are radical Kantians for whom inescapable temporality is transcendental, the encompassing horizon for the finitude of all human experience. See John D. Caputo, *Radical Hermeneutics: Repetition, Deconstruction, and the Hermeneutic Project* (Bloomington: Indiana University Press, 1987).

16. Derrida, "Force and Signification," in *Writing and Difference,* trans. Alan Bass (Chicago, Ill.: University of Chicago Press, 1978), 12–14.

17. Derrida, *Positions,* 3; cf. 45.

18. See Barthes, "The Death of the Author," 148; Foucault, "What Is an Author?" 119–20; and Derrida, *Positions,* 20, 63; "Structure, Sign, and Play in the Discourse of the Human Sciences," in *Writing and Difference,* 292; and *Of Grammatology,* trans. Gayatri Chakrovorty Spivak (Baltimore, Md.: John Hopkins University Press, 1976), 19.

19. Foucault, "What Is an Author?" 102. Emphasis added.

20. Derrida, "Edmond Jabès and the Question of the Book," in *Writing and Difference,* 70. On the theme of control as central to the question of authorship, see Manfred Frank, "Limits of the Human Control of Language: Dialogue as the Place of Difference between Neostructuralism and Hermeneutics," in *Dialogue and Deconstruction;* and Irene E. Harvey, *Derrida and the Economy of Différance* (Bloomington: Indiana University Press, 1986), 62–67.

21. Derrida, "Structure, Sign, and Play," 292; "The Ends of Man," in *Margins of Philosophy,* trans. Alan Bass (Chicago, Ill.: University of Chicago Press, 1982), 123–34.

22. "Structure, Sign, and Play," 292. Emphasis altered. In this context "center" and "origin" function synonymously.

23. Two of Kierkegaard's pseudonyms repeat the claim to write without authority, adding illuminating satirical comments in the process. Climacus asks that no one appeal to his book, since he is a humorist and not an authority, though he is comforted "that there are such great men who are able and willing to be the authority, from whom one has the benefit of accepting their opinion as a matter of course" (618–19); and Vigilius Haufniensis presents himself as "an author without any claims," though with regard to human authority "I am a fetish worshipper and will worship anyone with equal piety, but with one proviso, that it be made sufficiently clear by a beating of drums that he is the one I must worship and that it is he who is the authority and *Imprimatur* for the current year" (CA 8).

24. On the translation of *Styrelse* as "governance" rather than "providence," see PV 64n.

25. See the preface to Gregor Malantschuk, *Kierkegaard's Thought,* viii. The Hongs add that the purpose of pseudonymity is "to make the author of the authors irrelevant and to leave the reader alone with the works and the various positions presented" (EUD xx). Climacus says, with reference to the pseudonymous authorship, "The absence of an author is a means of distancing" (252; cf. 263 on the "gap between reader and author"), and Mackey states that the purpose of pseudonymity "was not mystification but distance" (*A Kind of Poet,* 247).

T H R E E | **Placing *Postscript* in
the Theory of the Stages**

The pseudonymous authorship finds its penultimate conclusion
in the works of Johannes Climacus, *Philosophical Fragments* and
Concluding Unscientific Postscript, and its ultimate conclusion in
the works of Anti-Climacus, *Sickness unto Death* and *Practice in
Christianity.* In either its shorter or its longer form it has the
theory of the stages at its center. In its simplest form it distinguishes the aesthetic, the ethical, and the religious as stages on
life's way; but, as we shall see, that simple schema gets complicated by refinements, especially in *Postscript.*

In the background of the theory of the stages (or existence
spheres, as they are called, even in *Stages on Life's Way*), is
Hegel's *Phenomenology of Spirit.* In its preface Hegel speaks of
"the stage [*Stufe*] which self-conscious Spirit has presently
reached." Speaking of the "new era" or the "new world" that he
believes to be dawning, he makes it clear that spirit's journey is a
historical journey.[1] But just as ontogeny recapitulates phylogeny,
so the individual whose substance would be the spirit in its
present mode must "also pass through the formative stages [*Bil-
dungsstufen*] of universal Spirit so far as their content is concerned, but as shapes which Spirit has already left behind, as
stages on a way that has been made level with toil." The *Phenomenology* thematizes both the abstract, structural stages of consciousness up to the level of spirit and the historical stages of the
development of the spirit that Hegel here calls "the World-
Spirit."[2] In a passage that the commentators regularly treat as
an allusion to the stations of the cross, Hegel describes the
individual's journey through these shapes of consciousness and of
spirit as "the way of the Soul which journeys through the series of
its own configurations as though they were the stations [*Statio-*

nen] appointed for it by its own nature, so that it may purify itself for the life of the Spirit, and achieve finally, through a completed experience of itself, the awareness of what it really is in itself."[3]

As the theory of the stages emerges through the entirety of the pseudonymous authorship, it embodies this double claim that the journey is grounded in human nature and that its goal is simultaneously the discovery and realization of one's true self.[4] But on another point it is sharply anti-Hegelian. Hegel speaks of the "necessary progression" through this "necessary sequence" and makes it clear that "Because of this necessity, the way to Science is itself already *Science*," so that "when consciousness itself grasps this its own essence, it will signify the nature of absolute knowledge itself."[5] Hegel regularly symbolizes this necessity with organic metaphors, describing the journey as that from bud to blossom to fruit, from acorn to oak, and from embryo to birth.[6]

These metaphors and the necessity they signify are repudiated in the theory of the stages. Neither developmentally nor conceptually is there any necessity to the movement from one stage to the next. The absence of both psychological and logical inevitability means that the stages are not part of "a way that has been made level with toil." Properly understood, the tasks set for the individual by the ethical and the religious are not made easier by the fact that others may have made them before. This is why Climacus will emphasize that his goal is not to make things easier for people but harder (not harder than they actually are, but harder than they often seem in a Christendom saturated with Hegelianism).

In his letter to the reader of *Stages on Life's Way,* Frater Taciturnus summarizes the stages as follows:

> There are three existence-spheres: the esthetic, the ethical, the religious. . . . The ethical sphere is only a transition sphere, and therefore its highest expression is repentance as a negative action. The esthetic sphere is the sphere of immediacy, the ethical the sphere of requirement (and this requirement is so infinite that the individual always goes bankrupt), the religious the sphere of fulfillment, but please note, not a fulfillment such as when one fills an alms box or a sack with gold, for repentance has specifically created a boundless space, and as a consequence the religious contradiction: simultaneously to be out on 70,000 fathoms of water and yet be joyful. (SLW 476)

The first step in unpacking this account is to get clear about what a stage on life's way or an existence sphere is. In his preface to *Either / Or,* Victor Eremita speaks of "an esthetic view of life" and "an ethical view of life" and describes them as two conflicting "points of view" (EO 1:13–14). We could call them *Weltanschauungen* if we remember that a worldview is less a theory, in the sense of a set of propositions, than a perception, a habit of seeing the world in a way that gives to my beliefs and practices whatever coherence they may have. Thus the stages are not in the first instance assertions about the world but modes of being-in-the-world.[7]

The identity and integrity of each stage—its essence, if you like—is the criterion it offers for successful living. Each stage is an answer to the question, What is the good life? in the classical sense in which it is equivalent to the question, Where is true happiness to be found? We know from Plato and Aristotle that in spite of the presence of the word "good" in the first formulation of the question, the ethical answer is only one possible answer. In fact, the aesthetic stage is perhaps best described as the attempt to define and live the good life without reference to good and evil. It is the generic name for those criteria for successful living that are pre-ethical.

The aesthetic stage is sometimes identified with hedonism. This will work only if we remember that there are pleasures of the mind as well as of the body. But this reminder is problematic, since those, for example, whose "delight is in the law of the Lord" (Psalm 1:2) would seem to be at the religious rather than the aesthetic stage. For "hedonism" to be a useful label, it will have to be qualified as the pursuit of pleasures that fall outside of the ethical and religious spheres and are unconstrained by ethical and religious norms. It is both easier and more to the point to define the aesthetic from the outset as the realm of pre-ethical norms.

Another advantage of this account is that it does not attempt to force a link between the aesthetic and either beauty or the arts. The young aesthete known to us only as A does indeed have musical and literary interests, especially when the erotic is involved; and the author of "The Seducer's Diary" writes, "What is glorious and divine about esthetics is that it is associated only with the beautiful: essentially it deals only with belles lettres and the fair sex" (EO 1:428). But alas, the link between the aesthetic and the beautiful, even in these two very different forms, cannot be maintained. For if there is a dominant category in *Either / Or*'s portrayal of the aesthetic sphere, it is not the beautiful but the interesting—even when belles lettres and women are the theme. Thus the analysis of ancient and modern tragedy in terms of an ancient and a modern Antigone comes down to the question, "How is the dramatic interest to be produced?" (EO 1:162). And

"The Seducer's Diary" makes clear his overriding concern with the interesting.[8] He insists that throughout the entire seduction he has been faithful—to his pact with the aesthetic; and he summarizes that pact with the question, "Has the interesting been preserved at all times?" (EO 1:437–38).[9]

But what are we to make of the regular identification of the aesthetic with the immediate, especially in the context of the standard dichotomy between immediacy and reflection? *In Either / Or* we have three especially vivid personifications of the aesthetic posture: A, the author of most of volume 1; Don Giovanni; and the seducer whose diary A finds and keeps with his own papers. Of the two seducers, Don Giovanni is truly an example of erotic immediacy. He comes, he sees, he conquers. Next! But the diarist is so highly reflective that most if not all of his delight in seducing Cordelia comes from watching himself do it and writing himself up. And A is so highly reflective that he reminds one more of the hyperconsciousness of Dostoyevski's Underground Man than of almost anyone else. How can both A and the seducer (if indeed they are not the same) be so far removed from immediacy and yet be paradigms of the aesthetic sphere?

Clearly they are not instances of the immediacy that excludes every reflection. But they are immediate in their reflection in the same way that Don Giovanni is immediate in his action: they are unmediated by ethical considerations of any sort. Their (non)relation to the ethical is summed up in the diarist's claim, "The ethical is just as boring in scholarship as in life. . . . Under the esthetic sky, everything is buoyant, beautiful, transient; when ethics arrives on the scene, everything becomes harsh, angular, infinitely *langweiligt* [boring]" (EO 1:367). Ethical categories are simply inoperative.

But what of A's observation that "a bad conscience can indeed make life interesting" (EO 1:304)? It might seem as if having a bad conscience presupposes that one is already operating in the ethical sphere. But if the only import of subjective guilt is as an alternative to boredom, two assumptions about conscience would seem to be at work: first, that it has no normative, revelatory significance; and second, that its presence is to be accounted for solely in terms of some psychological or sociological mechanism. All guilt is false guilt, but some guilt is interesting. Here, again, the ethical is simply inoperative.

It is precisely the normative, revelatory significance of conscience (though not its infallibility) that defines the ethical. I do not enter the ethical by choosing the good but by choosing to make good and evil the primary categories by which I define my existence. Thus Judge William, who represents the ethical in two (very) long letters to A, writes, "I only want to bring you to the point where this choice [between good and evil] has meaning for you. . . . Rather than designating the choice between good and evil, my Either/Or designates the choice by which once chooses good and evil or rules them out. Here the question is under what qualifications one will view all existence and personally live" (EO 2:168–69).

The confrontation between A and Judge William is a modern reenactment of the classical debate whether the highest good should be conceived as fortune or virtue.[10] So it is not surprising that in *Postscript* Climacus treats fortune as an aesthetic category (433–46).

The aesthetic sphere embodies a philosophy of self-choice. Judge William does not deny that this is a philosophy of freedom. But he complains that the aesthetic self chooses itself only in terms of its immediate interests and inclinations, where immediate means the whim of the moment. The result, he suggests, is an unstable self. He understands the ethical to enact a philosophy of self-choice, but it is a choice of the self in relation to the difference between good and evil, or, as he sometimes puts it, an *absolute* choice of the self in its *eternal* validity (EO 2:166–69, 178, 188–90, 214–19, 223–24).

These references to *absolute* choice and *eternal* validity should not lead us to think that Judge William understands the ethical in Platonic or Kantian terms as involving the apprehension of an abstract, formal principle by an intellect that has somehow become pure reason. Judge William is an Aristotelian, for whom right reason is to be defined in terms of the man of practical wisdom rather than the reverse,[11] and a Hegelian, for whom ethics is always a matter of *Sittlichkeit,* the laws, customs, practices, and institutions of a people. The right and the good are to be found, not abstractly in a rational principle but concretely within one's social order, which is, for each individual, the essential mediator of the absolute and eternal.

Accordingly Judge William immediately embeds his theory of self-choice in a theory of marriage, the first moment of Hegel's theory of *Sittlichkeit.*[12] It is the Hegelian character of his ethical thinking far more than A's fascination with sexual seduction (as expressed in his own essay on Don Juan, in Mozart's *Don Giovanni,* and in the now famous seducer's diary that he keeps with his own papers) that dictates marriage as the theme for his ethical appeal to the young aesthete.

Among the most important things Judge William says about marriage is that it should not and need not be boring. Thus his two letters bear the titles "The Esthetic Validity of Marriage" and "The Balance between the Esthetic and the Ethical in the Development of the Personality." Properly understood, the aesthetic and the ethical are not the eccentric circles of mutual exclusion but concentric circles of harmonious coexistence (EO 2:29–30, 47–48, 55–57). In marriage the sensuous, aesthetic moment "is by no means repudiated but is ennobled" (EO 2:61; cf. 21, 30, 57); "marriage is the transfiguration of the first love and not its annihilation" (EO 2:31; cf. 56–57, 94, 253).

There is a negativity in which the aesthetic moment is "dethroned" (EO 2:226); "but it by no means follows that the esthetic is excluded . . . the esthetic is absolutely excluded or it is excluded as the absolute, but relatively it is continually present. In choosing itself, the personality chooses itself ethically and absolutely excludes the esthetic; but since he nevertheless chooses himself and does not become another being by choosing himself but becomes himself, all the esthetic returns in its relativity" (EO 2:177). It is in terms of this relation of the relative to the absolute that the earlier formulas are to be understood, according to which the aesthetic is not repudiated or annihilated in the ethical but ennobled and transfigured.

The structure of this dialectical dethronement is pure Hegel. It is what he understands by *Aufhebung*. X is *aufgehoben* in Y when X is recontextualized, so that instead of standing by itself as self-sufficient, it belongs to Y, a wider frame of reference of which it is not the first principle. In its original solipsism it was of absolute import, but now it is only of relative significance. It has its place, to be sure, but it has been put in its place as well. Its dialectical tension consists in being very important but not all-important. In the context of the theory of stages or existence spheres, this relation obtains not only between sex and marriage[13] or, more generally, between the aesthetic and the ethical but also between each stage and the "next" stage, and thus between the ethical and the religious and between Religiousness A and Religiousness B as subdivisions of the latter. What makes any stage the "next" one in relation to some other stage is not some normal pattern of psychological development or some necessity of conceptual entailment but the value judgment that makes one stage the proper sphere for relativizing the other.

In developing all these themes, Judge William speaks easily and often of God. In the context of Kierkegaard's Denmark, it is not surprising to find so pious a jurist. But in the context of the theory of stages, it is a bit puzzling. After all, is he not the enactment of the ethical stage rather than the religious? What could the religious mode of being-in-the-world be if it is not what we find in Judge William?

In the pseudonymous writings there is a double *Aufhebung* of the ethical in the religious. The first involves personal repentance. Judge William speaks of the transition to the ethical in terms of repentance (EO 2:216), but elsewhere repentance signals the move beyond the ethical. Thus Johannes de Silentio writes, "As soon as sin emerges, ethics founders precisely on repentance; for repentance is the highest ethical expression, but precisely as such it is the deepest ethical self-contradiction" (FT 98n). And Vigilius Haufniensis adds, "Sin, then, belongs to ethics only insofar as upon this concept it is shipwrecked with the aid of repentance. . . . Repentance is the highest ethical contradiction, partly because ethics requires ideality but must be content to receive repentance" (CA 17, 117). This is what Frater Taciturnus meant earlier when he spoke of "the ethical [as] the sphere of requirement (and this requirement is so infinite that the individual always goes bankrupt)" (SLW 476).

If this were the main point, Judge William would fail to embody the religious sphere because of his moral complacency. He is not shy about calling his young friend, A, to repentance, but he gives the impression that he has never had to ask his wife for forgiveness for anything. By placing repentance at the entry into the ethical rather than at its exit, he presents himself as someone who has gone beyond the need for repentance. He is an example of what Nietzsche's Zarathustra calls the "wretched contentment" of "the good and the just."

But *Fear and Trembling* is the primary text for the transition from the ethical to the religious, and there the issue is not so much personal as collective repentance. According to Silentio's retelling of the Abraham story, Judge William falls short of the religious, not simply by virtue of his personal complacency but more deeply by virtue of the social complacency in which he participates.

Fear and Trembling presents the teleological suspension of the ethical in the religious. Now a teleological suspension is nothing but a Hegelian *Aufhebung,* in this case the relativizing of the ethical by recontextualizing it within the religious as its higher principle. But while the form of this teleological suspension is Hegelian, its content is anti-Hegelian, for it is an all-out assault on the Hegelian understanding of *Sittlichkeit*.[14] According to Silentio's understanding of the religious—which he does not purport to embody—religion allows the laws, customs, practices, and institutions of a people's ethical life to have only relative importance for the individual. The believing soul can pledge allegiance only with fingers crossed; because the social order is not absolute and eternal, it is not a reliable mediator of the absolute and the eternal. It can always be trumped by God.

Society tells Abraham that as a father he must preserve and protect his son, that the only conditions under which he could kill his son would be if a higher social need came into conflict with these family values. But when God asks Abraham to sacrifice Isaac, it is not in the name of any social benefit. The act that is sacrifice from the religious perspective is murder in society's eyes.

The point, of course, is not the claim that religion consists in child sacrifice. It is rather the claim that every social order has sinned and fallen short of the glory of God, that the believing soul will render unto Caesar only what is Caesar's in order to remain free to render unto God what is God's, to be able to say, "We must obey God rather than any human authority" (Rom. 3:23; Mark 12:17; Acts 5:29). Society's norms have a claim on the individual. But it is relative; only God's is absolute.

From the religious point of view, the ethical is the tendency of every society to absolutize itself, identifying as good those who meet its expectations and as evil those who are so irreverent as to defy them, whether from within (for example, the criminal) or without (for example, the enemy). In this mode society takes good and evil seriously, but by making itself their criterion, it fails to take God seriously, no matter how much it talks about God. Repentance thus signifies the transition to the religious, not simply for the individual but for the social order as well. The "attack upon Christendom" is not just a good title for the pamphlets that Kierkegaard produced during his last few years. It is a central theme of his authorship that begins at least as early as *Fear and Trembling,* which suggests that Hegelian philosophy fits European Christendom all too well as the ideology that legitimizes its powerful tendencies to talk much of God while deifying itself.

This account of the religious stage brings the Kierkegaardian text into direct contact with Marx. Silentio's account of the religious as the teleological suspension of every *Sittlichkeit* does not deny that religion can serve as an opiate, as the ideological legitimation of the status quo. But it sees religion, whenever it plays that role, as having backslid into the merely ethical, and it portrays religion as having its true essence in a critical refusal to identify the laws and customs of one's people with the divine will. *Fear and Trembling,* written in the same year as Marx's *Critique of Hegel's "Philosophy of Right,"* initiates a religiously motivated form of ideology critique.

It is the double *Aufhebung,* personal and corporate, of the ethical in the religious that Anti-Climacus has in mind when he writes,

> Strangely enough, this deification of the established order is the perpetual revolt, the continual mutiny against God. . . . [It] is the invention of the lazy, secular human mentality that wants to settle down and fancy that now there is total peace and security, now we have achieved the highest. . . . Every human being is to live in fear and trembling, and likewise no established order is to be exempted from fear and trembling . . . fear and trembling signify that there is a God—something every human being and every established order ought not to forget for a moment. (PC 88)

The teleological suspension of the ethical raises epistemological questions, and that is where Johannes Climacus comes in. If there is a good and a right higher than that which can be learned from the institutions and practices of my society, how can I know it? In *Philosophical Fragments,* the book to which *Postscript* is the postscript, Climacus presents two very different answers.

One is the Socratic theory of knowledge as recollection. Climacus sees a teleological suspension of the ethical in Socrates, whose questioning of Athens in the service of his god and the Idea clearly challenged the pretensions of Athens to be the ultimate enactment of wisdom. While the Spartans attacked her imperial pride militarily, Socrates attacked it morally.

But on what grounds? In the name of what law was Socrates willing to give honor, but only relative honor, to the laws of Athens as his teacher? Ignoring both the extrarational aspects of Socrates' *daimonion*—his god and the divine sign that sometimes restrained him[15]—and the Socratic ignorance motif, Climacus focuses on the recollection theme. In typically modern fashion, he takes this to be a theory of a priori knowledge quite apart from any explanation in terms of reincarnation and remembrance. The Platonic Idea stands for morally meaningful eternal truth, and recollection theory is the claim that human reason has the capacity to achieve direct awareness of this eternal truth, unmediated by nature (sense perception, bodily desire) or history (social practice). This knowledge is the transcendence of the world that makes possible Socrates' defiance toward his Athenian judges. The teleological suspension of the ethical is grounded in the fact that the truth is within us, that each individual has the capacity for this direct access to the eternal.[16]

Of course this account does not fit Abraham very well, and Johannes de Silentio goes out of his way to emphasize the paradoxical absurdity of Abraham's act (that he did not actually sacrifice Isaac is irrelevant) vis-à-vis human reason. Silentio's refusal simply to dismiss Abraham (and with it the Jewish and Christian traditions, according to which he is the father of the faithful) forces the question, What is human reason?

There seem to be three answers. First, human reason is now and always has been the ultimate standard of the good and the right; second, it is now, but has not always been such a standard; and third, it is not now and never has been such a standard.

The first of these we can call Platonic or ahistorical rationalism. It is the view we have just encountered as the recollection theory, of which there are many varieties, according to which human reason can disengage itself from its entanglement with the senses and its social context and attain a direct apprehension of eternal truth.

The second we can call Hegelian or historical rationalism. According to it human reason is inextricably tied to its sociohistorical perspective. It achieves absolute knowledge or ultimate authority only when the social order of which it is the expression has itself become absolute. Hegelian rationalism thus has a realized eschatology built into it, the claim that in modernity, history has attained its goal, that the Kingdom of God has come, and we are it. Complacent Christendom (Judge William) and triumphalist Hegelianism seem made for each other.

Perhaps it is because he has read *Fear and Trembling* and sees that neither of these two accounts fits Abraham very well that Climacus asks about a third possibility and formulates the question, What would it take to go beyond Socrates? By making Platonic rationalism his point of reference rather than Hegelian, he makes two points. First, so far as the present age is concerned, both involve the claim that human reason is the ultimate standard of truth and goodness. To go beyond one is to go beyond both. In this respect the two views are not essentially different.

But, second, in another respect they are. A teleological suspension of the ethical is possible according to the Platonic view, but not according to the Hegelian. According to the Platonic view, every historical society stands under the judgment of the Idea, and every Athens needs its Socratic gadfly.[17] But according to the Hegelian view, by the time human reason actually attains knowledge, the society to which it belongs has itself become the embodiment of reason and stands in no need of essential critique. Hegelian rationalism turns out not even to be religious but only, like Judge William, a version of the ethical that talks a lot about God. So much for its claim to be the only conceptually adequate expression of Christianity. It claims to be the best baseball team in town, while the game it plays turns out to be tennis.

Let us remember what Climacus's assignment is in the pseudonymous authorship. It is to present (not prove or promote) the religious stage. Now Platonic rationalism is a way of being religious, but it leaves Abraham in the lurch, and with him the Jewish and Christian traditions (with all their similarities and differences), according to which he is a paradigm of faith. It would seem that the religious stage must have some non-Platonic form. To be an alternative to Plato, this form will have to deny the recollection theory; but in order to be religious it cannot simply be the skeptical or historicist view that we have no access to eternal truth. (That view, too, would leave Abraham a murderer.) What is needed is an answer to the question, How are we in touch with the eternal? that keeps alive the possibility of social critique (contra Hegel) without confusing Abraham (and with him the Jewish and Christian traditions) with Plato. Just as Silentio's account of the religious is a challenge to the Marxian claim that it is nothing but ideology, so Climacus's account of the religious is a challenge to the Nietzschean claim that Christianity is nothing but Platonism for the masses.

Climacus finds his alternative in the biblical notion of revelation as presupposed by the Abraham story and developed throughout the Christian tradition. What unaided human reason cannot achieve for itself, God gives to us as a gift. Like Silentio, Climacus recognizes that this version of the religious will be offensive and paradoxical to the rationalist version. But that the two are at odds is an argument against the revelational view only on the assumption that human reason has been established as the ultimate arbiter of truth (PC 37–54, especially 52). But has that been established? Much like Socrates, Climacus asks this question without answering it.

These two versions of the religious will reappear in *Postscript* as Religiousness A and Religiousness B. This is not surprising, for *Postscript* is a postscript to *Fragments,* a further analysis of issues raised or suggested by the earlier work. It is time to turn to our main agenda, not overlooking the anti-Hegelian satire involved in Climacus's two titles. In an age when "science" and "system" were the philosophical buzzwords, only a nonconformist with a sense of humor would publish a philosophical treatise called *Fragments.* And then, to write a postscript to the tidbits (an alternative translation to "fragments"), and to make it several times longer than

the tidbits, and to go out of one's way to label it "unscientific"—
who said philosophy cannot be fun?

I N O T E S

1. *Hegel's Phenomenology of Spirit,* trans. A. V. Miller (Oxford: Clarendon Press, 1977), 4–7.

2. Ibid., 16–17.

3. Ibid., 49.

4. The "existentialism" of the authorship does not share the Sartrean view that existence precedes essence and its corollary that norms are always derivative from human choices. This is especially clear in *Sickness unto Death,* whose therapeutic point of view clearly invokes a normative understanding of human nature. See Jean-Paul Sartre, "Existentialism Is a Humanism," in *Existentialism from Dostoevsky to Sartre,* ed. Walter Kaufmann (New York: New American Library, 1975), 345–69.

5. *Hegel's Phenomenology of Spirit,* 50–51, 56–57.

6. Ibid., 2, 7, 12.

7. Here, as in §33 of *Being and Time* (trans. John Macquarrie and Edward Robinson [New York: Harper & Row, 1962]), assertion is a derivative mode of interpretation.

8. EO 1:304, 324, 328, 334–35, 339, 346, 351–52, 354, 362, 368, 380, 394, 415, 421, 434, and 445.

9. The aesthetic stage is closely linked to romantic irony, a target of critique in Kierkegaard's dissertation. There he writes, "Boredom is the only continuity the ironist has. Boredom, this eternity devoid of content, this salvation devoid of joy, this superficial profundity, this hungry glut. . . . That both Germany and France at this time have far too many such ironists and no longer need to be initiated into the secrets of boredom by some English lord . . . surely no one will deny" (CI 285).

10. See Charles Norris Cochrane, *Christianity and Classical Culture* (New York: Oxford University Press, 1957), 478–516.

11. If the man of practical reason (and in Aristotle's case the term "man" here is quite definitely not gender neutral) is not defined by his conformity to a right reason that can be specified without reference to him, he can only be defined by social approbation. Those men whom a particular society takes as its models become ipso facto the standard of virtue. There can be a moral critique of individuals who do not live up to the ideals embodied in these men, but there can be no critique of those ideals. Without realizing it, Aristotle gave to his ethics the conservatism and relativism that would later be known as historicism.

12. In both his *Philosophy of Right* (trans. T. M. Knox [Oxford: Clarendon Press, 1942]) and his *Philosophy of Mind* (trans. William Wallace and A. V. Miller [Oxford: Clarendon Press, 1971]) (a better translation of the German *Geist* would be *Spirit*), Hegel moves from two abstract understandings of the moral life, a Lockean theory of rights and a Kantian theory of conscience, to a concrete account of ethical life (*Sittlichkeit*) in terms of the institutions of family, civil society (the private economic sector), and the state. For illuminating accounts, see chapter 14 of Charles Taylor's *Hegel* (Cambridge: Cambridge University

Press, 1975) and Allen Wood's *Hegel's Ethical Thought* (Cambridge: Cambridge University Press, 1990), especially chapters 11–13. For Hegel's theory of marriage in particular, see chapter 3 of Westphal, *Hegel, Freedom, and Modernity* (Albany: SUNY Press, 1992).

13. Hegel's own account of marriage is built around this *Aufhebung* of sex as "the external embodiment of the ethical bond." See §§161–68 of *Philosophy of Right*.

14. For a detailed argument to this effect, see chapter 5 of Westphal, *Kierkegaard's Critique of Reason and Society*.

15. See chapter 2 of W. K. C. Guthrie, *Socrates* (Cambridge: Cambridge University Press, 1971); and chapter 2 of Paul Friedlander, *Plato: An Introduction* (New York: Harper and Row, 1964).

16. For a fuller account of this link between *Fear and Trembling* and *Philosophical Fragments,* see Westphal, "Johannes and Johannes: Kierkegaard and Difference" in Perkins, ed., *International Kierkegaard Commentary: Philosophical Fragments and Johannes Climacus.*

17. This is why Socrates can be Climacus's hero in *Postscript* while quite definitely not being the hero of *Fragments.*

P A R T
T W O

Commentary

Preface and Introduction (Pages 5–17)

Climacus praises the other pseudonyms for not misusing their prefaces to tell their readers what they are supposed to get out of their books (252). So it is not surprising that instead of using his own preface to tell the reader what the point of *Postscript* is and why it is important to the public, particularly at the present moment, he uses it to reflect further on his need as an author to keep his distance. This time, however, it is not from the reader individually but collectively, the reader as "the literary world," "the demands of the time," or "the present age" (6, 8).[1]

In keeping with his self-identification as a humorist, he does this ironically by expressing his unbounded delight that his first book, which he refers to throughout the preface and introduction as a "pamphlet," has "aroused no sensation . . . has remained unnoticed," has in fact not even been reviewed (5). This puts him in "the fortunate position of owing no one anything" (6). He has in mind the media, whose attention and approval can make a success, even a sensation, out of a book, but at a price: "One comes to owe them everything" and discovers that one has sold one's soul to "the demands of the times" (6).

Climacus points out that negative reviews do not interfere with an author's freedom. They create no debts. But affirmation tends to be addictive, and favorable notice tends to get its recipient hooked, that is, enslaved to what "they" say is "in" (at the moment, anyway).[2] In an ironic comment on the pride that the Danes were taking in their movement toward a liberal modernity, he writes, "The principle of sociality is precisely illiberal" (8).[3]

In other words, the voice of "the people" can be as absolute a monarchy as the voice of the king, and an age that prides itself on increasing freedom for the individual may have its own ways of taking back with one hand what it gives with the other. We are reminded of the words of Vigilius Haufniensis, who describes himself as a fetish worshipper who "will worship anyone with equal piety, but with one proviso, that it be made sufficiently clear by a beating of drums that he is the one I must worship and that it is he who is the authority and *Imprimatur* for the current year" (CA 8). Like his pseudonymous colleague, Climacus suggests that what distinguishes liberal society from traditional society is not that it has replaced authority with autonomy, but that its authorities are anonymous and rapidly replaced by new ones.

In the same spirit, the introduction introduces us not to the book's conclusions but to its task and to the dangers inherent to that task. The two key words are "dialectic" and "faith." At the conclusion of *Fragments,* Climacus had promised "that in the next section of this pamphlet, if I ever do write it, I intend to call the matter by its proper name and clothe the issue in its historical costume" (PF 109). Now he ridicules this task as absurdly easy, "since this costume is provided merely by mentioning the word 'Christianity'" (17). Climacus thinks "that not every young graduate in theology would have been capable of presenting the issue with even *the same dialectical rhythm* with which it is done in the pamphlet," but with regard to the sequel, he is sure "that every young graduate in theology will be capable of writing it— provided he is capable of imitating *the intrepid dialectical positions and movements.*" This is crucial, since "*the dialectical is nevertheless the vital power in the issue,*" and we fall into illusion if we ignore what "*naked dialectical deliberation shows,*" which is all too easy, since "*dialectical intrepidity is not easily acquired*" (10–12, my emphasis). The historical reference is easily supplied; the hard part is dialectical clarity.

Since Climacus immediately puts dialectic in opposition to "speculative thought" (13), it appears that the anti-Hegelian polemic for which *Postscript* is famous is already under way, as indeed it is. It may seem ironical that a polemic against Hegel should be waged in the name of the dialectical, but it is important to notice that Hegel, too, distinguishes dialectic from speculation and that Climacus's account is textbook Hegelianism, at least up to a point.

The Hegelian textbook, of course, is *The Encyclopedia of the Philosophical Sciences,* the first volume of which gives us Hegel's Logic.[4] Paragraphs 79–82 are devoted to developing the claim that "With regard to its form, the *logical* has three sides" (§79). These three aspects, or moments, are the understanding, the dialectical, and the speculative.[5]

The understanding is the attempt to comprehend finite things with abstract concepts, which it tries to make into the clear and distinct ideas of Descartes. Clarity is supposed to require distinctness; and so the understanding constantly draws distinctions in order to keep things (and concepts) "in isolation one from another" (§80A). The slogan on its flag is the epigraph of G. E. Moore's *Principia Ethica,* drawn from Bishop Butler, "Everything is what it is, and not another thing."[6]

The dialectical moment in thought and things undermines the urge of the understanding to rest in what is "fixed and ultimate" (§81A1, "ein Festes und Letztes"). It is a skepticism that is "complete despair about everything that the understanding holds to be firm" (§81A2). It sees that nothing finite can be fixed or final, since the nature of everything finite is "its own sublation" because it "passes over, of itself, into its opposite," or because, to speak more bluntly, "it contradicts itself inwardly" (§81A1).

Hegel stresses the internal character of finitude's instability. It passes over "of itself" into its opposite and "contradicts itself." Instead of being what it is and not another thing, it is the other of itself. Thus, for example, the proper understanding of mortality is that finite "life as such bears the germ of death within itself." Similarly, in his *Parmenides,* Plato "deduces the Many from the One, and, notwithstanding that, he shows that the nature of the Many is simply to determine itself as the One" (§81A1). The understanding's neat distinctions between life and death, one and many, tend to collapse. Hegel finds the dialectical spirit in such proverbs as "*Summum ius summa iniuria,* which means that if abstract justice is driven to the extreme, it overturns into injustice," "Pride goes before a fall," and "Too much wit outwits itself" (§81A1).

To use contemporary terms, we can say that as the realm of opposition and contradiction, the dialectical is the realm of difference, otherness, alterity; and as the region in which the fixed determinations of thought dissolve in a flux that permits neither immediacy (*alpha, archè*) nor ultimacy (*omega, telos*), it is a region of undecidability. It is the deconstruction of the desire to bring thought to closure and thus to the repose of eternity rather than the restlessness of time.[7]

It is just that desire, however, that is the strongest impetus in Hegelian thought. So it is not surprising that, unlike Socrates, whose irony and ignorance express the unsurpassability of the dialectical, he designates the speculative or the positively rational as the mode of thought that "apprehends the unity of the determinations of their opposition, the *affirmative* that is contained in their dissolution and in their transition" (§82). It does not deny the dialectical contradictions; rather "it expressly contains the very antitheses at which the understanding [does he not mean the dialectical?] stops short . . . sublated within itself; and precisely for this reason it proves to be concrete and a totality" (§82A).

Hegel does not use the familiar terms "thesis," "antithesis," and "synthesis" to describe the movement of philosophic thought as presented in his Logic.[8] But it is clear that the third moment, the speculative, involves a reconciling of the oppositions, differences, and contradictions that make up the dialectical moment. The centrality of this notion of reconciliation in Hegel's thought plays an important role in Hegel's claim to be an essentially Christian thinker.[9]

Climacus's account of the dialectical, then, is quite thoroughly Hegelian. Generically speaking, it belongs to logic as conceptual analysis in the search for conceptual clarity. Climacus will have a great deal to say about passion, but he makes it clear here that he does not view it as an alternative to conceptual rigor. Specifically, dialectic involves paying attention to conceptual difference, to the otherness and opposition without which no concept can be properly understood. To understand X is to understand what X is not. The underlying assumption is that finite things are not Spinozistic substances. They neither exist in themselves, nor are they conceived through themselves. Concepts can be understood only relationally—that is, in terms of their other—because things exist only in this way. As we have already seen, at the dialectical stage this relationality entails a restlessness for thought, which can find no fixed and final point of reference.

But according to Hegel, dialectical difference is surmounted in speculative identity, or, to speak more precisely, in totality. Thus thought has the character of classical music. Dialectic is the dissonance; speculation is the resolution. First there is tension, built to maximum intensity; then there is release and relaxation. By describing his task as dialectical rather than speculative, Climacus hints that he may not be as eager as Hegel to relax—or, perhaps, that he is as eager as anyone to relax but thinks that the dissonances of human existence are not as easily resolved as the system would lead us to believe. His quarrel with Hegel will not be about the nature of the dialectical but about the move from it to the speculative. He will play Stravinsky and even Schoenberg to Hegel's Mozart and Beethoven.[10]

We have seen an important element of synthesis or reconciliation in *Either/Or* and *Fear and Trembling,* and it may appear that these texts are more speculative than those of Climacus. Judge William, for example, argues that the ethical and the aesthetic modes of life are concentric rather than eccentric, that the ethical does not "detract from" or "annihilate" or "repudiate" or "destroy" the aesthetic, but is a "transfiguration" that will "ennoble" it (EO 2:30–31, 56–61, 253, 271). The aesthetic is not "excluded" but "returns in its relativity" as something "dethroned" (EO 2:177, 226). As in the Hegelian dialectic, the relativized moment is *aufgehoben,* denied the absolute self-sufficiency it at first pretends to, but it is preserved as an essential element in a larger totality.

Similarly, Johannes de Silentio argues that in the teleological suspension (*Aufhebung*) of the ethical, "that which is suspended is not relinquished but is preserved in the higher, which is its *telos*" (FT 54). The ethical is thereby "reduced to the relative," but "it does not follow that the ethical should be invalidated" (FT 70).

Is this a speculative reconciliation of the opposition between first the aesthetic and the ethical and then the ethical and the religious? Hardly. In the first case, the relation between the aesthetic, which takes itself to be absolute, and the ethical, which makes the aesthetic moment relative, is precisely the stark either/or that gives the book its title. The aesthete and Judge William continue to hear each other's life as a dissonant threat to whatever harmony they have found in their own paths. Similarly, when the ethical is relativized by the religious, it "receives a completely different expression, a paradoxical expression — such as, for example, that love to God may bring the knight of faith to give his love to the neighbor an expression opposite to that which, ethically speaking, is duty" (FT 70).[11]

Fear and Trembling is about the unresolved tension between the religious, which reduces the ethical to a relative moment, and the ethical, which takes itself to be absolute. Like *Either/Or* and the writings of Climacus, it is a dialectical rather than a speculative work. There is nothing necessary or inevitable, conceptually or developmentally or historically, about the transitions presented by the pseudonyms. For just this reason it is possible for Climacus to speak of the transition from one sphere to another as a "leap" (12; cf. FT 41–42; PF 43; JC 138).

Climacus's interest in dialectic, difference, and dissonance is the methodological side of his task. Its substantive theme is the nature of faith. When he refers to the "make-believe in which the system has made itself fancy that it knew what faith is" (15), he indicates his own central question, What is faith? In the historical context of a Europe that could still be referred to as Christendom and of a Hegelian philosophy that presented Christianity as the highest form of religion, the generic question *almost* immediately becomes the specific question, What is Christian faith? (In *Postscript,* this "almost" takes almost five hundred pages, throughout which Climacus reflects on faith generically.) Since this was the very thinly disguised central question of *Fragments,* the "sequel" consists not so much in providing the issue with "historical clothing" as in "a new approach to the issue of *Fragments*" (17). And since the nature of faith was also the theme of another Johannes, the pseudonymous de Silentio of *Fear and Trembling,* Climacus explicitly juxtaposes his pamphlet and its postscript to Silentio's emphasis on both the extraordinary difficulty of faith and the absurdity of assuming that one has mastered its movements and is now prepared to "go further."

Anticipating his own analysis, Climacus briefly sketches three approaches to faith that he finds insufficiently dialectical— that is, that reduce the tension of faith too quickly to relaxation. First, he warns against "changing faith into something else, into another kind of certainty," namely, the kind that only achieves probability (11). He is not saying that probability is not enough, that we must have certainty. Rather, he is echoing the Augustinian protest against a Platonic reduction of faith to simply a mode of cognition.

In the *Republic, pistis* (opinion or belief as distinct from knowledge) occurs on the lower half of the divided line and belongs to the sensible world, the cave cut off from the sunlight of reason (*episteme, noesis*).[12] If one brings this frame of reference to the New Testament, where *pistis* is the word for "faith," one easily comes to think of faith as nothing more than an inferior mode of knowing, one directed toward the wrong objects (the sensible as opposed to the intelligible world, or myth as opposed to science) and correspondingly lacking in the certainty and clarity of real knowledge. On the basis of such assumptions, it would make sense to try to "go further" than faith, namely, to knowledge.[13]

In the central books of Augustine's *Confessions,* we find a challenge to this framework, which comes from the central books of the *Republic.* In book 7 Augustine describes his intellectual conversion to Christian faith, a process of overcoming a series of confusions and uncertainties. One of the certainties with which he emerges is that evil "is not a substance [as the Manichees had thought] but a perversity of the will" (book 7, chapter 16). But if evil is a perversity of the will, it is not ignorance, as the Platonic scheme suggests; further, if faith is going to be linked to salvation from evil, it cannot consist simply in greater cognitive certainty and clarity but will have to involve a change of heart.

For Augustine, then, the question of faith and reason cannot be the question of opinion and knowledge but has to be, as he insists throughout the *Confessions,* the question of knowledge, whatever its mode, and that transformation of the will he most frequently identifies as humility. He uses himself as an example. By the end of book 7, he had completed the epistemological task, but he had not yet come to faith. "But I had ceased to have any doubt that there was an incorruptible substance from which came every substance. *I no longer desired to be more certain of you, only to stand more firmly in you"* (8.1, my emphasis). He says to himself, "Well, look. *Now the truth is certain, and you are still weighed down by your burden"* (8.7, my emphasis). What burden? "I was displeased with the worldly life which I was leading" (8.1). Augustine's breakthrough to faith in book 8 is not the movement from *pistis* to *episteme* or *noesis* but the opposite movement, from a certainty already achieved to faith as a whole new way of life, indeed, a whole new framework for interpreting and evaluating his life.

When Climacus warns against turning faith into "another kind of certainty," a lower stage on the divided line of theoretical cognition, he decisively sides with Augustine's understanding of *pistis* against Plato's. The Platonic analogue to faith is not to be found on the divided line but in that "conversion" of the soul (*periagoge*) whereby it turns from the darkness of the cave to the light of the sun.[14] The primary issue is not the degree of certainty but the direction of the will. Climacus has no objection to the epistemological distinction between certainty and uncertainty. He will use it himself. But he is unwilling simply to identify faith with uncertainty until we have taken a close look at the religious life to see whether the Platonic scheme, and its many historical variations, are adequate to what faith is.

A very different danger to the dialectician who would hold fast to the difficulty of faith comes from the orator. Because the orator is a "distinguished speaker" and has "rare gifts" by which to appeal to the imagination, there is the real possibility that he will overwhelm the "dialectical intrepidity" of the listener, which in any case is "not easily acquired." Filled with "admiration" for the great man (whose gender is probably not accidental here), the hearer is first filled with "terror" at the crisis the speaker produces. But then the orator "revives the troubled one, wrests him out of the terror as a mother her child, who feels reassured by the most affectionate caresses—and the poor dialectician goes home dejected" (12). The orator is a rhetorical version of Descartes, who first introduces his reader to a doubt so radical as to shake every foundation but then, just a few pages later, is happily building metaphysical schemes as grand as those which moments before had come tumbling down like the walls of Jericho.

Johannes de Silentio can remember when it was the task of a lifetime to learn how to doubt (FT 6–7), and Johannes Climacus begins his own career with a meditation on whether significant doubt comes as easily as Descartes suggests.[15] For with the speed of lightening Descartes not only doubts everything but goes beyond doubt to certainty. The doubt, it turns out, is only paper doubt, and the metaphysical edifice is a house of cards. The orator takes his hearers through an existential crisis as short-lived and superficial as Descartes's epistemic crisis in order to produce what he is paid for, a quick trip to existential relaxation.

There is more than a small dose of Platonic intellectualism (the first danger) in the work of the orator (the second danger). The way he gets his hearers from terror to the comfort of a mother's caresses is by getting them to agree with him about whatever he is discussing. Comfort is to be found in having the right opinions. About what? Undoubtedly Christianity, for the orator here is clearly not the political orator but the pastor, the priest, the preacher. We are at the beginning of a polemic that Climacus will carry on against the clergy throughout *Postscript.*

The third danger comes from the systematic philosopher, the master of speculative thought—in other words, the Hegelian. Here again there is a double danger, both that the would-be dialectician will be seduced by the "renown" of the philosophical "celebrity" (14) and that the content of the philosophical system will make faith too easy. This happens when "the system presupposes faith as given (a system that has no presuppositions!) Next, it presupposes that faith should be interested in understanding itself in a way different from remaining in the passion of faith" (14), in other words, that faith's chief goal is to surpass itself in knowledge.

In what sense does the Hegelian system presuppose faith as given, as something so automatic that its presence can simply be presupposed? Following contemporary usage, especially deriving from Friedrich Jacobi,[16] Hegel often uses *Glaube* (belief, faith) to refer to an intuitive, immediate knowledge of God. Prior to (that is, independent of) either catechetical instruction or philosophical reflection, everyone has a direct awareness of the divine. In his polemic against those who would elevate such faith against reason—namely, against conceptual analysis and critical reflection in matters of religion—Hegel does indeed treat faith as given. He does not deny the universal presence of faith in this sense but argues that it is so vague and indeterminate that apart from a reflective process in which it receives specific content, it is all but empty. Everything depends on moving from immediacy to the mediation that gives it determinacy.

Climacus's complaint fits Hegel's account of faith in this sense quite precisely. Faith is given, so we can relax on that front and concentrate on getting beyond it to something else. The problem is that Climacus is talking about specifically Christian faith, while in at least two places, Hegel quite explicitly distinguishes faith as this immediacy from Christian faith, which presumably is not treated as given.[17] So it is tempting to say that Climacus is quarreling with "the Danish Hegelians" but not with Hegel himself.

Still, there is an important sense in which Hegel does not escape Climacus's challenge so easily. Perhaps the best example is found in chapter 7 of the *Phenomenology*. Having used the term "faith" earlier, Hegel does not use it here but speaks of "revealed religion" (*die offenbare Religion*). No vague intuitive immediacy is at issue here but rather a Christianity sufficiently determinate to include such themes as incarnation and trinity in its content. Such faith is not explicitly said to be given, something whose presence can simply be presupposed, but there are two senses in which it is treated as if it were. First, there is the historical sense, in which Christian faith is presented as the *fait accompli* of the historical process, having established itself as the highest form of religion.[18]

Second, all the focus of chapter 7 of the *Phenomenology* is on getting from the "imperfect," "incomplete," and "defective" form (*Vorstellungen*), in which religion, even in its highest form, holds the truth, to the truly spiritual and perfected form (*Begriffe*), in which philosophy comprehends it.[19] This is the task; this is what calls for arduous effort. The impression is easily derived that getting to Christian faith, especially at this point in history, is indeed child's play, a task requiring so little effort that one is almost automatically a Christian (unless, of course, one happens to be Jewish). Here, as in the texts where faith means intuitive immediacy, faith is treated as effortless and virtually inevitable; the serious task is getting beyond it to knowledge. Since the deficiency of faith (both as immediacy and as *Vorstellung*) that makes this "going further" necessary is an epistemic deficiency, the Hegelian scheme is perhaps best understood as a modern version of Plato's divided line.

Hegel had already anticipated these results in his preface, where he links the notions of earnestness and serious effort to the work of speculative thought.[20] More importantly, he tells us that what was historically a major achievement becomes, with the passing of time, a mere exercise: "The individual whose substance is the more advanced Spirit runs through this past just as one who takes up a higher science goes through the preparatory studies he has long since absorbed . . . but he has no lasting interest in them. The Single individual must also pass through the formative stages of universal Spirit so far as their content is concerned, but as shapes which Spirit has already left behind, as stages on a way that has been made level with toil."[21]

The herculean achievements of Euclid, Galileo Galilei, and Isaac Newton have become for us the content of elementary highschool and college courses, all of which is presupposed as given (and inadequate) when modern physics goes in search of a unified field theory. This, Climacus fears, is how the faith of Abraham and Augustine is viewed as modern philosophy goes in search of its version of unified field theory, which Hegel calls systematic science. Like Johannes de Silentio, Climacus insists that he is not himself a man of faith. But as a dialectician, he will try to keep the difficulties and dissonances of faith clearly in view and to resist the reduction of faith to child's play.

He concludes his introduction with an important observation, namely, "that the issue is not about the truth of Christianity but about the individual's relation to Christianity" (15). The "objective issue" about the truth of Christianity is bracketed, as we would say today, in order to focus on the "subjective issue" of the individual's relation to Christianity (17). This means, first of all, that *Postscript* does not belong to the philosophy of religion as that discipline is usually conceived. What is most often presented under that name is the long debate in the Western tradition, both historical and contemporary, about the truth value of various religious claims, usually of a generically theistic nature but sometimes more specifically Christian. The debates over the proofs of the existence of God and over the problem of evil stand at the center of this discipline.

By bracketing all such questions, Climacus makes it clear that his project is phenomenological, descriptive rather than evaluative. Well before Husserl and the phenomenological movement of the twentieth century,[22] Climacus recognizes the value of temporarily setting aside certain ultimate truth-questions in order to focus more sharply on other questions. Consistent with this, he will never recommend that anyone should have faith; he will only demand truth in advertising, saying, in effect, If you are going to profess or recommend faith, make sure it is the real thing and not some unreasonable facsimile, a counterfeit faith from which all the difficulty (and greatness) has been removed.

At the same time, by describing his concern as "the subjective issue," he makes it clear that his will be an existential phenomenology, that is, one whose possible bearing on the life of each one who encounters it will be explicit. Phenomenology can be placed in the service of pure theory. But here the question, What is faith? is not being posed as a theme for disinterested and distanciated reflection; it is a question about oneself: "How can I, Johannes Climacus, share in the happiness that Christianity promises" (17)? Clearly Climacus hopes the reader will substitute his or her own name.

This means that Climacus eventually addresses a readership for whom Christian faith is at least, in the language of William James, a "live hypothesis . . . one which appeals as a real possibility to him to whom it is proposed."[23] Does this mean that Climacus (or Kierkegaard, who stages *Postscript* for us), is a religious thinker but not really a philosopher?

It is not easy to draw the line between philosophy and nonphilosophy. It is not even clear that such a project is appropriate, since attempts to draw such a line almost always show themselves to be power plays governed more by interest than by insight. Two facts, however, seem clear. First, Climacus is not writing for everyone. Those for whom Christian faith (or at least some form of religious commitment, since *Postscript* has a lot to say about the religious life generically) is not at least a live option are not those to whom he addresses himself, though they may well find some good reason to read his book and may conclude it was worth the effort.

Second, the fact that not every reader, or even every reader seeking or possessing a Ph.D. in philosophy, will find the issue posed here of interest and import does not tell us that it is not a genuinely philosophical issue. I find probability theory overwhelmingly boring, and I do not give a hoot about its debates. I do not present this fact as a virtue; perhaps it is a defect. But it is hard to see that it has any bearing on the philosophical status of probability theory, even if, as I suspect, many other philosophers share my disinterest. If Kierkegaard's writings are genuinely philosophical, it is because they pose the question that was utterly central for Socrates, namely, With reference to the possibility of eternal happiness, how should I live my life? It is no accident that the whole Kierkegaardian corpus and not just his dissertation on irony is written "with continual reference to Socrates."[24]

I NOTES

1. More or less simultaneously with the writing of *Postscript,* Kierkegaard wrote *Two Ages: The Age of Revolution and the Present Age, A Literary Review,* a lengthy review of a contemporary novel. The critique of "the present age" adumbrated here by Climacus is developed there in considerable detail. For an analysis, see "Kierkegaard's Sociology," in my *Kierkegaard's Critique of Reason and Society.* Johannes de Silentio opens the preface to *Fear and Trembling* with some caustic comments about "our age" (FT 5).

2. Kierkegaard's critique of the media in *Two Ages* and in *The Corsair Affair* can be fruitfully compared with Heidegger's analysis of *das Man* (the they) in *Being and Time* and with Max Horkheimer and Adorno's critique of the culture industry in *Dialectic of Enlightenment,* trans. John Cumming (New York: Continuum, 1982). See also *International Kierkegaard Commentary: Two Ages* and *International Kierkegaard Commentary: The Corsair Affair.*

3. For a magnificent account of the social context of Kierkegaard's writing, including the rise of liberalism in Denmark, see Bruce Kirmmse, *Kierkegaard in Golden Age Denmark.*

4. This version of Hegel's Logic, *The Encyclopedia Logic* (trans. T. F. Geraets et al. [Indianapolis, Ind.: Hackett, 1991]), is often called the "Lesser Logic" to distinguish it from the earlier, larger version, *Hegel's Science of Logic.* I shall cite the former by the paragraph numbers common to all versions. The letter A after a paragraph number signifies the addition, or *Zusatz,* to that paragraph, material from student notes included by Hegel's first editors. A number following the A identifies which of several *Zusätze* is involved in cases where there is more than one.

5. Hegel calls the dialectical the *"negatively rational side"* and the speculative the *"positively rational"* one. In other words, he is working here with Immanuel Kant's distinction between understanding (*Verstand*) and reason (*Vernunft*). The difference is that where Kant sees reason as ending in antinomies, Hegel posits a third moment in which oppositions are overcome or reconciled. There is something essentially Kantian in Climacus's resistance to this move by insisting on the unsurpassability of the dialectical moment.

6. Moore also quotes Butler's maxim on p. 206 of *Principia Ethica* (Cambridge: Cambridge University Press, 1959). The attractiveness of the maxim to Moore is surely related to his attempt to defend a metaphysics of external relations against the theory of internal relations he found in the "Hegelian" writings of F. H. Bradley. See "External and Internal Relations," in his *Philosophical Studies* (Patterson, N.J.: Littlefield, Adams & Co., 1959).

7. Like Climacus, Derrida thinks that Hegel's theory of absolute knowledge betrays this analysis of the dialectical. "Yet," he writes, "all that Hegel thought within this horizon [of absolute knowledge], all, that is, except eschatology, may be reread as a meditation on writing" (*Of Grammatology,* 26). The eschatological or teleological dimension in Hegel's thought is closely related to what he here calls the speculative, where reconciliation prevails over contradiction and the differences among the parts are overcome in the unity of the whole. Since Derrida's theory of writing is the denial of the possibility of such closure, he can be read, like Climacus, as a thinker who affirms Hegel's dialectical mo-

ment against his speculative moment. The same is true of Adorno in *Negative Dialectics.*

8. In the one place he uses this language, he both criticizes Kant for the "unspiritual" character of his thought and praises him for the triadic scheme as "a good introduction to Philosophy" (*Hegel's Lectures on the History of Philosophy,* vol. 3, ed. Robert F. Brown [Berkeley and Los Angeles: University of California Press, 1990], 477–78). Cf. Walter Kaufmann, *Hegel: Reinterpretation, Texts and Commentary* (Garden City, N.Y.: Doubleday, 1965), 168ff., and Hegel's own comment, "Of course, the *triadic form* must not be regarded as scientific when it is reduced to a lifeless schema, a mere shadow, and when scientific organization is degraded into a table of terms. Kant rediscovered this triadic form by instinct, but in his work it was still lifeless and uncomprehended; since then it has, however, been raised to its absolute significance, and with it the true form in its true content has been presented, so that the Notion of Science has emerged" (*Phenomenology,* 29).

9. See chapter 7 of the *Phenomenology* and *Lectures on the Philosophy of Religion,* ed. Peter C. Hodgson (Berkeley and Los Angeles: University of California Press, 1984–85), 3:290–347.

10. This feature of *Postscript* links it powerfully to the French poststructuralism of writers like Derrida, Foucault, and Lyotard. See note 7 above. It also links Climacus to Adorno, whose *Negative Dialectic* is a classic polemic against Hegelian speculation. His great appreciation of Schoenberg in *Aesthetic Theory* is surely no accident.

11. I have altered the punctuation of this passage in keeping with the earlier, Lowrie translation.

12. See the image of the divided line at the end of book 6 and its exposition in the allegory of the cave in book 7.

13. Since *Fear and Trembling* concerns the Jewish faith of Abraham, it might be better to speak of biblical faith; but *Postscript* will define its question in terms of Christianity. For the polemic against "going further," see FT 6–7, 9, 23, 32, 37, 121–23.

14. *Republic,* 515c–521c.

15. This passage appears in a manuscript Kierkegaard did not publish in his lifetime entitled *Johannes Climacus or De omnibus dubitandum est.*

16. See Hegel, *Faith and Knowledge,* trans. Walter Cerf and H. S. Harris (Albany: SUNY Press, 1977), 97–152; and *The Encyclopedia Logic,* §§61–78.

17. *The Encyclopedia Logic,* §63; and *Lectures on the Philosophy of Religion,* 1:159–61. Hegel is less explicit in his *Lectures on the Proofs of the Existence of God,* lectures 1–4, but the careful reader will not confuse faith as immediacy and Christian faith here, either. The *Lectures on the Proofs* are found in vol. 3 of *Hegel's Lectures on the Philosophy of Religion,* trans. E. B. Spiers and J. Burdon Sanderson (New York: Humanities Press, 1962).

18. This sense of historical givenness is perhaps even stronger in the *Lectures on the Philosophy of Religion* and the *Lectures on the Philosophy of World History.* For the latter lectures, see either *Lectures on the Philosophy of World History: Introduction,* trans. H. B. Nisbet (Cambridge: Cambridge University Press, 1975); or *The Philosophy of History,* trans. J. Sibree (New York: Dover, 1956).

19. *Phenomenology,* 462–63, 472, 477; cf. *The Encyclopedia Logic* §§ 1–5.

20. *Phenomenology,* 3, 19–20, 32–33, 35, 43.

21. *Phenomenology,* 16. Cf. 17, where the "enormous labor of world history" makes the individual's task dramatically easier.

22. See Herbert Spiegelberg, *The Phenomenological Movement* (The Hague: Martinus Nijhoff, 1971).

23. William James, "The Will to Believe," in *Essays on Faith and Morals* (Cleveland, Ohio: World Publishing Co., 1962), 33.

24. This is the subtitle of *The Concept of Irony.*

The Objective Issue of the Truth of Christianity (Pages 21–57)

Part 1, which is devoted to the objective issue of the truth of Christianity, takes up 37 pages in the Hongs' translation, while part 2, which is devoted to the subjective issue, requires 561 pages; so it should come as no surprise that part 1 does not address the objective issue for its own sake but only as a foil for introducing and identifying the subjective issue. Climacus develops the contrast in terms of the dialectical tension between *approximation* and *appropriation*.

In presenting the objective issue, he first distinguishes the question of historical truth from the question of philosophical or eternal truth (21). In so doing he evokes the distinction already drawn by Gotthold Lessing, and so central to his own *Fragments,* between historical and metaphysical truth. In the nineteenth century both history and philosophy claimed to be scientific, not because they imitated the experimental and quantitative methods of the natural sciences but because they developed methods that enabled them to achieve the same sort of disinterested objectivity, free from personal bias or communal ideology. The question of religion and science had meant religion and physics in the time of Galileo, and would shortly mean religion and biology in response to Charles Darwin. But in 1846 it was the question of the bearing of historical and philosophical scholarship on religion.[1]

Climacus recognizes that the question of Christianity's truth, usually thought to be a metaphysical question, has built into it the historical question of what Christianity is, what claims are essential to its identity. So the first two sections, devoted to "the historical point of view," address this question (23–24, 37). In a Lutheran context, where the Bible is held to be the standard of truth, this question, What is Christianity? immediately becomes the question, What does the Bible teach? It is the task of historical scholarship to provide the answer. But "with regard to the historical the greatest certainty is only an *approximation*" (23).

It is easy to think here in quantitative terms. Historical claims are never absolutely certain but only more or less probable. The greater the evidence in favor of a hypothesis and the less the evidence against it, the more probable it is. An 80-percent chance of rain will produce more umbrellas than a 20-percent chance.

Climacus, however, treats the problem of probability or approximation as a qualitative problem. Objectivity requires that one withhold judgment until the evidence is in, but it is never in in any final and definitive sense. The process of historical scholarship is open-ended, passing from generation to generation, laying aside old questions only to take up new ones. Climacus uses the image of a parenthesis to signify the gap between promise and fulfillment in relation to historical scholarship, which always tells us it is not yet finished (26–32). During the process the odds in favor of any particular hypothesis may rise or fall quantitatively, but the qualitative gap between an ongoing temporal process and its completion is never closed. Or, to put it a little differently, the issue is not about the amount of evidence but about the temporal character of human existence. The problem is not out there in the world (Is there enough evidence out there?) but in here, in the observer (Can I ever bring the debate over the evidence to a conclusion?). The need for decision remains. As John D. Caputo puts it, "Undecidability does not detract from the urgency of decision; it simply underlines the difficulty."[2]

But what if the question, What is Christianity? could be answered not by turning to the Bible but by turning to the Church? "The difficulty with the New Testament as something past now seems to be canceled by the church, which is indeed something present" (38–39). The Catholic Church has a theory of this kind (34), but writing in Lutheran Denmark, Climacus turns to a Protestant version associated with the contemporary church leader N. F. S. Grundtvig (36, 44).[3] Can one in this way avoid the "not yet" and "parenthesis" of dependence on interminable historical scholarship?

No, says Climacus. For as soon as the unavoidable question arises, Is this the true, apostolic church? the historical question is opened on another front. We are suspended once again within an open-ended parenthesis because "the approximation is never finished" (38–41, 44).

It is natural, Climacus tells us, to want "to have something really firm and fixed that can exclude the dialectical" (35n), the

tension of unresolved oppositions.[4] Church theory (and by implication any theory that seeks to ground faith in objective knowledge) is rooted in such a need "for something firm with which the
dialectical can be held at bay" (44). In other words, objectivity is
subjectively motivated. Its disinterestedness arises from an interest in avoiding or resolving dialectical dissonance. What is
worse, it is a lapse into superstition. In both of the passages just
cited, Climacus challenges the Enlightenment concept of religious superstition by offering an alternative definition: religion is
superstitious just to the degree that it flees the dialectical, seeking to tame the flux of temporal existence by imposing something
firm and fixed upon it.[5]

Not surprisingly, Climacus accuses these objectivist theories
of confusing faith with knowledge (29). But he adds a special
twist to this when he adds "that faith is abolished in eternity"
(30). This means both that, as we have begun to see, he will suggest that the nature of faith is linked to the temporal structure of
human existence, and that the flight from the dialectical tensions
of temporality is the attempt to flee the human condition, or
worse, the pretense of already having done so. Since he presents
himself as a humorist, we can expect Climacus to find comedy in
this attempt and this pretense.

Before doing so, however, he poses a second problem for objectivism. In the first instance faith does not result from scholarship (23, 25–26) because the scholarly task is essentially and
thus permanently incomplete. But suppose that it could be completed. Climacus is willing to concede this for the sake of argument in order to see what follows. But nothing follows, he claims,
so far as faith is concerned. "Faith does not result from straight-
forward scholarly deliberation, nor does it come directly; on the
contrary, in this objectivity one loses that infinite, personal, im-
passioned interestedness, which is the condition of faith" (29).

It is at this point that the discussion of objectivity becomes
the stage for the presentation of subjectivity. In order to show the
comical misrelation or incongruity between objectivity and faith
(24, 25n 43), it is necessary to specify further what faith is. Climacus makes three suggestions.

First, faith is rooted in interest. This puts it immediately at
odds with objectivism in all its forms, since what they have in
common is the ideal of disinterested reflection (22). Climacus
regularly identifies the interest of faith as *infinite, personal, passionate, interest.* To call it infinite is to say that it is, in the language of Paul Tillich, one's ultimate concern, an interest superior
to, and unconditioned by, all other interests. What makes this

interest infinite for the (potential) believer, as for Socrates of old, is its object, eternal happiness. The assumptions here are that happiness is in any case our highest aspiration and that an eternal happiness would have an absolute value in relation to any temporal happiness.

What makes this interest personal, of course, is that in each case it is the meaning and destiny of *my* life that is at issue. *I* am the one who must live it with some at least implicit relation to the question of eternal happiness, and *I* am the one who must die either with or without the hope of eternal happiness beyond the grave.[6] And since what is at issue is the *meaning and success of my life* — now, in death, and (perhaps) beyond death — this interest could hardly be anything but passionate. One could say that all interests are passions, but an interest that is infinite and personal is bound to be conspicuously passionate if it understands itself with any clarity.

Second, faith is a decision (27, 31, 33–34). As with Augustine, its home lies fundamentally in the will rather than in the intellect. This does not mean that Climacus espouses the problematic notion that we simply decide what we believe. Rather, his point is that in the light of whatever beliefs we may have, however derived and however strongly held, we have to decide whether we will live our lives in the hope of eternal happiness and, if so, on what we will base that hope. We are still in the theory of the stages, exploring the choices open to us among various ways of structuring our lives.

Finally, faith is subjectivity or inwardness. These two terms are introduced as virtually interchangeable and as essentially synonymous with spirit (33, 43). Inwardness or "inward deepening" (37) is "the subject's transformation within himself" (38). In other words, it is the self's relation to itself rather than to that which is outside itself. As such inwardness, subjectivity is the root of decision (33–34).[7]

Faith as interested decision rising out of the self's inner relation to itself is the religious act of appropriation. Here the objective content of religion is transmuted into the very form of personal existence; doctrine becomes lifestyle. Far from providing support to faith, objectivism leads the individual to the place where faith is not even possible. While faith is interested, objectivism teaches the self to become disinterested (21–22, 29, 31). While faith is decision, objectivism teaches that the decision must be postponed until the final results are in (27, 31). And while faith is subjectivity and inwardness, objectivism confuses faith with knowledge and teaches that faith is one's relation to "a sum total of propositions" (37).

Objectivism assumes that the hard part is its chosen task and that "if only the objective truth has been obtained, appropriation is an easy matter; it is automatically included as part of the bargain" (22; cf. 46). Following Augustine, Climacus disputes this, suggesting that making faith as appropriation an effortless result of knowledge as an approximation that never terminates is simply a clever ruse for avoiding the "risk" involved in "choice" (42) and for holding dialectical tension "at bay" (44). For if faith does not automatically result from knowledge as the (hypothetically conceded) completion of the tasks of objective scholarship, it surely does not automatically result from the most recent, controversial, and incomplete stage of that process.

Climacus concludes his discussion of the objective issue by addressing two attempts to establish objectively the truth of Christianity. The first keeps us in the realm of historical knowledge. It is called "the evidence of the centuries for the truth of Christianity." Since this matter was treated at length in chapters 4 and 5 of *Fragments,* the reader is referred to that discussion after only the briefest of treatments.

Finally we get to "the speculative point of view," an attempt to establish the metaphysical truth of Christianity metaphysically. With regard to historical truth, Climacus had raised two objections: the approximation process is never completed, meaning that there are never any final, assured results of research on which to base faith; and faith as appropriation is not the sort of thing that results from objective knowledge, even if we could achieve it. With regard to the Hegelian system, Climacus never tires of tweaking its nose for not being finished (13, 76–77, 106–9, 119–24, 145), and in a footnote to the passage we have just been considering, he suggests that speculative thought is the same comical attempt to deny its own essentially temporal incompleteness that we found in examining historical knowledge as the alleged ground of faith (33–34n).

But here he focuses on the second point, the incommensurability of faith as infinite, personal, passionate interest and speculative thought, even if it could be what it claims to be (51–56). Thus, if someone says "that he builds his eternal happiness on speculative thought, he contradicts himself comically, because speculative thought, in its objectivity, is indeed totally indifferent to his and my and your eternal happiness" (55). Here the problem is not that the system is not finished but that it never

raises the question of the choice confronting each individual concerning the categories in which to build his or her life or the question of personal life after death.

The "misrelation" (55) between speculative thought and faith
shows itself when the former assumes that we are all Christians
and, instead of concerning itself with whether this or that individual accepts Christianity, devotes itself entirely to "going further" by "permeating it with thought" (52, 50).[8] Here we get the
first concrete satire of *Postscript*. An unfortunate fellow begins to
doubt whether it is "quite right for him to call himself a Christian." His friends become hostile at his making "so much ado
about nothing; why can't he be like the rest of us, who are all
Christians. He is just like F. F., who does not want to wear a hat,
as the rest of us do, but has to be eccentric" (50). His wife is even
more emphatic. "You are Danish, aren't you? Doesn't the geography book say that the predominant religion in Denmark is
Lutheran-Christian? You aren't a Jew, are you, or a Moham-
medan? What else would you be, then? . . . Don't you tend to your
work in the office as a good civil servant; aren't you a good subject
in a Christian nation, in a Lutheran-Christian state? So of course
you are a Christian" (50–51).

Since it is not obvious that these friends and this wife are speculative thinkers, we might wonder how this joke is at the expense of
the speculative point of view, as it purports to be. So Climacus immediately explains, "Lo, we have become so objective that even the
wife of a civil servant argues from the whole, from the state, from
the idea of society, from geographic scienticity to the single individual" (51). In other words, whether or not she has heard of Hegel,
she thinks like a Hegelian, reducing the individual to a function of
the social totality to which he or she belongs.

At least two things are going on here. First, Kierkegaard likes
to present philosophies of life concretely in personages who show
what it would be like to live them. So in *Either/Or,* he stages the
aesthetic and the ethical by having A, the seducer, and Judge William enact them, while in *Fear and Trembling* Silentio presents
faith in the person of Abraham. Here Climacus does the same by
having the friends and the wife act out the Hegelian perspective
as he understands it. If we are to choose intelligently among the
forms of life available to us, we must not represent them to ourselves as verbal slogans or abstract concepts but as the most concrete possible modes of human action. Climacus presents
Hegelianism to us as the wife who argues that her husband must
be a Christian because he is a respectable civil servant living in

Denmark. The presentation is like a political cartoon. It is caricature, but to the degree that it rings true, it is devastating critique.

Second, in the footnote on Hegel mentioned earlier, Climacus
refers to "a speculative and almost Hegelian public" (34n). The
suggestion, and we find it throughout the Kierkegaardian corpus,
is that there is an important isomorphism between Hegelian
thought and Danish society. The point of drawing this parallel is
not to call attention to the obvious fact of Hegel's strong impact on
Danish culture at this time.[9] In terms of explaining the relationship, the movement might be in just the opposite direction; that
is, Danish culture might have reached out to Hegel because it recognized itself in his thought. The point is about congruity, not
about causality. It is to suggest that Hegelian thought is a powerful ideological reflection of Danish society, a mirror in which the
latter can see itself presented as the embodiment of reason.

This means that, as in *Fear and Trembling,* the critique of
the speculative point of view is already an attack upon (Danish)
Christendom. Climacus is engaged in an ideology critique very
similar to that of Marx, except that according to his diagnosis the
pathology of modernity does not lie in capitalism; it is a spiritual
rather than a material disease.[10]

This has a consequence overlooked in those interpretations
of Kierkegaard's writings that view them as embodying an apolitical or asocial individualism, a privatistic withdrawal of interest from the public domain.[11] Ideology critique is a political act.
Its diagnostic negations of the established order are always at
least implicitly prescriptive affirmations of an alternative. The
fact that one affirms the importance of the individual (as Climacus has already done in his analysis of faith as interest, as decision, and as subjectivity or inwardness) does not mean that one
does not care about community or that one devalues the public
sphere. Classical political liberalism, for example, is a clearly political affirmation of the individual.

Climacus is neither a Lockean nor a Marxist. From his point
of view, it would be dogmatic liberalism to talk as if the "possessive individualism" of Locke were political theory, while the religious individualism he juxtaposes to Hegel and an "almost
Hegelian" public is not; just as it would be dogmatic Marxism to
talk as if materialist ideology critique were a form of social theory,
while his spiritual ideology critique is not.[12] Of course, if my eternal happiness is my ultimate concern, then our temporal welfare
cannot be my ultimate concern. But then again, would it not be
dogmatic to say that only those accounts that make political life

our highest destiny are to count as political theory? According to that account, Plato's *Republic* would be a piece of apolitical individualism.

Before concluding the brief section on speculative objectivism, Climacus introduces two more very concrete images, one expressive of the speculative, the other contrastingly expressive of faith. The first image is that of the gods, whose "blissful pastime of thinking" Aristotle presents as the paradigm of happiness (56). Hegel's system culminates in a quotation of the passage from Aristotle's *Metaphysics* (21.7) that portrays God as thought thinking itself,[13] and Climacus suggests that the speculative thinker tries to be an Aristotelian-Hegelian god: If "the question of his personal eternal happiness cannot come up at all, [this is] precisely because his task consists in going away from himself more and more and becoming objective and in that way disappearing from himself and becoming the gazing power of speculative thought. . . . But note that the blessed gods, those grand prototypes for the speculative thinker, were not in the least concerned about their eternal happiness." In other words, the speculative thinker "wants to be exclusively eternal within time" in spite of the fact that "a human being is a synthesis of the temporal and the eternal" (56; cf. SUD 13).[14] Hegel represents a flight from the reality of the human condition as temporal.

The other image reintroduces as central to *Postscript* a trope that was crucial to *Fragments,* the metaphor of faith as erotic love (PF 25–36; and offense as unhappy love, 49). Objectivity is as inappropriate to faith as it is to erotic love, not because it presupposes an "object" where there is none but because it takes up an attitude, disinterested and detached, that is foreign to the relationships in question and thus fatal if elevated above the passion and commitment essential to both (53). A marriage, of course, is a historical phenomenon, something outward and observable; but the love that gives it whatever life it has is an inwardness not available to someone primarily given over to the objectivity of observation (54). Thus, if a social scientist were to treat his or her marriage more as a datum for psychological or sociological analysis than as a relationship to be built and a task for spiritual growth, it would be hard to know whether to laugh or cry. But we would surely have before us a parody and not a true marriage. Climacus suggests that in the same way, to make the essential task of faith a cognitive one is to make a joke out of faith. If we want to understand what it means to be a believer, we will have to think carefully about what it means to be a lover.

∎ N O T E S

1. Perhaps the best contemporary equivalent would be Carl Sagan's belief that we come to know who we are and what our destiny is by means of natural science. I am indebted to Steve Evans for this suggestion.

2. John D. Caputo, *Against Ethics* (Bloomington: Indiana University Press, 1993), 4.

3. See 2:189n. 44. For a thorough treatment of Grundtvig, see chapter 13 of Kirmmse's *Kierkegaard in Golden Age Denmark.*

4. Derrida's critique of the philosophical aspiration for presence, origin, center, etc., is a critique of the attempt to replace the dialectical with the speculative. See "Structure, Sign, and Play in the Discourse of the Human Sciences," in *Writing and Difference.*

5. John Caputo develops precisely this interpretation of Kierkegaard's *Repetition* in his *Radical Hermeneutics.* He then goes on to link this understanding of Kierkegaard with Derridean deconstruction. The themes of deferral and undecidability in Climacus's account here can equally be related to those themes in Derrida's account of *différance* as developed, among other places, in his essay "Différance," in *Margins,* in spite of the fact that the former is developed in terms of truth, while the latter is developed in terms of meaning.

6. In *Being and Time,* Heidegger shows that both these dimensions of the question can be developed generically, without specific reference to the Christian context in which Climacus places them. See §§9, 12, 46–53.

7. The linkage between the self's relation to itself and the self's freedom is developed by Anti-Climacus in *Sickness unto Death.*

8. See the discussion in the previous chapter of the system presupposing faith as given.

9. For detailed analysis, see Kirmmse, *Kierkegaard in Golden Age Denmark.*

10. For a more detailed analysis of ideology critique in the writings of Climacus, see chapter 7 of my *Kierkegaard's Critique of Reason and Society.*

11. For example, see Martin Buber, "The Question to the Single One," in *Between Man and Man,* trans. Ronald Gregor Smith (New York: Macmillan, 1965); Adorno, *Kierkegaard: Construction of the Aesthetic;* and Mark C. Taylor, *Journeys to Selfhood: Hegel and Kierkegaard* (Berkeley and Los Angeles: University of California Press, 1980).

12. For Lockean "possessive individualism," see C. B. Macpherson, *The Political Theory of Possessive Individualism* (London: Oxford University Press, 1962). For an example of a tendency to insist that ideology critique must be materialist in order to count as such, see Stephen Best and Douglas Kellner, "Modernity, Mass Society, and the Media: Reflections on the *Corsair* Affair," in Perkins, ed., *International Kierkegaard Commentary: The Corsair Affair.* For a brief introduction to "spiritual" ideology critique in Albert Camus, see my *Kierkegaard's Critique of Reason and Society,* 40–42.

13. *Hegel's Philosophy of Mind,* 315. This is the third part of the *Encyclopedia of the Philosophical Sciences.*

14. In this context "synthesis" does not have the Hegelian meaning of reconciliation, resolution, and relaxation but rather the opposite meaning of a "spiritual tension" from which we can flee but never (in this life) escape. See Taylor, *Journeys to Selfhood,* 172–79; and John Elrod, *Being and Existence in Kierkegaard's Pseudonymous Works,* 29–71.

CHAPTER

S   I   X | The Subjective Issue—
Something about Lessing
(Pages 63–125)

A partial outline of *Postscript* would look like this, with the numbers showing the number of pages in the Hongs' translation:

Part 1 (37)

Part 2 (561)

    Section 1 (63)

    Section 2 (494)

It is clear that Climacus loves wildly unequal dyads, with the second of two elements being many times longer than the first.

In both cases the two unequal divisions might be compared to the exposition and development sections of a musical movement in sonata-allegro form. The first introduces the main themes, while the second continually repeats them in somewhat altered form (A returns as A'), in different keys, and in different contextual relations to each other, so that one is always hearing the same motifs but never in quite the same way. To say that Climacus composes his text musically is to say that repetition belongs to his artistry as much as it does to that of Haydn, Mozart, and Beethoven. This is not to say that his repetitions are all equally successful or that his text would not have benefited from some hardnosed editing. But it is to suggest an approach to a text that continually reworks a relatively small number of basic ideas.

The brief first chapter of section 1, "An Expression of Gratitude to Lessing" (once again much shorter than chapter 2, which develops four theses related to Lessing), opens with a satire on holding to ideas because some famous person, in this case Lessing, has espoused them, and insists that Climacus is not using Lessing as an authority figure to appeal to as "a first step toward getting the majority vote on one's side" (63, 66). But Climacus admits to being powerfully drawn to the clarity with which Lessing understands that people can relate to the Deity "only one at a time" and that no one's God-relation can be in any essential way mediated by another human being, much less by "the jostling crowd" (65–67).

But a pang of uncertainty interrupts his enthusiasm—"if only it is certain that this is how it is with Lessing—if" (65). So he makes it clear that his reflections do not claim to be what Lessing actually intended, as a question of objective scholarship, but are expressions of what he finds by way of subjective appropriation when he reads Lessing. In effect, he makes the historical Lessing into a pseudonym in order to read him as he (Climacus) and others, including Kierkegaard, suggest reading the pseudonymous literature. Authorial intention is supplanted by the reader's appropriation when Climacus says, "I now intend to present something that I shall, what the deuce, ascribe to Lessing, without being certain that he would acknowledge it" (72). Kierkegaard, who wrote that what matters is appropriating the truth "whether it is spoken by Balaam's ass or a sniggering wag or an apostle or an angel," would approve (JP 5.5646). As in *Fragments* and in the discussion about to occur in *Postscript,* the human teacher bears only a maieutic relation to the human pupil. Lessing "teaches" Climacus about subjectivity as Socrates "teaches" the slave boy in the *Meno* a version of the Pythagorean theorem. This kind of teaching becomes the opening theme, which Climacus wishes to develop.

The first of the four theses attributed to Lessing in chapter 2 is brief: *The subjective existing thinker is aware of the dialectic of communication* (72). This means that such a thinker will consciously avoid relying on direct communication. In attending carefully to what Climacus says about the difference between direct and indirect communication, we must be careful not to confuse him with Kierkegaard. Both are intensely interested in this difference, and on this—as on so many points—they are often in agreement, as can be seen by comparing what Climacus says with what Kierkegard writes under his own name. But Kierkegaard often speaks as if the two forms of communication correspond to the difference between pseudonymous and nonpseudonymous writing. This makes his nonpseudonymous religious writings a form of direct communication, including both the *Eighteen Upbuilding Discourses,* which were written and published alongside the pseudonymous authorship, and such postpseudonymous texts as *Works of Love* and *Purity of Heart.* But this is clearly at odds with the way Climacus here defines direct communication.[1]

We see this immediately when we see Climacus equate direct communication with objective thinking, "completely indifferent to subjectivity and thereby to inwardness and appropriation" (75). This kind of thinking and communication, the antithesis of all of Kierkegaard's writings, is oriented toward certainty, security, and comfort (74n) and is therefore much more concerned with results than with process (73–74, 78). It is governed by the notion of transferring information from one place to another. Communication has occurred when "one person states something and another acknowledges the same thing verbatim" (74). (See Climacus's scorn for "reeling off the results and answers" [73] and the critique of learning "by rote" in chapter 2 above.) Learning consists in "ignorance liquidation" rather than "consciousness formation."[2]

Objective thinking has its place (76n), but it is a social event linking two selves in the act whereby one directly gives to the other what is essential. When it comes to the religious and the God-relation, appropriation cannot have this form but requires an inwardness that is a form of isolation vis-à-vis other selves (73 and 73n). In this context the (human) communicator must focus everything on "setting the other free" (74) for a God-relationship that is "a secret" free from the "meddling busyness of a third person," since it is a mistake to think "that some other human being needs one's assistance in his God-relation, as if God were not able to help himself and the person involved" (77–78).

What kind of communication is it whose goal is to set the other free, that knows that "individuals must be held devoutly apart from one another and must not run coagulatingly together in objectivity" (79)? Its name, given here only by implication, is indirect communication. But what does that mean? In a journal entry from 1847 on "the dialectic of communication," Kierkegaard gives three headings under which "instruction in the ethical as an art" is to be grasped (JP 1.649, p. 273):

Indirect Communication

Double Reflection

The Maieutic[3]

Perhaps he learned this linkage from Climacus, who here explains indirect communication in terms of both the maieutic and double reflection. Already in *Fragments* Climacus had drawn attention to Socrates' insistence that he is only a midwife and cannot give birth to wisdom in another, a claim closely related to his admission that he is never a teacher but always only a fellow learner.[4] According to Climacus, he held this view "because he perceived that this relation [of midwife] is the highest relation a human being can have to another" (PF 10). Thus, "the person who by Socratic midwifery gave birth to himself . . . in a more profound sense owed no human being anything" (PF 19).

Based on both of the hypotheses explored in *Fragments,* the human "teacher" can at most be the occasion of learning. According to the Socratic assumption that knowledge is recollection and the truth is already within the learner, the slave boy from the *Meno,* for example, must see for himself that the diagonal will generate a square with twice the area of the given square. Socrates cannot see this for him, and if boy merely memorizes the answer and recites it by rote, this will not count as knowledge. According to the contrary assumption—that knowledge is revelation and the truth is not already within the learner but must be given by God as the teacher-savior, along with the condition for recognizing it as the truth—the human teacher is equally impotent. Thus either no one or only God can give the truth to the learner. While the first learner is epistemically self-sufficient and the second learner anything but, the human teacher remains in both cases no more than a midwife whose assistance always falls short of giving knowledge to another. But this, put in other words, is simply the impossibility of direct communication.[5]

Although Climacus does not repeat all this here, he reminds us of it by suggesting that when Socrates, "on account of his daimon, isolated himself from any and every relation and . . . presumed that everyone had to do it that way, such a life-view would essentially become a secret or an essential secret, because it could not be communicated directly; at most he was capable of artistically, maieutically helping another person. . . . Everything subjective, which on account of its dialectical inwardness evades the direct form of expression, is an essential secret . . . [because] such a form of communication [namely, indirect or maieutic] corresponds to and renders the existing subject's own relation to the idea" (80).

In *Fragments* the goal was to find a way of going beyond Socrates; but in *Postscript* Socrates emerges as a hero, and for quite understandable reasons. Who better to throw a monkey wrench into the self-containment of Hegelian spirit or the comfortableness of Danish Christendom than a Socrates who maintains a private, essentially secret relation to the god (his daimon) and to the idea. Like Abraham in *Fear and Trembling,* whose God-relation disrupted the linguistic community he normally shared with Sarah and Isaac (see problema 3), Socrates disrupts the Athenian *Sittlichkeit.*

In other words, the theory of indirect communication as explicated in terms of the maieutic is a form of social critique directed against an all too Hegelian Christendom that views itself as a linguistic or cognitive totality, self-sufficient and thereby immune from anything outside it. It is only the critique of epistemic-social totality that is developed here, and it is easy to think that what we have is an existentialist individualism set against the various forms of modern mass society. This may be the case for Climacus, whose fictional status allows him the luxury of being one-sided. But if Kierkegaard uses Climacus to deconstruct the totalizing tendencies of modernity in one of its modes, it is not to leave the individual, thus reflected out of the universal, alone with a secret relation to the idea. Virtually simultaneously with the writing of *Postscript,* Kierkegaard begins to develop under his own name in *Two Ages* the notion that precisely the individual's private relation to the idea is an essential foundation for an authentically human community (TA 62–63).[6] We are reminded of Kierkegaard's plea that we not identify him with his pseudonyms.

The other part of Climacus's commentary on indirect communication is the notion of double reflection. In immediacy we live our lives thoughtlessly, allowing instinct or habit, inclination or drive, to dictate our actions. Sigmund Freud captures this powerfully, following Georg Groddeck in putting the verb "to live" in the passive voice: "we are 'lived.'"[7] In reflection, by contrast, we become thoughtful. We disengage from our instincts, habits, inclinations, and drives so as to step back from life and take a look at it. It is appropriate that the term "reflection" should make us think of seeing ourselves in a mirror or in a calm lake, for in reflection we do indeed manage to look at ourselves. Reflection is reflexive and is sometimes even called reflexion.

Climacus introduces the notion of reflection into his account of communication in order to underscore in a slightly different way the limits facing the communicator when personal appropriation is at issue. The introduction of "another kind of reflection," so that we then speak of "double reflection," is entirely a matter of "inwardness" and "possession, whereby it belongs to the subject and to no one else" (73).

Climacus gives two descriptions of the first mode of reflection. On the one hand, it is the moment in which the subject "thinks the universal" (73). To become thoughtful about my life is inevitably to employ concepts, to recognize the moment of universality in my particularity. On the other hand, first reflection also includes the moment in which "a thought has gained its proper expression in the word" (76). Without this expressive moment the

theory of reflection could not belong to a theory of communication. First reflection is the double movement from particularity to
universality and from thought to word.

We need not attribute to Climacus the theory that thought is
a realm of prelinguistic meaning and that expression is the trans-
porting of this meaning from inside the self to outside, as if the
two moves just mentioned were sequential rather than simultaneous.[8] A more charitable reading would be that he is using everyday language without intending any theoretical commitments on
that issue. His point is simply that in language reflective universality has the publicity required for communication. Is that all
that is needed? Have I communicated when I have spoken?

Climacus's question does not arise out of the possibility that
one might be misunderstood. He assumes that when thought
gains its "proper expression" in the word, the listener understands what is said. But suppose that what is said is not just a
piece of information, first to be understood and then processed in
the usual way as my instincts and habits, inclinations and drives,
dictate. Suppose, rather, it is a challenge not only to my normal
modes of information processing but also to the modes of behavior that arise out of them. That is what Climacus assumes the religious to be, with the result that the communication process just
described remains radically incomplete if the content has religious import.

What is left out, obviously, is the act of personal appropriation that distinguishes subjectivity from objectivity and indirect
communication from direct communication. A second reflection is
called for, this time on the part of the listener, who must step back
from the normal processes of information processing and decide
how to respond to this challenge. Thus the second reflection is a
matter of "acquiring [the universal content of the communication]
in . . . inwardness" (73), since "it bears upon the intrinsic relation
of the communication to the communicator and renders the existing communicator's own relation to the idea" (76). We may be surprised to read "communicator" instead of "communicatee," but if
the "idea" in question has religious import, it puts both the
speaker and the listener in question. This is why Socrates insisted
that he was not really a teacher but a fellow learner.

This double movement of reflection, first from particularity
and privacy to universality and publicity, and then back to the
inwardness where personal appropriation takes place, is found in
Maurice Merleau-Ponty's famous reinterpretation and reappro-
priation of Husserlian phenomenology. Husserl insists not only

that phenomenology is science but also that it is an eidetic science. The move from fact to essence is fundamental, and phenomenological insight is the intuition of essence [*Wesenserschauung*].[9] Merleau-Ponty affirms this phenomenological essentialism: "Every reduction, says Husserl, as well as being transcendental is necessarily eidetic. That means that we cannot subject our perception of the world to philosophical scrutiny without ceasing to be identified with that act of positing the world, with that interest in it which delimits us, without drawing back from our commitment which is itself thus made to appear as a spectacle, without passing from the *fact* of our existence to its *nature,* from the Dasein to the Wesen."[10]

One can imagine how nervous Climacus would be on hearing this description of how our interest and our commitment "appear as a spectacle" before us. That is the problem with speculation, in his view; it makes disengaged, theoretical observers of us and keeps us so busy trying to comprehend our interests and our commitments that we forget that we are responsible for them, that reflection, always an open-ended and unfinished task for temporal selves, needs to be interrupted by decision.

But Merleau-Ponty agrees that it would be a mistake to end our account of reflection at this point. "The need to proceed by way of essences does not mean that philosophy takes them as its object"—now it is Husserl and Hegel who are getting nervous—"but, on the contrary, that our existence is too tightly held in the world to be able to know itself as such at the moment of its involvement, and that it requires the field of ideality in order to become acquainted with *and to prevail over its facticity.*"[11]

If essences are not my object, this is because knowing myself or becoming acquainted with myself is not an end in itself but a means toward prevailing over my facticity. In other words, in reflection I step back from my life not simply to take a look at it but to take an attitude toward it and to take a shot at presiding over it. If Merleau-Ponty's formulation does not sound particularly religious, that is because there is no hint that presiding over my existence might involve submission to something transcendent, like the idea or the daimon of Socrates. But he does clearly subordinate reflection to self-choice, and that is the point of double reflection for Climacus.

The second thesis that Climacus attributes, "what the deuce," to Lessing is this: "*In his existence-relation to the truth, the existing subjective thinker is just as negative as positive, has just as much of the comic as he essentially has of pathos, and is continually in a process of becoming, that is, striving"* (80). It is clear that Climacus has made technical terms out of the verb "to exist" and the noun "existence." Has he become an "existentialist" while we were not looking?

Perhaps. But the technical use to which he puts these terms is surely not that of Jean-Paul Sartre, who wants to claim that for humans existence precedes essence, that we choose who we are in the sense of having no nature or identity prior to such a choice.[12] By contrast, the account that Climacus gives here (82, 89, 92) of the human self as a synthesis[13] of finite and infinite, temporal and eternal, sounds very much like an account of human nature to which it behooves our choices of self to conform if they are not to represent "an attempt to cease to be a human being" (93). As such, it sounds very much like a philosophical anthropology, something anathema to Heidegger, even when he designates *Dasein* as existence (*Existenz*) and says, *"The essence of Dasein lies in its existence."*[14]

What links Climacus with such "existentialists" as Sartre, Heidegger, and Karl Jaspers is that all make a technical term out of "existence." But each does so in a way distinctively different from the others. Climacus introduces "existence" as a philosophical category in order to protect the question, What is the thinker's relation to the truth? from misunderstanding. So he specifies that the thinker's relation to the truth is an *"existence-relation,"* and he identifies the thinker as *"the existing subjective thinker."*

The previous section has tightly linked the notions of subjectivity with personal appropriation. What is the point of further qualifying the subjective thinker as *"the existing subjective thinker,"* whose relation to the truth is an *"existence-relation"*? Quite simply that the task of appropriation is carried out in time by a thoroughly temporal self, a self that *"is continually in a process of becoming, that is, striving."*

In spite of his own warnings to the contrary, Climacus becomes didactic. "One who is existing is continually in the process of becoming; the actually existing subjective thinker, thinking, continually reproduces this in his existence and invests all his thinking in becoming. This is similar to having style. Only he really has style who is never finished" (86). Existence so construed is expressed by Eros as presented by Socrates in the *Symposium,* where "Poverty and Plenty begot Eros, whose nature is made up of both. But what is existence? It is that child who is begotten by the infinite and the finite, the eternal and the temporal, and is therefore continually striving" (92).

The model of the erotic thinker who has style is Socrates himself. "Even in his seventieth year, he was not finished with his striving" (88). Accordingly, the paradigm of an "existence-relation" to the truth is "a Socratic tryst with the god in the idea on the boundless sea of uncertainty" (88). The assumptions that Climacus shares with Socrates are that there is an infinite and an eternal truth, that the human thinker has an essential relation to it, and that this relationship is severely restricted by virtue of the finitude expressed in the temporality of the thinker as human. It is the first two of these assumptions that distinguish Climacus's postmodernism from the French versions discussed in chapter 2 (as well as from that of Richard Rorty) and that distinguish Kierkegaard, who shares these assumptions, from Nietzsche.

This severe restriction means, for Climacus, that the existing subjective thinker *"is just as negative as positive."* Here the positive stands for certain and final knowledge, the philosophical touchstone of philosophical modernism from René Descartes to Hegel. Whether one seeks to ground such knowledge in sense experience, in historical research, or in philosophical speculation, Climacus claims that "this positive is precisely the untrue" because all forms presuppose "a fictive objective subject," which succumbs to "an illusory termination" of the thinking process and wants, most especially in its speculative mode, to see the world *"sub specie aeterni."* Such a thinker "fancies himself to have a certainty that can be had only in infinitude, in which, however, he cannot be as an existing person but at which he is continually arriving" (81).

The human thinker is a "synthesis . . . an existing infinite spirit. The infinite and the eternal are the only certainty, but since it [this certainty] is in the subject, it is in existence [*Tilvæ-relse*], and the first expression for it is its illusiveness and the prodigious contradiction that the eternal becomes, that it comes into existence [*blive til*]. . . . The existing subject is eternal, but as existing he is temporal. Now, the illusiveness of the infinite is that the possibility of death is present at every moment" (82).

There are several things to note about this remarkable passage. First, the synthesis that makes up the human self as existing infinite spirit is expressed as a "prodigious contradiction." A synthesis that is a contradiction is clearly a dialectical rather than a speculative synthesis (see note 13), a whole whose parts remain in conflict with one another. One moment is not *aufgehoben* in the other, nor is the opposition of the parts *aufgehoben* in the synthesis that unites them. Their endless contention gives rise to permanent tension.

Second, it is the human self in the first instance, and not the incarnate God of *Fragments* and (later in *Postscript*) of Religious-ness B, who is "the prodigious contradiction that the eternal be-comes, that it comes into existence." Already with Socrates, whose ignorance, whose perpetual striving, and whose insistence that the teacher is just another learner all express "the wound of negativity" with shining clarity (84–85), we have the paradox that wisdom appears as madness (83–84) by virtue of the anti-thetical union of time and eternity.

Third, if we, living on the far side of modernity, are all too fa-miliar with the finitude and temporality of all human thought, we may be wondering what all the fuss is about. What is more obvi-ous to us than "the wound of negativity" and, to speak more con-cretely, the primacy of death in everything human? Brought up on John Dewey and Ludwig Wittgenstein and Heidegger, we have abandoned the quest for certainty and the illusions of finality that accompany it. We can scarcely conceal the smile of self-satisfac-tion, for Climacus's polemic against speculative hubris sounds like congratulations to us. "I knew that," we say, not noticing how close our skepticism is to cynicism and nihilism.

But Climacus may be as disruptive to our postmodern com-placency as to that of Hegelian modernism. By insisting on the presence of the infinite and eternal within us (without allowing the Hegelian interpretation that identifies these with *our Sitt-lichkeit*), he resists our attempt to be the one-sidedness that is equal but opposite to modernism. Hegelian complacency requires that one never seriously consider the implications of the fact that the thinker is one who may die at any moment. The equal but opposite complacency of secular postmodernism resides in the confidence that death is the ultimate fact about life. But what if it is not? What if, as Climacus and Socrates suppose, this self, who will surely die, nevertheless has a destiny beyond death? What if our inability as existing selves to transcend the cave does not mean that there is no life in the sunshine toward which we are ordered? What if Kant is right in suggesting that our questions about God, freedom, and immortality are as inescapable as final answers to them are unavailable, that the question, For what may I hope? is as basic as the question, What may I know?[15]

Suddenly Climacus remembers the poor civil servant who became unsure whether he was a Christian. He never wants his philosophical reflections to get too far removed from prephilo-sophical everyday life, so he presents us with the quotidian ver-sion of "illusory termination": "For most people, life changes when they have come to a certain point in their searching. They marry, they enter occupations, in consequence of which they must out of decency finish something, must have results. . . . So they believe that they themselves actually have arrived." It may be that "off and on they also engage in a little striving, but the last is merely a skimpy marginal note to a text finished long ago. In this way, one is exempted from becoming aware in action, of the strenuous difficulties contained in the simplest statement about existing *qua* human being, whereas in the capacity of a positive thinker, one knows all about world history and our Lord's most private thoughts" (85).

We are in the world of the fairy tale. "Once upon a time" is far behind us, for we have gotten to the place where "they lived happily ever after," being finished with all witches, giants, and trolls—in short, with all striving. The closing comments about world history and "our Lord's most private thoughts" are an unmistakable reference to Hegel, implying that "most people" are practicing Hegelians, whether they have heard of Hegel or not. But if one changes these references to refer to the certainty that human history enacts no purposeful metanarrative and that there is no Lord—and hence, no divine thoughts—it is not difficult to envisage a situation in which "most people" are practicing postmoderns, whether they have heard of Derrida and Foucault or not. In either context, the point is that "the urge to have something finished . . . is of evil and must be renounced" (86). Both the certainty that one is in full possession of the divine and the certainty that there is nothing divine to worry about allow one to be "finished" with the "striving" that was the heart of philosophy for both Socrates and Climacus.[16]

The notion that the subjective existing thinker is the intersection of certainty and uncertainty, of knowledge and ignorance, and thus of positive and negative "can also be expressed by saying that he has just as much of the comic as of pathos" (87). The pathetic here is the pitiful, not in the sense of "That was a pitiful attempt" but in the sense of that which properly evokes pity—the tragic. At the root of both the comic and the tragic is "the misrelation, the contradiction between the infinite and the finite, the eternal and the becoming" (89). (Later on Climacus, the humorist, will develop this notion that contradiction lies at the heart of laughter; see chapter 11 below.) There is something inherently tragic about the erotic character of human striving, oriented toward plenty (presence, certainty) but never able to overcome its origin in poverty (absence, uncertainty), as writers as different as Blaise Pascal and Sartre so eloquently have shown. But Climacus insists that for exactly the same reason human life is comical.

Just as we think that politicians who are able to laugh at themselves are somehow more human than those who take themselves with utter and unrelieved seriousness, so Climacus portrays the existing thinker as having what we might call a metaphysical sense of humor, an appreciation of the inherent incongruities of being human.

The third thesis attributed to Lessing comes directly from the text that gives rise to *Fragments: "Lessing has said that contingent historical truths can never become a demonstration of eternal truths of reason, also that the transition whereby one will build an eternal truth on historical reports is a leap"* (93).

In his introduction, Climacus speaks of "the qualitative transition of the leap from unbeliever to believer" (12), but it is only here that he begins to thematize this category, so central to his thinking. Although in the passage just cited and in the section currently before us Climacus is clearly interested in the transition to Christian faith, Kierkegaard does not let him use the term "leap of faith," surprising as this may be to some readers. It is important to notice this fact, for in the wider context of Kierkegaard's authorship, "the leap" is a generic category referring to all qualitative transitions, of which the transition to faith is but one specific example.[17] Thus in his journals Kierkegaard gives as examples of the leap the transitions from water to ice, from good to evil, from the aesthetic to the ethical, from the ethical to the religious, and from reading the Bible as a human book to reading it as Holy Scripture, that is, as God's word (JP 3.2345, 2358).

Lessing had argued that while the evidence for a historical claim might be greater or less, the transition from a historical claim (more or less strongly supported) to a metaphysical claim was not quantitative but qualitative, a μετάβασις εἰς ἄλλο γένος, a move to a thoroughly different sort of thing. He was referring to a point in Aristotelian logic according to which one cannot, for example, prove a geometrical theorem from arithmetical premises. It was in this context that Lessing spoke of "the ugly, broad ditch which I cannot get across, however often and however earnestly I have tried to make the leap."[18] With this in mind Kierkegaard defines the leap as that "whereby I burst the whole progression of reason and define a qualitative newness . . . a newness ἄλλο γένος" (JP 3.2358).

According to Gregor Malantschuk, Kierkegaard recognizes "that it is impossible to carry through a continuous movement *either in thought or in existence. Thought and existence encounter very definite limits,* and the next level or next sphere cannot be

reached without a leap." But in addition to "dialectical" (epistemic) leaps and "pathos-filled" (existential) leaps, "there are also
the leaps from each of these to the other, of which the leap from
thought to existence is the more important" (JP 3, page 794, my
emphasis). We need these distinctions if we are to read Climacus
attentively, for he discusses all three kinds of leaps without carefully distinguishing them. Most obvious are the leaps within existence. The transitions from one stage to another fall into this
category, including the move from objectivity to subjectivity already introduced, and the still to come move from Religiousness
A to Religiousness B.

Lessing, of course, was interested in a leap within the realm
of thought, from one (kind of) belief to another. Climacus accu-
rately paraphrases his claim *that contingent historical truths can
never become a demonstration of eternal truths of reason* as the
claim that *the transition where one will build an eternal truth on
historical reports is a leap.* Both formulations designate a move
from one cognitive location to another.

But Climacus also points us to the leap from thought to existence. He notes that Lessing's issue arises "precisely because one
wants to base on [historical reports relating to Jesus of Nazareth]
the acceptance of a [metaphysical] doctrine that is the condition
for an eternal happiness, that is, to base an eternal happiness on
them." So Lessing asks "who, on the basis of this belief, would risk
anything of great, permanent worth, the loss of which would be
irreparable?" (96). To accept a doctrine is to make a move on the
epistemic playing field. But to base the whole meaning of my life
on this doctrine, to risk my eternal happiness on it, is to move to
another game altogether. It is like the difference between making
a move I think will win a chess match for me and betting my house
on the outcome of that move. Like Martin Luther, Climacus assumes that religious faith always includes cognitive assent to the
truth of certain propositions, but it also always overreaches that
assent in an act of commitment that is more than belief and whose
source is deeper than the intellect.

The theory of the leap is perhaps best understood by a consideration of two objections that have been raised against it. One
is that it involves an indefensibly voluntaristic account of belief,
that it rests on the false assumption that we can directly will or
simply choose our beliefs, that at least for some beliefs, we believe
p if and only if we *just decide* to believe *p*.

In *Postscript,* Climacus constantly affirms that "the leap is
the category of decision" (99; cf. 95–96, 100, 102, 105, 381, 384;
and chapter 5 above). This is in keeping with Kierkegaard's own

claim that the leap "is essentially at home in the realm of free-dom" (JP 3.2352). This linkage of the leap with freedom and deci-sion is not especially puzzling in relation to two of the three kinds of leap we have just distinguished. Leaps within existence (for example, from the aesthetic to the ethical sphere) or from thought to existence (for example, from believing that this move will win the chess match to betting the house on the outcome, or from the belief that the Gospel narratives about Jesus have a high degree of historical reliability to the practice of the Chris-tian life) have in common the fact that the far side of the ditch, the place to which one leaps, is not a new belief but an action or even a new way of life. Sartre would speak of a new fundamental project, and Heidegger would speak of a new mode of being-in-the-world.[19] To speak of adopting a new life-style, in the deepest sense of the term, as a matter of freedom and of decision is not, to repeat, especially puzzling.[20]

But it is problematic to speak in these terms about leaps in thought, for where the landing is a new belief, the claim seems to be that we simply choose what to believe. Thus Louis Pojman finds in the Kierkegaardian texts an unacceptable view, which he calls direct volitionalism, according to which "we can obtain be-liefs and withhold beliefs directly upon performing an act of will."[21]

It might be tempting to say that in *Postscript* Climacus shifts attention away from Lessing's concern about the logical gap be-tween one (kind of) belief and another (kind) to his own concern with existential self-choice, set in the theory of the stages on life's way. As just noted, however, Climacus holds that while faith as existential self-choice is more than mere cognitive assent, it is not less, but it includes belief. Thus he takes Lessing's leap to involve both acceptance of a doctrine and basing one's eternal happiness on it (96), and later, while discussing Jacobi's relation to the leap, says the issue is "to decide whether he will by virtue of the absurd accept in faith that which indeed cannot be thought" (100). So the question of epistemic volitionalism is un-avoidable, especially in light of what Climacus has already said on the subject.

In *Fragments* he asserts quite clearly that some beliefs de-pend upon the will. In chapters 4 and 5, he argues that with re-gard to the historical content, which is an essential ingredient in Christian faith, faith is as risky for the contemporaries of Jesus as for those who live one or even many generations later. As Lessing helps us see, there is a gap between what an eyewitness could know directly (that Jesus said this and did that) and what a believer claims to be true (that Jesus is God incarnate). The leap is as necessary for the eyewitness as for those separated from the events by centuries. Neither is faith easier for those who come later; the historical impact of the Christian church is not a bridge that eliminates the need for a leap.

The interlude that separates these two chapters is directed against the Hegelian view that there is some kind of necessity at work in history. There are neither necessary events in history nor necessary truths of history. History's modality, both as occurrence and as proposition, is contingency. At the same time, since history is by definition past and not present, there can be no immediate knowledge of historical truths. In the absence of either necessity or immediacy, there is a radical uncertainty to all historical belief grounded in the gap between what we can know in the strong senses, made possible by either immediacy or necessity, and what is claimed by the belief.[22] Sounding quite Platonic, Climacus says that history is the object of belief, not of knowledge (PF 79–84). It is important to note here that while the word he uses for belief, *Tro,* like the German *Glaube,* is used both for ordinary, everyday beliefs of various sorts and for religious faith, he is here speaking about the logic of ordinary historical beliefs, such as the belief that Caesar crossed the Rubicon.

The logic of the situation is the same one that David Hume identified in his famous analysis of inductive inference, for what is at issue is not the peculiar nature of religious belief but the nature of any belief in contingent matters of fact not directly present to us.[23] Climacus seems to hold the Humean view of Kierkegaard, who writes, "By analogy and induction the conclusion can be reached only by a LEAP. All other conclusions are essentially tautological" (JP 3.2321). What is directly present or can be tautologically inferred can be known with certainty, but beyond that lies risk and uncertainty. How do we bridge the gap, leap across the ditch, between what we can be certain of and what we believe in spite of its uncertainty? Hume's answer is custom. Climacus's answer is will. He tells us that "belief is not a knowledge but an act of freedom, an expression of will. . . . The conclusion of belief is no conclusion but a resolution" (PF 83–84).

There is no need to follow Pojman in interpreting these statements as an expression of direct volitionalism. We might consider the situation of a jury presented with conflicting testimony about the matter before them. Let us assume that they are serious about their task and act responsibly throughout the trial.

The facts in question are clearly historical facts, past events not available to their immediate observation. Neither can they be inferred with logical necessity from anything the jurors can know with the certainty of immediate presence. In such a case we say quite naturally that the members of the jury will each have to *decide* whom to believe.

But in saying this we have not espoused direct volitionalism. We do not mean that they will decide between the defense and prosecution witnesses as I would choose between scallops and calamari at a seafood restaurant, and this for at least two reasons. In the latter case, assuming that I like both, I might well be said to *simply choose* between them, while in the former case we would not be likely to say this at all. The jurors will carefully consider everything that has been presented to them; they will have crucial parts of the testimony read to them again; and they will listen to the arguments presented by their fellow jurors. Yet we might still speak the language of decision in order to indicate that (how else to say it?) the decision of whom to believe was not made for them by the evidence available to them. Yes, she cried while telling her story, and yes, the three brothers all told essentially the same story, but these facts are, unfortunately, compatible with both the truth and the falsity, even deliberate falsity, of what they said. No rational process is available to transport the jurors passively and impersonally from what they know (she cried, they agreed, etc.) to what they must (how else to say it?) decide, namely, whom to believe.

We should note that while my restaurant choice is oriented toward personal pleasure, the jurors' decision is oriented toward the truth. The juror analogy suggests a way of making sense out of Climacus (and Descartes) when they find no conflict between a commitment to the truth and deciding what to believe.[24] It shows how someone who speaks of decision in connection with believing might not espouse the direct volitionalism that Pojman attributes to Climacus (and Descartes). It gives us reason to look closely at the text to see just what role freedom plays in Climacus's account of believing. Perhaps it is better described as indirect than as direct.

His own example in *Fragments* is that of the ancient skeptics, and it is of the highest importance when he tells us that before reading Lessing he had encountered the theory of the leap in *Fear and Trembling* (105). There Johannes de Silentio not only interprets both the knight of infinite resignation and the knight of faith (Abraham) in terms of the leap (36, 42n)[25] but also develops a parallel between the believer and the ancient skeptic that Climacus, having read it, will develop further.

In his preface, Silentio develops a satire against the view, so popular among his contemporaries, especially among Hegelians, that the task of the modern age is not to arrive at faith but to go beyond it. He likens them to the Cartesians, who do not stop at doubt but immediately go further. Against the latter he invokes the Greek skeptics, who assumed doubt to be "a task for a whole lifetime, because proficiency in doubting is not acquired in days and weeks" (FT 6). Against the former he invokes the ancient believers, for whom faith was also "a task for a whole lifetime, because it was assumed that a proficiency in believing is not acquired either in days or in weeks" (FT 7).

Returning to the interlude in *Fragments,* we find Climacus drawing a similar parallel between belief and the doubt of the Greek skeptics. He argues that the skeptic is not compelled to doubt by knowledge (since one does not know the proposition in question to be false any more than one knows it to be true), concluding that the Greek skeptics "doubted not by virtue of knowledge but by virtue of will. . . . This implies that doubt can be terminated only in freedom, by an act of will" (PF 82). By the same token, the decision (is this language inevitable?) to believe is equally uncompelled by knowledge, so that "belief is not a knowledge but an act of freedom, an expression of will" (PF 83).

Climacus clearly wants us have the ancient skeptics in mind as we interpret his account of belief. Three points are worthy of careful attention:

1. What was at issue for the skeptic is not doubting this proposition or that one but rather a general policy about belief and doubt, a policy whose goal was the formation of a certain kind of disposition or habit. This policy/disposition was for them an Aristotelian ἕξις (*habitus*), which they considered to be at once the highest virtue and the highest happiness for mortals. According to Aristotle, such states of character arise out of activities that are voluntary and even deliberate. Thus it would be quite natural to say that the will and not just the intellect is involved in their formation and in the particular acts, intellectual or moral, that arise from them.

The ancient skeptics "used cognition only to preserve the cast of mind, which was the main consideration" (PF 83). The "dialectical arguments" they presented were to them "nothing more than outer fortifications, human accommodations" (PF 84)—in other words, means deliberately employed to build and maintain the habit of suspending judgment, just as the Buddhist uses various meditational practices to build and maintain the habit of seeing everything as suffering and nothing as substantial.

These passages lead C. Stephen Evans to write, "Climacus wishes to claim that the skeptic is a skeptic in the final analysis because he wills to be a skeptic, [but] there is no claim here that belief states are always or even ever under the direct control of the will. On the contrary, there is the clear statement that at least in some cases the control exercised by the will is indirect. Though the ultimate source of doubt is the will, doubt is achieved through cognitive *means* . . . there is a logical gap between whatever totally objective, certain evidence we have for matters of fact, and our beliefs about these matters. It is this gap which makes skepticism as a willed life-stance possible. It provides room, as it were, for the skeptic to do what he needs to do to arrive at a state of suspended judgment, though this is not necessarily easy and will certainly not be successful in all cases."[26]

If, as Climacus suggests, our ordinary historical beliefs are analogous to the rather extraordinary doubt of the ancient skeptics, it is not because they represent isolated acts of "sheer wilful acceptance."[27] It is because they stem from a belief-forming disposition over which we have significant control and for which we have substantial responsibility. As Evans puts it, Climacus thinks "that what we want to believe and think ultimately plays a decisive role in what we do believe and think."[28]

2. A second feature of Climacus's account of the ancient skeptics does not match up with belief (*Tro*) in its "direct and ordinary meaning" but only with faith "in the wholly eminent sense," the religious faith that is his ultimate theme in any case (PF 87). This is the difficulty involved in suspending belief. Johannes de Silentio, as already noted, insists that "proficiency in doubting" is not easily acquired and was understood by the ancient skeptics to be "a task for a whole lifetime" (FT 6). He says precisely the same about religious faith. Climacus echoes this theme when he notes that the would-be skeptic needs to employ means toward his end. Thus he has the skeptic say, "If I can only avoid drawing conclusions, I shall never be deceived" (PF 82), expressing the realization that wanting to suspend judgment is one thing, succeeding in this enterprise another.

Like Climacus, Hume emphasizes the inadequacy of intellect alone to produce the belief-forming disposition or habit that concerns him. But it is so naturally and easily formed that he can call it custom. The belief-suspending ἕξις of the skeptic is neither natural nor easy. It goes deeply against the grain of spontaneous human development. In this respect it is like the belief-generating "mechanism" that belongs to faith as explored by Johannes de Silentio and Johannes Climacus. Kierkegaard has both Johanneses present biblical faith to us as a steep, uphill climb, cognitively as well as practically. They unite in seeking to eliminate any temptation to think that faith is "something one can acquire simply by fiat."[29] The decision involved in the leap begins to look less like the decision to have calamari rather than scallops and more like the decision to climb Mount Everest.

3.   Finally, right after telling us that belief and doubt are expressions of will (PF 82–83), Climacus tells us that both are passions (PF 84). Frequently in the Kierkegaardian corpus, passion functions as the opposite of reflection (for example, FT 42n in connection with the leap). Thus this language reiterates the claim that we are dealing with human activities that cannot be fully determined by intellect alone. But it does more than that; it reinforces the notion that the role of the will is indirect. If we think of other passions, such as love and hatred, it is clear that we do not simply choose to love or to hate. Thus Evans writes, "Passions are things that must be slowly cultivated and constantly renewed. Acts of willing play a role in this cultivation, and Kierkegaard regards the higher ethical and religious passions as things we are responsible to achieve. However, by and large, passions are formed on a long-term basis, and they are not simply willed into existence, but formed indirectly through a process of willing to do other things."[30]

Even passions like anger and sadness, which often seem to appear without being "slowly cultivated," need to be "constantly renewed." If we want to cling to them, there are things we can choose to do, as every child knows who refuses to smile in order to remain in a pout. If we wish to nurse our anger, we can continually rehearse to ourselves and to others the events that gave rise to it; or we can direct our attention to factors in the situation that will tend to loosen the hold our anger has on us.[31]

My conclusion is that when Climacus represents the leap to faith as including a decision to believe, and when his colleague Anti-Climacus, in the same spirit, represents Christianity as saying, "Thou shalt believe in the forgiveness of sins" (SUD 115), we understand them to be saying that the will has an impact on what we believe—neither direct nor total, but sufficient to make possible both an ethics of belief whereby questions about our doxic responsibilities can be discussed and a therapy of spiritual formation whereby strategies can be developed for shaping our cognition of the world as well as our conatus and our comportment in it.

If we ran a word-association test, asking people to give us the first word they think of when they hear of the leap in Kierkegaard's writings, the most frequent response would surely be "faith." Although the crucial phrase is not to be found in the corpus, everyone knows that the leap is the leap of faith. I suspect that the second most frequent response would be "blind." For everyone also knows that the leap is a blind leap in the dark. This is another standard objection to the theory of the leap, for a blind leap is held to be irrational.

A leap could be described as blind either if it occurred without the awareness that a leap was involved, or if one had no idea what one was jumping toward. But in neither sense is the Kierkegaardian leap blind. Who does more than Kierkegaard and the authors he creates to call attention to the leaps involved in human existence, including the leap to religious faith? And who tries harder than Kierkegaard and the authors he creates to clarify the alternatives, making as clear as possible what is involved in such choices as between the aesthetic and the ethical, between the religious and the speculative, and between Religiousness A and Religiousness B? The assumption underlying the entire authorship is that leaps can be blind but need not and ought not to be. One could do much worse than summarize the authorship as a sustained effort to lead the reader out of the cave, in which all leaps are blind, and into the sunlight, where one leaps in the full knowledge of both the leap itself and its hoped-for destination. Even in the case where the landing site is held to resist conceptual mastery by virtue of its paradoxical character, authors like the two Johannes do everything they can to make the paradox as conspicuous as possible. The landing site is highly problematic, they keep reminding us. Nothing could be less blind than the leap as they present it.

While Climacus would vigorously resist all talk about a blind leap of faith, he does qualify the leap with two not entirely reassuring adjectives. It is risky and desperate. "Without risk, no faith" (204; cf. 210). Climacus will develop this central motif in his understanding of faith later on. In the passage before us, he commends Lessing for portraying this risk with the vivid image of a not so grand canyon, the "ugly broad ditch" that makes the leap necessary (96, 98). At its core the risk of faith is the epistemic uncertainty that attends both the belief and the mode of life that it informs. Faith includes belief that lacks the certainty of tautological reasoning and perceptual immediacy. Because the object of judgment is not present to the intellect or to the senses, there are no guarantees that one is not mistaken. (Climacus al-

ways sees the quest for certainty as a need for security, an epistemic requirement grounded in an existential demand.)[32]
It is this incurable uncertainty that leads to talk about the
blind leap of faith. But it does so only if awareness of this uncertainty is combined with a Cartesian foundationalism or a Hegelian holism or some third equivalent that leads one to believe
that in common sense, in the sciences, even in philosophy (but
not in religion), one can have the certainty that eliminates risk.
If, on the other hand, one recognizes with Climacus the uncertainty involved in ordinary historical judgments or, with Hume,
the uncertainty involved in everyday inductive inferences, one is
not likely to call faith a blind leap. By the same logic one would
have to call beliefs that Caesar crossed the Rubicon and that the
sun will rise tomorrow blind leaps of faith, and that does not
seem very illuminating.

Long before contemporary attacks on foundationalism and
totalizing holism, as developed in both the "analytic" and "Continental" philosophical traditions, Hume and Climacus highlight
the epistemic riskiness of much of what counts as secular knowledge. What distinguishes Climacus from Hume is his unwillingness—although he is not a believer—to repudiate religious faith
on the grounds of its uncertainty while accepting secular knowledge in spite of its uncertainty.[33]

Climacus also describes the leap as desperate (105–6). He
thus joins Johannes de Silentio in seeing faith as necessarily accompanied by fear and trembling. But what is the nature of this
despair? Our best clue here, I think, is to remember how deeply
Hegelian Climacus is. In the famous introduction to his *Phenomenology,* Hegel describes the movement from natural consciousness to absolute knowledge as "the way of the soul which
journeys through the series of its own configurations as though
they were the stations appointed for it by its own nature . . . this
path has a negative significance for it, and what is in fact the realization of the Concept, counts for it rather as the loss of its own
self; for it does lose its truth on this path. The road can therefore
be regarded as the pathway of *doubt,* or more precisely as the
way of despair."[34]

There is a nice word play here, since doubt is *Zweifel* and
despair is *Verzweiflung.* This despair is an intensified form of
doubt, a "thoroughgoing skepticism" that is "the conscious insight into the untruth of phenomenal knowledge," not to be confused with superficial, momentary, Cartesian doubt.[35] And yet,
the language of despair and the images of a *via dolorosa* for the
soul give existential overtones to this doubt. "Thoroughgoing

skepticism" is not merely a matter of cognition but of self-formation through suffering.

This is not the only place where Hegel links doubt and despair. In the discussion of the dialectical, as distinct from the speculative, moment of reason (see chapter 4 above), he identifies the former as a special kind of skepticism, one "completely certain about its central point, i.e., the nullity of everything finite. The person who simply doubts still has the hope that his doubt can be resolved. . . . Skepticism proper, on the contrary, is complete despair about everything that the understanding holds to be firm . . ."[36] This is the same "high ancient skepticism" to which Johannes de Silentio appeals, and Hegel again sharply distinguishes it from modern—in this case, Humean and Kantian—skepticism.

If we read Climacus against this background, his description of the leap as a desperate act becomes a restatement of his earlier claim that human reason can be dialectical but not speculative.[37] We move from A to B not because of rational insight into the necessity of B but because we have come to despair over A; we move to a cognitive/affective sense of its limits, of its inability to satisfy the requirements that led to its adoption. As true skepticism for Hegel is a certainty about the nullity of the finite, this despair is a certainty that A is not working for me. (Given Climacus's emphasis on the open, temporal character of human experience, this is not to be confused with the certainty that it *will not* or *cannot* work for me. Later I might return to that from which I now find it necessary to leap away.)

If we reply that despair over A does not tell us whether to jump to B or to C, Climacus will reply something like this: "That's the point. Reason cannot provide us with the assurances and guarantees we have been taught by speculative philosophers to expect. This is a very risky business." That is what the fear and trembling are all about. Thus, in addition to the material despair over a particular project that we can no longer sustain, there is a formal despair over the claims of reason to enable us to walk by sight and not by faith, to have the truth and justification of our move plainly present to us. Climacus would call this despair over the speculative; contemporary postmodernism would call it despair over the metaphysics of presence. In either case it involves insight into our inability to fill the "broad ugly ditch" that makes leaping necessary.

The leap is thus a doubly desperate act, rooted in the desperate conviction that my present project is a failure and the desperate conviction that the move to an alternative is highly risky, since reason cannot guarantee its success. I must make a decision in a situation that is (objectively) undecidable.

The final thesis attributed to Lessing is drawn directly from an essay of 1778. *"If God held all truth enclosed in his right hand, and in his left hand the one and only ever-striving drive for truth, even with the corollary of erring forever and ever, and if he were to say to me: Choose! — I would humbly fall down to him at his left hand and say: Father, give! Pure truth is indeed only for you alone!"* (106).[38] It is not clear that Lessing believed in the kind of personal God who might confront a human being with such a choice, but he has no trouble using such an idea of God to make a point about the finitude of human knowledge. In this respect he is somewhat like Kant, who, in the First Critique, is not entitled to assume the existence of God, but who defines human knowledge in its receptive finitude by contrast with the idea of God's knowledge in its creative infinity. The thing in itself is not defined just negatively, as the thing apart from the conditions of our apprehension, but positively, as the thing (possibly) known by the creative mind of God.[39]

Hegel keeps the connection between the divine and absolute knowledge, but by making the latter a human achievement at a certain point in history and at a certain level of philosophical sophistication, he eliminates the gap between the human and divine, which is so central to Lessing, to Kant, and to Climacus.[40] In the *Phenomenology,* Hegel describes the achievement of human community as reciprocal recognition in these terms: "The reconciling Yes, in which the two 'I's let go their antithetical existence, is the existence of the 'I' which has expanded into a duality . . . and, in its complete externalization and opposite, possesses the certainty of itself: *it is God manifested in the midst of those who know themselves in the form of pure knowledge.*"[41] This post–French Revolution, post-Enlightenment event is what he had in mind when he said that "it is not difficult to see that ours is a birth-time and a period of transition to a *new era.* Spirit has broken with the world it has hitherto inhabited. . . . The gradual crumbling that left unaltered the face of the whole is cut short by a sunburst which, in one flash, illuminates the features of the *new world.*"[42]

The religious import of this event can be put in traditional religious language: "This incarnation of the divine Being . . . is the simple content of absolute religion. . . . The divine nature is the same as the human, and it is this unity that is beheld." But this religion is wildly different from historical Christianity, for not only does this unity of the human and divine not occur uniquely in Jesus of Nazareth, but it occurs only "now" (Hegel is writing in 1807) and only in Hegelian philosophy: "God is attainable in pure speculative knowledge alone and *is* only in that knowledge, and is only that knowledge itself, for He is Spirit. . . . It is precisely this that the revealed religion knows. The hopes and expectations of the world up till now had pressed forward solely to this revelation, to behold what absolute Being is, and in it to find itself. The joy of beholding itself in absolute Being enters self-consciousness and seizes the whole world . . ."[43] This is the meaning of the absolute knowledge with which the *Phenomenology* concludes, the standpoint from which the Logic and, indeed, the entire system of Logic, Philosophy of Nature, and Philosophy of Spirit is written.

By contrast, Kant begins the *Critique of Pure Reason* with the words "human reason" (A vii), and at the end, pure reason is still human, all too human. His distinction between understanding (*Verstand*) and reason (*Vernunft*) is between two dimensions of a human cognition that is positively (the Transcendental Analytic) or negatively (the Transcendental Dialectic) phenomenal in contrast with God's knowledge. In the Analytic he portrays the understanding as the successful constitution of the world of common sense and Newtonian science, a world of appearances but not of things as they truly are. In the Dialectic he portrays reason as the unsuccessful attempt to achieve the unconditioned totality, which the understanding never attains, only to fall into paralogism and antinomy.

These two moments correspond to Hegel's distinction between the understanding and the dialectical. But Hegel immediately goes on, as we have seen (chapter 4 above), to posit a third mode of human cognition, the speculative, whereby our aspirations for totality and ultimacy are achieved. This positive fulfillment of reason is the location of that incarnation in which the human becomes divine. The distinction between human and divine knowledge is not simply obliterated, but it is reinterpreted as a distinction within human cognition between understanding (and dialectic, as the negative side of reason) on the one hand and reason (in its positive, speculative mode) on the other.

This conception of human knowledge in its highest, philosophical form, as absolute knowledge, as the self-consciousness of spirit in its absolute and thus divine character, is first clearly spelled out in the *Phenomenology,* but it lives on at, and as, the heart of Hegel's later work. It is to resist this self-deification of post-Kantian philosophical self-consciousness and of post–French Revolution modern society (in Denmark, Christendom) that Climacus turns to Lessing. He translates the claim that "Pure truth is indeed for [God] alone" into the claim that only God could write or understand the system (118–19), for the claim that truth requires totality and that philosophy therefore can and must be a system are closely linked.[44] It is as producers and consumers of the system that Hegelian humanity takes itself to be divine.[45]

Rather than see this apotheosis as a long-awaited promotion, Climacus sees it as pure loss, the loss of our humanity, our true self. He writes, "I, Johannes Climacus, am neither more nor less than a human being; and I assume that the one with whom I have the honor of conversing is also a human being. If he wants to be speculative thought, pure speculative thought, I must give up conversing with him, because at that moment he becomes invisible to me and to the weak mortal eye of a human being" (109). He pleads, "Let us be human beings" (114). He exhorts others not to forget that they are human beings (117, 120), and he complains, "To be a human being has been abolished, and every speculative thinker confuses himself with humankind" (124).

Climacus has moral objections to this abolition and this confusion. He charges Hegel with having "behaved irresponsibly" toward the youths who believed in him (118). He charges that the system has been completed "without having an ethics" (121), apparently because it directs the individual's attention away from the task of simply being human and choosing how to do so. Whereas pantheistic systems have been seen as a threat to morality because of their denial of freedom and of a real difference between good and evil, Climacus replies that "every system must be pantheistic simply because of the conclusiveness. Existence must be annulled in the eternal before the system concludes itself" (122). What is at issue is not whether a philosophy agrees with, say, Spinoza, on this or that theorem, but whether by virtue of its claim to finality a philosophical system denies or distracts attention from the temporal conditions of the moral life.

But almost immediately, Climacus reins himself in: "Let us not do the wrong of calling the objective tendency impious, pantheistic self-worship but rather view it as a venture in the comic" (124). Here he behaves like the lawyer who asks a question, knowing that the other side will object and that the judge will sustain the objection and instruct the jury to disregard what they just heard. The item in question will be stricken from the record but not from the memory of the jurors, who, after all, heard it.

Climacus scolds himself for raising moral objections to philosophy's claim to completion, but only after having done so three times. And he does not even strike them from the record.

Still, he begins this section with a running satire on the question of whether the system is finished (106–8), and he concludes it with the appeal to the comic just cited. He is serious in wanting to make his primary charge against the system that it is "fantastical," "ludicrous," and "farcical" (119; cf. 117, 121, 125). "If a dancer could leap very high, we would admire him, but if he wanted to give the impression that he could fly—even though he could leap higher than any dancer had ever leapt before—let laughter overtake him (124; cf. 118). In other words, if Hegel wants to claim that he has given us the most comprehensive and illuminating philosophy since Aristotle, let us acknowledge his greatness, but if he presents his system as absolute knowledge, let us greet this claim with roars of laughter.

If the most appropriate response is laughter rather than refutation, this is because the fundamental problem is not error but forgetfulness. The problem with modern speculative thought is "that it has not a false presupposition but a comic presupposition, occasioned by its having forgotten in a kind of world-historical absentmindedness what it means to be a human being . . . what it means that we, you and I and he, are human beings, each one on his own" (120; cf. 117, 119, 124). The cure for this absentmindedness is to direct our attention decisively toward the fact that one is an existing human being and toward what this means (120–21). Climacus clearly considers this directing of our attention as something we decide to do. This either/or is an example of the role of the will in shaping how we think: "*either* [the existing individual] can do everything to forget that he is existing and thereby manage to become comic . . . *or* he can direct all his attention to his existence" (120, my emphasis).[46]

Here we encounter again the use of "existence" as a technical term for the human mode of being-in-the-world (117–20). "Don't become comical by forgetting that you are human" is interchangeable with "Don't become comical by forgetting that you exist." Our expectation that the theme of temporality cannot be far away will shortly be confirmed.

But first we must ask the question, What do we take ourselves to be when we forget that we are existing human beings? Climacus gives three answers: "pure speculative thought" (109, 117), "the pure I-I" (117), and "humankind" (124). To confuse oneself with pure speculative thought is a kind of grammatical mistake. It involves moving from "I am a philosopher engaged in philosophizing" to "I am philosophy." It is the same kind of mistake a president makes when, under attack, he replies by accusing his critics of dishonoring the presidency, as if he were the presidency, and not merely the president. Editorial writers, in high moral dudgeon, will doubtless lament this "cynical, manipulative appeal to the Constitution," but Climacus will look for the best responses in *Doonesbury* or on *Saturday Night Live*.

Climacus's question, "How, if at all, is the empirical *I related to the pure I-I?*" (117) is offered as a gloss on the slide from the philosophizing philosopher (who has a Social Security number) to philosophy itself (which does not). The reference is to Johann Gottlieb Fichte (cf. CI 273), whom Climacus takes to have laid the essential foundation for the post-Kantian speculative philosophical systems that we know as classical German idealism: his own, Friedrich Schelling's, and Hegel's. The pure or transcendental ego in Kant is, as transcendental apperception (a priori self-consciousness), the formal principle of merely phenomenal knowledge. To know it through the kind of reflection carried out in the First Critique is neither to know the self in itself nor to enable the self to know anything else as it is in itself. But Fichte's theory of the transcendental ego presents itself as the overcoming of the thing in itself. To know the first principle of philosophy, expressible either as A=A or as I=I, is both to know the self in itself and to have the key to knowing everything else as it truly is.[47] The pure I-am-I is the self-positing, self-identical, a priori, and absolute starting point for speculative philosophy. Accessible to intellectual intuition,[48] this deepest self knows itself to be and thus to stand at the origin of the world. It is the *archè*, the alpha both of being and of thought, and thus of their identity. No doubt this Fichtean I=I is the boldest version of the "fictive objective subject," to which Climacus referred earlier (81).

Hegel acknowledges a deep debt to Fichte but in the end finds him too Cartesian and too Kantian.[49] In the *Phenomenology* and in the Logic, he tries to show that any attempt to start with intuitive certainty, sensible or conceptual, is bound to fail, since to achieve the desired immediacy we must leave behind all determinacy. We buy certainty at the cost of content, and absolute certainty along this path is sheer emptiness. Since Hegel is no Buddhist, his strategy for absolute knowledge is holistic rather than foundationalist. The true is the whole, and we achieve the absolute standpoint necessary for speculative philosophy, not at the outset, but only at the end of a journey that stops at all ports.

This totality ultimately means the entirety of human experience, and it is the phenomenological recollection of that experience rather than the intellectual intuition of the pure I=I that makes the system possible. The philosopher who has become the repository of the totality of human experience (recollection = *Er-Innerung*) has arrived at the point where the Logic can begin. The philosopher is the alpha only by virtue of standing at the omega point of human experience. The *archè* is found only in the *telos*. This is the familiar argument of the *Phenomenology of Spirit*.[50]

Enter Climacus. Laughing. When we talk this way, we confuse ourselves, in a comical fit of absentmindedness, with humankind (124–25). This is the point at which Climacus introduces us to the dancer who, instead of claiming to be able to leap higher than anyone before, wanted us to think he could fly (124). To philosophize on the basis of human history to this point is one thing (leaving aside quibbles about whether everything to this point gets adequately included; does Hegel's philosophy of history, for example, have a European bias?); but to profess to embody the totality of human experience, and thus to satisfy the Hegelian criterion that only the whole is true, that is something altogether different. Lessing would call it a μετάβασις εἰς ἄλλο γένος. Climacus merely adds that whoever writes the system is surely "a human being—and surely a living, that is, existing, human being" who becomes "the comical contradiction of wanting to be what one is not" by professing to be the voice of world history (120).

There appear, then, to be two ways in which we might comically confuse ourselves with "pure speculative thought"—the foundationalist, Fichtean way; and the historically holistic, Hegelian way. The existing self is too thick to be the former and too thin to be the latter. Or, to put it differently, while the existing self is always *in medias res,* pure speculative thought is possible only to those who stand outside the world, either as its origin or as its culmination.

Climacus sets his invitation to laugh at the would-be speculative philosopher in the context of an analysis of why the existing individual cannot stand at either of these divine locations. After insisting that he and, presumably, his interlocutor are "neither more nor less than a human being," he writes, "Consequently, *(a) a logical system can be given; (b) but a system of existence cannot be given*" (109).

The logical system that Climacus has in mind has much more in common with Alfred North Whitehead and Bertrand Russell than with Hegel. It defines a realm of pure being whose relation to actuality is merely hypothetical, and it resists any attempt by (Hegelian) ventriloquists to sneak reality into logic (109–11). What he seems to have in mind is something like the propositional calculus of twentieth-century symbolic logic, a system demonstrably both complete and consistent, but one whose theorems are stubbornly noncommittal about which possible facts are actual. Thus, for example, $(p \cdot (p \supset q)) \supset q$ is an entirely hypothetical statement about the world, compatible with the truth and falsity (existence and nonexistence) of both p and q. Climacus may be reading the mind of his maker, who sounds like a formal logician when he says that apart from tautology, everything is a leap (JP 3.2341).

Hegel has a much more ambitious view of his own Logic. He writes, "Thus *logic* coincides with *metaphysics,* with the science of *things* grasped in *thoughts* that used to be taken to express the *essentialities* of the *things.*" He even claims that his Logic "is the exposition of God as he is in his eternal essence before the creation of nature and a finite mind."[51]

Such a system does not purport to be about existence in Climacus's sense, as the inward, temporal subjectivity of the ethical-religious self; but it does purport to give us substantive knowledge about God and the world. It seeks to be the culmination of the metaphysical tradition, not the inauguration of existentialism.

In light of the system's not even attempting to include individual inwardness, we might expect a reprise of Climacus's complaint that the system has no ethics. But he chooses to waive that objection, having already made it to his own satisfaction, and to ask whether the system that Hegel has in mind is possible, and whether or not it would be a good thing. Thus when Climacus says that a system of existence cannot be given, he is alluding above all to the Hegelian system that begins with the Logic and continues with the Philosophy of Nature and the Philosophy of Spirit. Not even in its Logic is it the kind of formal system that Climacus takes to be quite possible.

The question is not whether someone can give a very impressive and illuminating theory about God and the world. The question is whether such a theory can be a system according to the criteria that Hegel himself gives. Can it be all-inclusive, and thus without presuppositions? Climacus's conclusion is doubly negative. Hegel's kind of system cannot get started, and if it could get started, it could not get finished.

Climacus poses the question of getting started as the question of movement in logic. His claim is that "logic cannot explain movement" (109–10). Perhaps this is an expression of the view that logic deals only with tautologies. In a tautological proposition or a tautological inference (which can be construed as a complex tautological proposition), it can be said that we go nowhere, that the predicate is already "contained" in the subject, and in affirming it we are merely repeating to ourselves what we have "already thought." Such judgments do not provide "a genuinely new addition to all previous knowledge."[52] Thus "All bachelors are unmarried" becomes, by substitution of a definition, "All unmarried males are unmarried"—which has the form "All AB is A," the predicate merely repeating part of the subject.

By contrast, nontautological propositions and their inferential equivalents, arguments by induction and analogy, involve a movement from one location in logical space to another. The predicate, or conclusion, is not contained in the subject, or premises. This movement cannot be explained, this "leap" cannot be justified by the resources of formal logic. Put in twentieth-century language, we can say that Climacus is pre-Quinean. He takes the distinction between the synthetic and the analytic to be as sharp as Hume and Kant did before him.[53]

All this might have led him to a discussion of the dialectical transitions in which every finite thought "flips over into its opposite by itself" (115).[54] Instead he focuses on the first move, the one that gets the system under way. The question of a beginning for the system is one that concerned Hegel considerably. First, he wrote the *Phenomenology* to try to show that the philosopher could achieve the standpoint of absolute knowledge, from which the system could be written. Then he began his *Science of Logic* with a chapter on how to begin, entitled "With What Must the Science Begin?" Climacus's doubts about the beginning have the genuinely Hegelian character of immanent critique. He asks, in effect, whether Hegel's Logic can live up to the criteria that it gives itself in this famous opening.

There Hegel writes, "Thus the beginning must be *absolute,* or what is synonymous here, an *abstract* beginning; and so it *may not presuppose anything,* must not be mediated by anything nor have a ground; rather it is to be itself the ground of the entire science. Consequently, it must be purely and simply *an* immediacy, or rather merely *immediacy* itself. . . . The beginning therefore is *pure being.*"[55] This account is meant explicitly to repudiate the view—held chiefly by Karl Reinhold—that "philosophy can only begin with a *hypothetical* and *problematical* truth and therefore philosophizing can be at first be only a quest." Against this Hegel insists that the true beginning "is neither an arbitrary and merely provisional assumption, nor is it something which appears to be arbitrarily and tentatively presupposed . . . as is the case with the constructions one is directed to make in connection with the proof

of a theorem in geometry, where it becomes apparent only after-
wards in the proof that one took the right course . . ."[56]

The reason that Hegel cannot accept Reinhold's account is
because of the conceptual tie between immediacy and absolute-
ness. To be absolute is to be not relative to, and thus dependent
(either causally or conceptually) upon, something other than oneself, such as a hypothesis that is either "arbitrary" or "provisional" or "tentative." To be mediated is precisely to be so related
to one's other, by which one is mediated. Hegel thus speaks of
pure being as the immediacy with which the Logic must begin,
since "at the beginning we have as yet no other."[57] To be absolute
or to be immediate here means the same thing: to stand alone,
self-sufficient and independent of any other.[58]

After giving an impeccable summary of the Hegelian position, Climacus then asks (and answers) a question he thinks crucial: "The system begins with the immediate and therefore
without presuppositions and therefore absolutely, that is, the beginning of the system is the absolute beginning. . . . *How does the
system begin with the immediate, that is, does it begin with it immediately?* The answer to this must certainly be an unconditional
no. . . . The beginning of the system that begins with the immediate *is then itself achieved through reflection*" (111–12).

Hegel accepts this shift of attention from the objective to the
subjective, from the content of the beginning to the act by which
it is posited as the beginning, insisting that "the *subjective* act
has also been grasped as an *essential* moment of objective truth."
He also agrees that the starting point of the Logic is indeed mediated by reflection, a long reflection known as the *Phenomenology
of Spirit*. It has this "science of manifested spirit" as its presupposition, just as this science, in turn, has "empirical, *sensuous* consciousness" for its presupposition. But in spite of this double
mediation and these two presuppositions, "*Logic is pure science,*
that is, pure knowledge in the entire range of its development."[59]
How is this possible?

Hegel's reply to this question is plainly that the system does
not begin with the immediate immediately but as a result of reflection. In addition to the reflection of the *Phenomenology* that
leads from the realm of ordinary, natural consciousness to the
realm of pure thought, there is the reflection of "With What Must
the Science Begin? which tells us what the first moment of pure
thought has to be: pure being. If philosophy were a chess game,
we would be talking first about the decision to play chess rather
than some other game and then about the decision to begin with
this chess move rather than some other.

At least Climacus would be talking this way, for he wants to insist that decisions are involved here, decisions, like the ones he has already been talking about, that have to be made by particular individuals without the certainty and security that would accompany them if they could be described as having been made for us by some sort of rational necessity. It is not always clear when he talks about the beginning whether he is talking about the decision to play chess (*The Phenomenology of Spirit*) or about the decision to begin the chess game with this particular move ("With What Must the Science Begin?"). Probably we understand him best if we apply his critique to both.

Its character is clear. Reflection, once started, does not stop of its own accord. Only a "resolution," a "leap," a "μετάβασις εἰς ἄλλο γένος," can terminate reflection by undertaking speculative philosophy or in the act of beginning the system with pure being rather than, say, the transcendental ego. Reflection is one thing, decision is another. Climacus reminds us of Hamlet to underscore this point (112–17). As a thinker, I must draw a conclusion. Thought does not do this for me, so it does me no good to confuse myself with thought. It only makes me comical.

In spite of the argument of the *Phenomenology* that there is something both natural and necessary about the transition from everyday experience to speculative philosophy, Hegel seems prepared to concede the first "decision": "All that is present [at the beginning of the Logic] is simply the resolve, which can also be regarded as arbitrary [*eine Willkür*], that we propose to consider thought as such."[60] But he vehemently insists that once we have decided "to consider thought as such," beginning with pure being is absolute and without presupposition, relative to no resolve and presupposing no personal preference. His support for this claim is the argument that pure being is the only possible starting point for a science of pure thought.[61]

While Climacus notes that this argument is an act of reflection, a point that Hegel concedes in acknowledging that we do not begin with the immediate immediately, he does not discuss its content in detail. A full-fledged debate does not occur. But the issue is clear. Unless reflection can transport the existing individual to a place outside of time, from which it would be possible to see the world *sub specie aeterni,* then either all conceptual necessity would be itself contingent, as philosophers as diverse as Willard Van Orman Quine and Derrida would argue, or at least all nontautological necessity would be contingent, as Kant insists and Climacus seems to suggest. In either case, the Hegelian philosophy would have to present itself, not as *the* system, but as *a* system, one of an indeterminate number of possible conceptual interpretations of the world. And this would be a public-relations defeat of major proportions.[62]

Climacus's second argument against the possibility of a system of existence is that even if it could somehow get started, it could not get finished. If we ask why this is impossible "for any existing spirit," we get a blunt answer: "Existence is the spacing that holds apart; the systematic is the conclusiveness that combines. . . . The systematic idea is subject-object, is the unity of thinking and being; existence on the other hand, is precisely the separation. From this it by no means follows that existence is thoughtless, but existence has spaced and does space subject from object, thought from being" (118, 123).

If this spacing sounds a lot like the parenthesis we encountered at the beginning of chapter 5, and if we suspect that, here as there, space serves as a symbol for time, we are on the right track. What stands in the way of "the conclusiveness that combines" subject and object or thought and being for the existing spirit is simply time. To complete the system, we would need "a conclusiveness that corresponds to the eternity into which the past has entered. . . . Existence must be annulled in the eternal before the system concludes itself" (118–19, 122). The decision between "a continued striving" and "systematic conclusiveness" is a decision about one's relation, as an existing, human self, to the eternal. When evoking Platonic contexts (121–22), Climacus speaks of a kind of pretemporal eternity, an eternity behind one, so to speak. But in the Hegelian context of reality as essentially historical, eternity lies ahead as the completion of the temporal. The appeal to the Greeks disguises the thrust of his argument, in a way, which is simply this: As long as the story of my own life is incomplete, and as long as the larger story of human history, to which it belongs, is also incomplete, I have no access to the conclusiveness that the system requires. Any interpretation of concrete actuality, my own or the world's, can only be penultimate and tentative, awaiting support or refutation (even in the weak form of amendment) by the way the stories, mine and the world's, actually turn out. It is the temporality of the thinker's existence that makes totality and system impossible, and that in turn makes the claim to a finished system comical.

In the final analysis, it is existence in Climacus's sense (as the temporal subjectivity of the human self) that makes impossible a system of existence in Hegel's sense (as the totality of actuality); or, to put it a bit differently, it is Climacus's existentialism that makes him a postmodernist. A central theme of the thinkers to whom this latter term is applied is the very impossibility of immediacy (an absolute beginning) and totality (a totalizing closure), which is the Achilles' heel of traditional metaphysical systems. The postmodern description of these systems as the metaphysics of presence indicates an agreement with Kierkegaard that human temporality is the fly in the ointment.

But Climacus is a distinctive kind of postmodernist, as we see the moment we ask the question, For whom is a system of existence impossible? Contemporary postmodernists often argue that it is impossible for us humans and proceed as if they had established its impossibility per se. In assuming that what we cannot have simply is not, they exhibit, in spite of their protests against anthropocentrism, an anthropocentric assumption, never argued for, that the limits of human experience are the limits of reality. Ironically, this assumption has Hegelian fingerprints all over it.

Climacus clearly does not make this assumption. He writes, "A system of existence cannot be given [to us]. Is there, then, not such a system? That is not at all the case. Neither is this implied in what has been said. Existence itself is a system—for God, but it cannot be a system for any existing spirit. . . . But who, then, is this systematic thinker? Well, it is he who himself is outside existence and yet in existence, who in his eternity is forever concluded and yet includes existence within himself—it is God" (118–19).

Of course, Climacus does not purport to have established the reality of such a God or of such a complex relation between God and the world. If we take his claim that reality is a system for God at face value, we will conclude that although he tells us he is not a Christian, he is nevertheless a theist. But a weaker interpretation is sufficient for him to make his point, namely, that we are not in a position to rule out the theistic possibility and therefore not in a position to give up on the notion of truth, even when recognizing our own inability to possess it and preside over it.

Climacus's assault on the system is not an abandonment of the idea of truth. He loves Lessing (just as he loves Socrates) both because he recognizes that pure truth is for God alone and because he recognizes as his own vocation "*den einzigen immer regen Trieb nach Wahrheit* [the one and only ever-striving drive for truth]" (106, 108).[63] He even identifies this continuous striving as "striving for a system" (108). His point is not that we should stop writing systems, only that the advertising copy with which we present and promote them should embody a humility appropriate to the human condition.

| N O T E S

1. Kierkegaard came to see indirect communication as the essential meaning of pseudonymity, though the two are not synonymous. As Mackey reminds us, the latter is not his only tactic in developing the former (*Kierkegaard: A Kind of Poet,* 255). Moreover, Kierkegaard says of one pseudonymous text, *The Concept of Anxiety,* that "its form is direct and even somewhat didactic" (CUP 269). Still, the linkage is so close that he often suggests the equation just noted, even if it makes it all too easy for us to pay insufficient attention to the way Climacus defines direct communication.

2. I owe this apt distinction to a lecture by Paul Holmer.

3. From the Greek *maieuesthai,* to act as midwife; and *maieutikos,* of midwifery.

4. *Theaetetus,* 149–51.

5. Kierkegaard writes in a journal entry, "It may be said that there is something Socratic in me. Indirect communication was my native element" (JP 6.6532).

6. See chapter 4 of my *Kierkegaard's Critique of Reason and Society.*

7. Sigmund Freud, *The Ego and the Id,* chapter 2.

8. In chapter 2 we saw a bit of the contemporary critique of this notion in the critique of *mens auctoris* by Gadamer and French postmodernism. For a closer look at the issues involved, see "Expression and Meaning," investigation 1 of Husserl's *Logical Investigations,* trans. J. N. Findlay (New York: Humanities Press, 1970); and Derrida's detailed critique in *Speech and Phenomena.* Some of the same issues are raised in a Wittgensteinian context in the "private language" debate. See John Turk Saunders and Donald F. Henze, *The Private-Language Problem* (New York: Random House, 1967).

9. See especially part 1, "Essence and Eidetic Cognition," in Husserl's *Ideas, First Book,* trans. F. Kersten (The Hague: Martinus Nijhoff, 1983) and the index items on pp. 379 and 397.

10. Merleau-Ponty, *The Phenomenology of Perception,* trans. Colin Smith (New York: Humanities Press, 1962), xiv.

11. *Phenomenology of Perception,* xiv–xv, my emphasis.

12. See Sartre's "Existentialism Is a Humanism," in Kaufmann's *Existentialism from Dostoevsky to Sartre.*

13. It is important to remember that for Climacus, as a dialectical rather than a speculative thinker, synthesis means tension rather than resolution. The elements conjoined do not dissolve into a (re)solution but continue to oppose one another. See chapter 5, note 14.

14. See *Being and Time,* §§9–10, and the constant attempts to distinguish fundamental ontology from philosophical anthropology, pp. 37, 170, 227, 238, and 244. For Anti-Climacus, the syntheses of infinite and finite, eternal and temporal, and freedom and necessity clearly function as a normative anthropology (SUD 13ff.)

15. For these questions, see, respectively, *Critique of Pure Reason,* B xxiv–xxx and A 805 = B 833ff. In the introduction to his *Logic,* Kant says the three questions that express the "interests of my reason" in the Critique, namely, "What can I know?" "What ought I do to?" and "What may I hope?" are all aspects of a fourth, "What is man?" (*Logic,* trans. Robert S. Hartman and Wolfgang Schwarz [Indianapolis, Ind.: Bobbs-Merrill, 1974], 29).

16. Caputo expresses postmodernism's agreement with Climacus this way: "Deconstruction issues a warning that the road ahead is still under construction. Ethics [as speculative theory], on the other hand, hands out maps which lead us to believe that the road is finished and there are superhighways all along the way" (*Against Ethics*, 4). Rorty makes the point linguistically. Irony stands against the desire of metaphysical theory to find "a vocabulary final in every sense—a vocabulary which is no mere idiosyncratic historical product but the last word, the one to which inquiry and history have converged, the one which renders further inquiry and history superfluous" (*Contingency, Irony, and Solidarity* [New York: Cambridge University Press, 1989], 96). Ironically, that seems a good description of his own atheism.

17. In *Fear and Trembling* the leap is to infinite resignation rather than to biblical faith (FT 34–37). In *Fragments* it is from the premises of a proof for the existence of God to the conclusion (PF 43). And in *Johannes Climacus* it is to modern philosophy, which begins with doubt, from premodern philosophy, which does not (JC 137–38).

18. "On the Proof of the Spirit and of Power," in *Lessing's Theological Writings*, trans. Henry Chadwick (Stanford, Calif.: Stanford University Press, 1957), 55. For Aristotle, see *Posterior Analytics*, 1.7. In *Fragments*, Climacus describes coming into existence, the transition from possibility to actuality as a μετάβασις εἰς ἄλλο γένος (PF 73).

19. These categories are developed in Sartre's *Being and Nothingness*, trans. Hazel Barnes (New York: Philosophical Library, 1956); and Heidegger's *Being and Time*, respectively.

20. It does, however, challenge the claim of Hegel's *Phenomenology* that transitions from one shape of consciousness or one world of spirit to another have about them the kind of necessity that makes organic metaphors, such as the tadpole becoming a frog and the acorn becoming an oak, appropriate ways of describing qualitative transitions as natural and somehow inevitable. Hegel distinguishes shapes of consciousness from shapes of a spiritual world on page 265. For his own organic metaphors, see 2, 6, and 12; for his account of this transitional necessity, see 32 and 55–57. The two come together on pages 34–36. J. N. Findlay makes a heroic attempt to make sense out of Hegel's claim that dialectical transitions are necessary in chapter 3 of *Hegel: A Re-examination* (New York: Collier Books, 1962). The theory of the leap denies that new modes of human existence are necessary, either ontogenetically (developmentally) or phylogenetically (historically).

21. Louis P. Pojman, *Religious Belief and the Will* (New York: Routledge and Kegan Paul, 1986), 143. When combined with the view that the paradox is a logical contradiction, faith is seen as "the sheer wilful acceptance of the logically impossible by an act of will" (Terence Penelhum, *God and Skepticism: A Study in Skepticism and Fideism* [Dordrecht: Reidel, 1983], 82). Illuminating refutations of this interpretation of Climacus can be found in C. Stephen Evans, *Passionate Reason*, 128–42; and M. Jamie Ferreira, *Transforming Vision*, 7–40.

22. Climacus distinguishes his view of the leap from Schelling's theory of intellectual intuition and Hegel's theory of method (105). In other words, for metaphysical beliefs, he reads them as seeking to render the leap unnecessary by providing, respectively, the immediacy or the necessity that would leave the intellect fully in charge.

23. *An Enquiry Concerning Human Understanding*, sections 4–5.
24. Pojman finds the kind of epistemic volitionalism he attributes to Climacus incompatible with our duty to believe, as best we can, only what is true (*Religious Belief and the Will*, 158, 189–92). In his fourth meditation, Descartes argues just the opposite, that in the service of truth we must use our freedom to control our believing. Kierkegaard sides with Descartes, who holds "that freedom in man is superior to thought" (JP 3.2338). So does Climacus (PF 83n). Thomas Aquinas also links faith to will in the service of truth (See *Summa Theologiae*, II–II, q. 2, a. 9). Pojman interprets him, along with Descartes and Kierkegaard, as a direct volitionalist (145–49), but his emphasis on the necessity of grace in this connection makes that matter anything but clear. For an account of Aquinas that points to surprising affinities between his account and that of Climacus (without mentioning the latter), see Laura L. Garcia, "Natural Theology and the Reformed Objection," in *Christian Perspectives on Religious Knowledge*, ed. C. Stephen Evans and Merold Westphal (Grand Rapids, Mich.: Eerdmans, 1993), 122–27.
25. Climacus writes, "In that book I had perceived how the leap, according to the author, as the decision κατ' ἐξοχήν becomes specifically decisive for what is Christian" (105), in spite of the fact that neither the knight of infinite resignation nor Abraham represents Christian faith. But Climacus's reading is in keeping with his own understanding of the role of the reader's rights in relation to the author (see chapter 2 above).
26. Evans, *Passionate Reason*, 135–36.
27. This formulation comes from Penelhum. See note 21 above.
28. Evans, *Passionate Reason*, 136; cf. Kierkegaard's own analysis in *Christian Discourses*. Each of us knows from his or her own experience, he claims, "that at the bottom of his heart a man has a secret dread and mistrust of the truth, a fear of getting to know too much. Or dost thou really believe that it is every man's sincere wish to get to know effectually what self-denial is . . . but even a man of the better sort, one who has overcome the first shudder at the truth . . . will indubitably admit that over and over again he has had reason to suspect himself of hiding from the truth, as Adam hid among the trees" (CD 178).
29. This is Evans's formula (*Passionate Reason*, 135), intended to express an implication of the Pojman-Penelhum interpretation of Climacus as a direct volitionalist.
30. Evans, *Passionate Reason*, 134. In *Transforming Vision*, Ferreira seeks to refute a direct volitionalist reading of Climacus almost entirely on the basis of his identification of faith as a passion. She says that "the category of passion substantively qualifies what decision means in the case of faith." This seems right to me, but I find it misleading to say that the concepts of the leap and of passion are "in tension with each other" and need to be seen "as parallel and as mutually and substantively correcting or qualifying each other" (9). The text suggests to me that the notion of faith as a passion is an integral part of the theory of faith as a leap, incompatible with direct volitionalism but not in tension with an indirect volitionalism that will still speak of will and of decision. The great strength of Ferreira's analysis is her sustained development with reference to the imagination of the notion that the transition to a passion, whether fear or anger or love or faith, is best construed as a kind of *Gestalt* switch, free because, among other things, it is not determined by the intellect but is not simply chosen, either.

31. Spiritual writers, whether seeking to inculcate Buddhist skepticism or Christian faith, place great emphasis on attending, on deliberately directing the mind in a certain direction. In her analysis of passional transitions in terms of *Gestalt* switches, Ferreira emphasizes the indirect character of this control of cognition: "As in the case of a *Gestalt* switch, the disciplined effort of 'attending' can be thought of as an act of will, but it is not at all the direct willing of the acceptance of a conclusion. The *attending* is active and free, yet the recognition we have is not achievable by fiat" (*Transforming Vision*, 51).

32. For Derrida's similar analysis, see "Structure, Sign, and Play."

33. A similar kind of argumentation can be found in contemporary American philosophy of religion quite independently of Kierkegaard. See *Faith and Rationality*, ed. Alvin Plantinga and Nicholas Wolterstorff (Notre Dame, Ind.: University of Notre Dame Press, 1983); William P. Alston, *Perceiving God* (Ithaca, N.Y.: Cornell University Press, 1991); and Plantinga, *God and Other Minds* (Ithaca, N.Y.: Cornell University Press, 1967). The collapse of classical foundationalism is central to all these projects.

34. Hegel, *Phenomenology*, 49. The best account of the process by which various forms of consciousness deconstruct themselves is found in Joseph C. Flay, *Hegel's Quest for Certainty* (Albany: SUNY Press, 1984).

35. *Phenomenology*, 49–50. For a fuller analysis of Hegel's phenomenological doubt, see Westphal, *History and Truth in Hegel's Phenomenology* (Atlantic Highlands, N.J.: Humanities Press, 1979), 8–14.

36. Hegel, *The Encyclopedia Logic*, §81A2.

37. Cf. Kierkegaard's own claim, "No doubt it is because *Christianity is a radical cure* from which men shrink . . . they no doubt lack the strength to make the despairing *leap*" (JP 3.3247). This comes from an 1835 journal entry that opens with the claim that Christianity and philosophy are dialectically rather than speculatively related. "I have attempted to show why Christianity and philosophy cannot be united."

38. In an 1849 journal entry, Kierkegaard criticized Lessing on this point "insofar as this is a little too erotic and smacks a little too much, also in relation to truth, of wanting to regard the price as being more valuable than the truth. But this is really a kind of selfishness and can easily become a dangerous, yes, a presumptuous error" (JP 4.4375). We do not find a hint of such criticism from the pen of Climacus. Did Kierkegaard change his mind about Lessing? Perhaps. But I think we would do better to take this as an example of Kierkegaard's freedom to allow a pseudonym to develop a point as strongly as possible, even if he becomes somewhat one-sided in doing so. We are reminded again of Kierkegaard's plea not to attribute to him what his pseudonyms say.

39. For the textual evidence that Kant's theory of the thing in itself is an essentially theistic theory, see Westphal, "In Defense of the Thing in Itself" *Kant-Studien* 59, no. 1 (1968): 118–41. I have argued that the heart of the theory involves the contrast between the temporality of the human and the eternity of the divine (precisely the point that Climacus wants to make) in "Christian Philosophy and the Copernican Revolution," in *Christian Perspectives on Religious Knowledge.*

40. That the finitude of human knowledge is defined by its contrast to divine knowledge is central to both Kantian thought and that of Climacus (along with several other pseudonyms). Although Ronald

Green represents Kierkegaard as a "back to Kant" thinker in *Kierkegaard and Kant* (Albany: SUNY Press, 1992), 77, he has surprisingly little to say about this linkage.

41. Hegel, *Phenomenology,* 409, my emphasis replacing Hegel's.

42. *Phenomenology,* 6–7, my emphasis. For the prevalence of this theme of the new era in Hegel's thought, see Schlomo Avineri, *Hegel's Theory of the Modern State* (Cambridge: Cambridge University Press, 1972), chapter 4.

43. *Phenomenology,* 459–61. For more detailed analysis, see my *History and Truth in Hegel's Phenomenology,* chapter 7.

44. The *locus classicus* for this claim is the preface to the *Phenomenology.* For Hegel's holism, see especially 2, 7, 11, 20, and 28. For the concept of system, see 13–14.

45. This way of putting it has the advantage of permitting us to see how easily social systems, such as democracy, capitalism, and Western civilization, can replace philosophy as the basis of human claims to be final and ultimate. See Francis Fukuyama, *The End of History and the Last Man* (New York: Free Press, 1992).

46. See note 31 above.

47. See Fichte's *Science of Knowledge,* trans. Peter Heath and John Lachs (New York: Appleton-Century-Crofts, 1970), especially 93–102. Helpful commentary from Fichte's own pen can be found throughout *Fichte: Early Philosophical Writings,* trans. Daniel Breazeale (Ithaca, N.Y.: Cornell University Press, 1988), especially 124–25, 147–50, 247–56, and 322–25. For the transition from Kantian to speculative idealism, see Frederick Beiser, *The Fate of Reason* (Cambridge, Mass.: Harvard University Press, 1987); and George di Giovanni and H. S. Harris, eds., *Between Kant and Hegel* (Albany: SUNY Press, 1985). For Kierkegaard's earlier discussion of Fichte's I-I, see "Irony after Fichte," especially 272–74, in CI.

48. See Fichte, *Science of Knowledge,* 38–47; and *Early Philosophical Writings,* 204–6.

49. Hegel's early critique of Fichte is found in *Faith and Knowledge,* 153–87. His mature appreciation and critique are found in *Lectures on the History of Philosophy,* 3:229–36.

50. For Hegel's account of phenomenological recollection, see the final paragraph of the *Phenomenology,* and Westphal, "Johannes and Johannes: Kierkegaard and Difference," in Robert L. Perkins, ed., *International Kierkegaard Commentary: Philosophical Fragments and Johannes Climacus.* Climacus refers explicitly to the much discussed "question of the importance of the Hegelian phenomenology for the system" (117).

51. *The Encyclopedia Logic,* §24; and *Hegel's Science of Logic,* trans. A. V. Miller (New York: Humanities Press, 1969), 50. Cf. *The Encyclopedia Logic,* §85.

52. This is the language with which Kant describes the difference between synthetic and analytic judgments in the First Critique, B10 to B16.

53. See Willard Van Orman Quine, "Two Dogmas of Empiricism," in *From a Logical Point of View,* by Willard Van Orman Quine (New York: Harper & Row, 1963), 20–46.

54. Concerning the famous first move in his Logic, Hegel writes that "being—does not pass over but has passed over—into nothing" (nicht übergeht—sondern übergegangen ist) (*Science of Logic*, 82–83). Cf. 411 and 836; also 433, where he says that contradiction "*resolves itself*" (*löst sich auf*) because of the "self-transposition of [positive or negative] into its opposite" (jedes ist schlechthin das Übergehen oder vielmehr das sich Übersetzen seiner in sein Gegenteil). On the notion that the self-movement of the subject matter is the essence of philosophical method, see 53–54 and *Phenomenology*, 28–34, 49–55. In the former Hegel speaks of "the method which I follow in this system of logic—or rather which this system in its own self follows." In the latter he says that consciousness, the subject matter of the *Phenomenology*, provides its own criteria and examines itself, so that "all that is left for us to do is simply to look on" (53–54). Climacus notes the close link between movement and method in Hegel (109n).

55. *Science of Logic*, 70.

56. *Science of Logic*, 70–72. On Reinhold, cf. *The Encyclopedia Logic*, §10A, and *The Difference between Fichte's and Schelling's System of Philosophy*, trans. H. S. Harris and Walter Cerf (Albany: SUNY Press, 1977), 174–95. For discussion, see George di Giovanni, "The Facts of Consciousness," in di Giovanni and Harris, eds., *Between Kant and Hegel;* and Beiser, *The Fate of Reason,* chapter 8.

57. *The Encyclopedia Logic*, §86A1.

58. The *Phenomenology* and the Logic begin with the failed attempts to find a sensible and a conceptual immediacy, respectively. At each level philosophy begins with the insight that "there is nothing in heaven or in nature or mind or anywhere else which does not equally contain both immediacy and mediation, so that these two determinations reveal themselves to be *unseparated* and inseparable and the opposition between them to be a nullity" (*Science of Logic*, 68). In other words, this "failure" is the insight that leads to the realization that nothing can be absolute but the totality, that "the true is the whole" (*Phenomenology*, 11). Against every foundationalism, Hegel insists on this holism.

59. *Science of Logic*, 67–69.

60. *Science of Logic*, 70. For a helpful discussion of the issues raised here, see Tom Rockmore, *Hegel's Circular Epistemology* (Bloomington: Indiana University Press, 1986), 85–90, 100, and 107. Gabriel Marcel defines philosophy as "reflection of the second degree" that moves, in a Hegelian manner, from abstraction back to concretion. But like Climacus, he emphasizes the contingency of this activity: Truly philosophical reflection "exists only for and by means of freedom; nothing external can force me to exercise it. . . . My undeniable ability to pursue or not a sequence of thoughts, is, in the final analysis, only a mode of attention, and can be immediately exercised . . ." (*Creative Fidelity,* trans. Robert Rosthal [New York: Farrar, Straus and Giroux, 1964], 22–23). Husserl would agree that we perform the phenomenological reduction by virtue of a decision to do so. Climacus would want to press the question whether Hegel's justification of the starting point in terms of the result applies to this act of beginning and not just to the content with which I begin.

61. This argument is analogous to the argument of the *Phenomenology,* namely, that the phenomenological journey of consciousness to absolute knowing is through "stations appointed for it by its own nature" (49), thus constituting a "necessary sequence" (56).

62. It would turn Hegel into a Rorty, a kind of atheistic Climacus who stresses the contingency of our interpretations and choices, but in a context from which God and immortality had already been excluded with an ironically Cartesian certainty. See Rorty, *Philosophy and the Mirror of Nature* (Princeton, N.J.: Princeton University Press, 1979), and *Contingency, Irony, and Solidarity* (New York: Cambridge University Press, 1989). Derrida makes the point this way: "We must begin *wherever we are* and the thought of the trace . . . has already taught us that it was impossible to justify a point of departure absolutely" (*Of Grammatology*, 162).

63. Climacus comments on "einzig." He might well have focused on "rege" as well, which signifies, among other things, "in motion," "lively," "alert," "active," "industrious," "enthusiastic," and "zealous."

CHAPTER
S E V E N | **The Subjective Issue—
Becoming Subjective
(Pages 129–88)**

This chapter might have been entitled "the ethical and the world-historical." In the previous chapter we watched Climacus raise a moral objection to the Hegelian system—which had been completed "without having an ethics" (if indeed it had been completed at all)—only to withdraw it and to turn to satire instead, giving only the briefest of hints as to the meaning of that objectivism (119–22). Here he returns to that issue and explores it at more leisure.

It might seem that by focusing on the world-historical, Climacus is directing us away from the system, as expressed in Hegel's published works, to the lectures on world history that were published from student notes after his death.[1] But he does not see the theme of the world-historical as external to the system (133), and for good reason. In the last chapter we saw how deeply embedded the *Phenomenology* is in a philosophy of history, so that Hegel's claim that "now is the time for philosophy to be raised to the status of a Science" is to be understood in terms of his kerygmatic announcement of a "new era" and a "new world."[2]

Not surprisingly, Hegel's philosophy of objective spirit culminates in a philosophy of world history, both in its *Encyclopedia* version (§§548–52) and in the *Philosophy of Right* (§§341–60). What is surprising is that even the Logic, which purports to present "God as he is in his eternal essence before the creation of nature and a finite mind," is presented not as a peek out of time into eternity but as the wisdom of the new age.

As Hegel undertakes his task, he complains that "logic shows no traces so far of the new spirit which has arisen in the sciences no less than in the world of actuality," but he assures us that "once the substantial form of the spirit has inwardly reconsti-

tuted itself," a new logic is as inevitable as the new buds that replace the withered leaves on a tree.[3] His Logic is a work "belonging to the modern world."[4] Kant may be satisfied with a logic that
has not changed since Aristotle, but "if logic has not undergone
any change since Aristotle . . . then surely the conclusion which
should be drawn is that it is all the more in need of total recon-
struction; for spirit, after its labours over two thousand years,
must have attained to a higher consciousness about its thinking
and about its own pure, essential nature."[5]

The system is itself a world-historical event, possible only at
this point in history. To show a tension between the objectivity of
the world-historical and the subjectivity of the ethical would be to
illuminate the claim that the system has no ethics.

Climacus begins with two warnings. First, there is the difficulty in talking about subjectivity. To do so is an act of reflection
that makes subjectivity its object, its "case in point" (129), its
Sache, its theme. Since the question about ethical subjectivity is
a question about decision,[6] and since thematizing it is just as
much an act of theorizing as thematizing any other "case in
point," there is always the ironic possibility that talking about
subjectivity renders me less subjective, helping me "to evade
some of the pain and crisis of decision," postponing anything decisive until "one more book" or "one more paragraph" or "one more
argument" is produced. Thus, for example, reading or writing a
book about prayer may become an alternative to prayer itself, the
decisive act of bringing myself explicitly before God.[7]

The second warning is against "perdition's illusion" that the
subjective act of acceptance or appropriation follows "directly of
its own accord" from the objective determination of the truth, so
that we can forget about the former in order to concentrate on the
latter (129–30). We are intended to recall the earlier discussions
of the leap and of objectivity as endless approximation.

Climacus understands Christianity as wanting "to give the
single individual an eternal happiness, a good that is not distrib-
uted in bulk but only to one, and to one at a time" (130). Because
acceptance or appropriation of this gift necessarily involves decision, there is an inescapable subjectivity involved in becoming a
Christian. Climacus describes this moment as a "development or
remaking" of subjectivity, "the developed possibility of the
subjectivity's first possibility" (130). It is a kind of second-order
freedom.

Every human person is "something of a subject . . . a so-called
subject of sorts" (130–31). Every day we make decisions that give
content to our life. We decide whether to have Wheaties or Corn

Flakes for breakfast, whether to major in English or chemistry, whether to marry N. N., and so forth. These decisions range from trivial to momentous, and we may make them casually or carefully. By making these decisions, we preside over our lives to a limited but very real degree. They represent freedom's first possibility.

We make such decisions based on criteria that have been given to us. We inherit them from our family; we find them in our environment; or we invent them in moments of resistance to our social milieus. In Aristotle's sense, they are voluntary but not deliberate. No doubt it is the deliberate adoption of the criteria by which we make our everyday choices that represents the "remaking" or "developed possibility" of subjectivity's first possibility.[8] Here we are not so much choosing which move to make in a game already begun but are deciding which game to play, which makes all the difference in terms of the goals we will pursue and the rules we will have to obey. At this point we are asking Nietzsche's question, What is the value of our values?[9]

In terms of Kierkegaard's authorship, it may seem that we are talking about the conscious choice of one of the stages on life's way. But it is not quite that simple. Judge William, for example, wants A to choose the ethical life over the aesthetic life, but instead of saying, "Choose the ethical!" he says, "Choose yourself!"[10] He wants him to choose the ethical in a way in which he has not chosen the aesthetic. In the act of choosing a new set of criteria by which to live and judge his life, and as a transcendental condition for the possibility of making *that* choice, he wants the young man to accept responsibility for that choice, to posit that choice as a choice. I can adopt the aesthetic lifestyle without acknowledging my responsibility for having done so, but I cannot adopt the ethical in that way, for what I adopt *in that way* is simply not the ethical. The ethical involves a *how* as well as a *what,* and the name of that *how* is subjectivity. It is subjectivity, so understood, that takes us beyond being "a so-called subject of sorts."

It is this adverbial sense of the ethical to which Climacus appeals in the text before us. Although it is the speculative rather than the aesthetic that is his target, he stands much closer to Judge William than to Johannes de Silentio.[11] The question to be addressed to Hegelian ethics here is not the question of *Fear and Trembling,* whether the laws and customs of my people can be absolute for me, but whether the Hegelian understanding of ethics as *Sittlichkeit* involves enough subjectivity to deserve the name of ethics at all. That is the meaning of the question that structures the first part of the present chapter, *"what ethics would have to judge if becoming a subjective individual were not the highest task assigned to every human being"* (133). Since Climacus speaks of becoming and of a task, it is clear that the subjectivity he has in mind is not that by virtue of which each of us is "a so-called subject of sorts."

In Climacus's view Christianity (like Socrates) presupposes the adverbial-ethical as the condition of the possibility of the spiritual life that it sets forth (131). This creates a tension with the system, for, while Christianity does not deny that we should discard those subjectivities that can be described as "the accidental, the angular, the selfish, the eccentric, etc. . . . science and scholarship want to teach that becoming objective is the way, whereas Christianity teaches that the way is to become subjective, that is, truly to become a subject" (131). In this context, of course, "science" means the Hegelian system as philosophical science.[12]

These competing claims about "the way" represent a disagreement about the highest task for those who are "subjects of sorts." To be objective is to be an observer, and the system is seen as presenting "the objective trend toward becoming an observer" as "the *ethical* answer to the question of what I am to do ethically. (To be an observer, that is the ethical! . . .) And it is supposed to be certain that world history is the task assigned to our observing nineteenth century—the objective orientation is the way and the truth" (133).

If we were to summarize by saying that the first and greatest commandment of the system is, Thou shalt observe world history, we would capture the unmistakable element of satire in this account. To what degree does this caricature hit home? First, we have already noted that the linkage of the Hegelian system to the world-historical perspective is no caricature but its own pride and glory. Second, as philosophy, as the system of the philosophical sciences, Hegel's thought puts forth the strongest of claims to be *Wissenschaft*. Just as he concludes the *Phenomenology* with a claim to absolute knowledge, so he concludes the *Encyclopedia of the Philosophical Sciences* by assimilating the result to the divine thought that thinks itself.[13]

Finally, and most important, according to Hegel, *Sittlichkeit,* the ethical life of a people, belongs to the realm of objective spirit. This is the sphere where spirit objectifies itself as the historical development of social life, something quite different from the theoretical objectivity of *Wissenschaft,* which comes only at the next, higher level of development. As absolute spirit, the spiritual life that has externalized itself in the historical world returns to itself in self-knowledge, first as art and religion, which are not scientific, and finally as philosophy, which is. Philosophy, as the scientific self-knowledge of spirit, is presented as the highest manifestation of spirit. Although his style has something of the cartoonist, Climacus is not caricaturing when he presents the highest human task, according to the system, as becoming philosophical, which means becoming scientific, becoming objective. Since there is nothing in the Hegelian account to suggest that this becoming presupposes the adverbial-ethical as its transcendental condition, Climacus sees becoming objective as an alternative to (and thus an escape from) becoming subjective.

Although Climacus will joyfully satirize any talk about world history that pretends to see it whole, as if from outside it, he does not find anything intrinsically wrong with thinking world-historically as such. He rather views it as a "temptation" (135–36) "because this easily becomes a trap, a demoralizing esthetic diversion for the knowing subject" (134). The temptation is to allow my preoccupation with the world-historical, including, perhaps, the desire to become world-historical myself (135, 139), to divert me away from the highest, ethical task, that of becoming subjective. This is demoralizing, not because it weakens my morale but because it undermines my morality. As such it belongs to or is akin to the aesthetic stage. So we should not be surprised to find Climacus raising the question of criteria. He complains that "the absolute ethical distinction between good and evil is world-historically-esthetically neutralized in the esthetic-metaphysical category of 'the great,' 'the momentous,' to which the bad and the good have equal access" (134).[14]

This sustained assimilation of the system to the aesthetic sphere represents a recasting of the theory of the stages central to *Postscript*. It now begins to look like this:

> Objectivity
>> the aesthetic
>> the speculative
>
> Subjectivity
>> the ethical
>> the religious

What links the two moments of objectivity is the absence of the adverbial-ethical, while it is precisely its presence that links the ethical to the religious (in both of the modes that Climacus distinguishes, the immanent Religiousness A and the transcendent Religiousness B).[15]

Like Judge William, Climacus finds himself easily speaking about God in this discourse on the ethical. As the one who can "require everything of every human being" (136), God is the source of moral obligation. Climacus would agree with Kant that religion is, at least in part, "the recognition of all duties as divine commands."[16] Here religion is the presupposition of ethics. On the other hand, freedom is like the wonderful lamp of fairy tales: "When a person rubs it with ethical passion, God comes into existence for him" (138). Here ethics (in the adverbial sense) is the presupposition of religion. In the ontological order, God comes first; in the transcendental order, the ethical is prior. Together they define the domain of subjectivity.[17]

Having introduced God into the discussion, Climacus concludes the first part of the chapter with a reference to a famous line of Schiller and Hegel, "die Weltgeschichte ist das Weltgericht" (the history of the world is the judgment of the world).[18] "Perhaps," he comments, "it is this way for God. . . . But the human mind cannot see world history in this way" (141). Later, to be sure that we do not miss the point, he will add, "But to God, world history is the royal stage where he, not accidentally but essentially, is the only spectator, because he is the only one who *can* be that. Admission to this theater is not open to any existing spirit" (158).[19] In these passages he repeats, in the language of the world-historical, the point insisted upon earlier, namely, that reality is a system for God but not for any existing spirit (118).

The second part of the present chapter is shaped by the question, *What must be disregarded in a closer understanding of this task?* (141; cf. 130). What must be disregarded, it turns out, are certain objections to the world-historical project. The reason they must be disregarded is "lest attention be drawn away from the ethical" (141) by getting too involved in theoretical analysis. This is a version of the earlier warning that thematizing the ethical may be a way of avoiding it.

The first objection concerns the quantitative character of the world-historical. This is a reminder that when "the great" and "the momentous" is at issue, the operative categories concern the size of an action's impact rather than its inner form. This is why the ethical becomes, in the face of the world-historical point of view, "as shy as a sparrow in a dance of cranes" (142).

Climacus sees the Hegelian theory of *Sittlichkeit* as the view that "the ethical is supposed to find its concretion first in the world-historical, and only then in this concretion is it a task for the living." In other words, only when and insofar as a moral ideal has become the "moral substance" of the age, its "world-historical moral idea," does it have normative force for the individual. In this way the ethical is confused with the world-historical "by pertaining to millions rather than by pertaining to one" (143–44).

According to one form of this idea, the age requires "a prophet with a world-historical eye on world history" to tell it what its moral idea is; otherwise "we can all call it a day, for then no one knows what the ethical is" (144).[20] This, it could well be argued, is not Hegel's view at all. He is fond of the story of the father who asked how to give his son an ethical education, to which "a Pythagorean replied: 'Make him a citizen of a state with good laws.'"[21] Quite possibly it is this story he has in mind when he writes, "The wisest men of antiquity have therefore declared that wisdom and virtue consist in living in according with the customs of one's nation."[22] He clearly thinks that there is no need for philosophers or prophets as moral experts, since the normal socialization processes will provide all the moral training that any society is capable of providing.

Climacus anticipates the objection: "Now, if someone says that this is a pettifogging overstatement, that those who are occupied with world history gladly allow normal-school graduates and parish clerks [school teachers and Sunday School teachers] to lecture on popular ethics and do not mind that the lower classes in particular seek to live according to it, but that the world-historical interest designates only something superior, the much greater tasks—then this answer adequately shows that it was no pettifogging overstatement" (145). The quotidian ethics taught by parents and teachers may, on the first, ludicrous (145) assumption, require a world-historical genius to teach to the parents and teachers; but its requirements might well be passed on as the highest task for each individual to whom they are taught. But on the second, authentically Hegelian assumption, the movement from the ethical tasks of objective spirit (and even of the religious stage of absolute spirit) fall below the higher tasks of the philosophical, scientific, world-historical self-comprehension of spirit, at least for all who are sufficiently cultured to get excited about the system. Perhaps for the lower classes, the ethical, with help from the religious, remains the highest task.

It is in this context that Climacus speaks of the ethical as "to be discovered by the individual's becoming immersed in himself and in his relationship with God" (144) and, waxing hortatory, presents the ethical as saying, "dare to renounce everything [world-historically speaking] . . . dare to become nothing at all, to become a single individual from whom God ethically requires everything" (149; cf. 155, 157). Like Johannes de Silentio, Climacus affirms the individual alone with God not as a piety indifferent to the suffering of the world but as an almost desperate defense against a dual Hegelian threat: the claim that the customs and laws of one's people are the highest ethical criteria for anyone, and that at least for the cultured, the ethical task is surpassed by the higher task of philosophical comprehension. Against the ethnocentrism of the first notion and the cultural elitism of the second, Climacus pleads for an ethical-religious egalitarianism.[23] The priority of the ethical to the world-historical means "that first of all the wise person ought to understand the same thing that the simple person understands and ought to feel bound to the same thing that binds the simple person, and that only then should he pass on to the world-historical" (159–60).[24]

As we turn to the second objection, Climacus reminds us that it must once again be disregarded, not in the sense of discounting it but in the sense of not getting so wrapped up in discussing and debating it that our discourse on subjectivity renders us hopelessly objective. The objection is simply that world-historical knowledge, like all objective knowledge, is a matter of approximation.[25] As such it is *subject to the same dialectic as every dispute between idea and experience, which at every moment will prevent the beginning and, once begun, at every moment threatens a revolt against the beginning"* (149–50).

Against any claim to an absolute beginning grounded in intuitive immediacy, Climacus points to the gap between idea and experience. His critique of the metaphysics of presence claims that what the idea signifies is never wholly and simply present in experience. He does not linger long on this point because he is aware of Hegel's own critique of immediacy and of his appeal to his method against Schelling's intellectual intuition (150n). Hegel's strategy for surpassing approximation is not immediacy but totality, to which Climacus immediately turns.

Waiving the objection that the comprehension of world history is not possible until the occurrence of its denouement, he assumes that world history concerns itself with the past. But even here the materials are endless, generating "ever-new observation and research." Moreover, the general scheme for ordering these materials "depends upon arbitrariness and leaps." So it is not entirely clear "where China is to be placed in the world-historical process. . . . But then the system is not entirely finished yet" (150, 150n). Suppose, for example, that the general scheme assigns to Asia and Africa roles in the story that are more determined by Eurocentric colonial assumptions than by philosophical insight. If the cognitive task remains unfinished, the *Sache* is not fully present to knowledge by means of the totality strategy any more than by means of the immediacy strategy.

Climacus has a second totality objection, this one ethical rather than epistemological. Suppose one were to undertake the world-historical project with greater epistemological humility. One would see the story of the race rather than the story of the individual. This means the loss of the ethical, because the operative categories are the metaphysical, speculative categories of cause and effect rather than the ethical categories of good and evil. Correspondingly, one looks for the effects of human action rather than its intentions (154–56).

In other words, the actions of individuals are "traced away from the individuals and to the totality," a totality that can be described as "the immanence of cause and effect" (155). Climacus is picking up on the Spinozism at the core of Hegel's philosophy. Hegel says that "to be a follower of Spinoza is the essential commencement of all Philosophy" and that "You are either a Spinozist or not a philosopher at all."[26] He distinguishes himself from Spinoza in terms of the priority of spirit over substance as the primary category but affirms the latter's ontological holism. *Deus sive natura* has become *Gott oder Weltgeschichte*.

Climacus recognizes that the totality is no longer nature but world history. Still, as a totality construed in speculative rather than in ethical categories, it displaces the world of good and evil and the God who is the creator, law-giver, judge, and savior of that world. "Therefore God does not play the role of the Lord in the world-historical process as it is seen by human beings. Just as one does not see the ethical in it, so also one does not see God . . . in a fantastical sense God is the moving spirit in a process. In the world-historical process, God is *metaphysically* laced in a *half-metaphysical, half-esthetic-dramatic,* conventional corset, which is *immanence*. What a devil of a thing to be God in that way" (156, my emphasis).

If, on the contrary, God is the only spectator of the world-historical because, by transcending it he alone is able to see it as a totality, then the highest task for human beings would be the ethical task, one "sufficient for even the longest life" (158).[27]

Climacus begins the final section of this chapter by reflecting on the fact that while simple folk seem to understand this task, the wise find it extraordinarily difficult to do so, precisely because of its simplicity (159–60). Consistent with his self-appointed mission to point toward rather than away from difficulties (130, 187, 213, 241), he gives several "examples of thinking oriented to becoming subjective" (129), designed to show "how the simplest is-

sue is changed . . . into the most difficult" (165).[28] They concern
what it means to pray (162), what it means to die (165),[29] what it
means to be immortal (171), what it means to thank God for the
good he gives me (177), and what it means to marry (179).

Since Climacus devotes most attention to the issues of death
and immortality—as if to remind us that the issue from *Fragments* that gives rise to *Postscript* concerns the possibility of eternal happiness—we can focus on these two. He insists that about
these topics he knows "what people ordinarily know" (165, 171).
But that falls short of really understanding, for my certain death
and possible immortality are not exactly "topics." We are not
dealing with learned questions, which can be answered objectively and systematically, because the questions that he has in
mind cannot be asked that way (173–74). To make them into
themes for reflection and knowledge is to put them out in front of
me and to distance myself from them as a subject over against an
object. But what is at issue is the meaning of my own subjectivity,
and to pose the question objectively is to pose a different question
from the meaning of my death, my immortality.[30]

There is another way in which the issue of my death and my
immortality is not properly understood as a theme for cognition.
Any theme can become my intentional object when I turn my attention to it. To use Gestalt language, it then becomes the fore-
ground of my consciousness against a background of "surrounding"
themes. Thus, when I focus attention on these texts in *Postscript,*
I do so against the background of my knowledge of the rest of
Postscript, the other writings of Kierkegaard, the Hegelian corpus, and so forth. But my beloved, bumbling Chicago Cubs are
not to be found within this horizon, which provides the background that I inevitably "think with" this portion of *Postscript.*
They are, to return to Gestalt language, more like the objects
that fall entirely outside of my field of vision by being, for example, behind my back.

Of course, this can change. Just as I can redirect my vision to
objects that were part of the background or to objects that were
entirely outside my field of vision, so I can direct my thought now
to this and now to that. The problem with being a theme is that it
gets to be the center of attention, but not for long. It is like the
fame that Andy Warhol says each of us will get for fifteen min-
utes. And this, for Climacus, is the problem. To understand my
death or my immortality is not to comprehend it "once and for all,
or once a year" (166; cf. 176), as if we were dealing with Gödel's
theorem. Once upon a time I understood it, but now I can go for
months, even years at a time, without ever thinking of it. Truly to

understand my death or my immortality would be "to think it into every moment of my life" or "to think it every moment" (167–68). The question becomes "in what sense [I] must have the consciousness of [my death or of my] immortality present in [me] at all times" (175).

To have such consciousness present in me at all times cannot mean to have my death and my immortality before me at all times as the object of each intentional act. Under this impossible, morbid, and no doubt immoral scenario, whenever offered a penny for my thoughts, I could answer, "I am thinking about my death and immortality." So Climacus's formula, "to think it into every moment of my life," is perhaps less misleading than the formula "to think it every moment," for the former is easily expanded into "to think it into every moment of my life no matter what else I may be thinking about."

Such a thought, copresent with every thought, is not a theme, the noematic correlate of a noetic act. It is much more like the "I think" of Sartre's prereflective cogito. In reflection, the self becomes its own theme; but most of the time the self is not turned in on itself but out to the world, and the object of its consciousness is other than itself. But, insists Sartre, in every such consciousness, whose intentional structure as "consciousness of . . ." can be designated with such terms as "positional" or "thetic," the self has a "non-reflective," "non-positional," "non-thetic" consciousness (of) itself. Sartre puts the "of" in parentheses as a reminder that it does not signify the aiming of an intentional act at its intentional object but rather an awareness that accompanies every such aiming.[31] Without necessarily thinking about myself, I am always aware that I am the one who is thinking. Climacus seems to be groping for something like this, for a mode of thinking that is not the thematizing of some knowable but the silent accomplice of all such thematizing. To thematize my own death or immortality is both to distance or disengage myself as observer and to make my disengaged engagement with them occasional and episodic rather than ongoing. This is objectivity. Becoming subjective, so far as my death and my immortality are concerned, means allowing them to cross the moat that separates subject from object and to enter into the castle of my consciousness, becoming a permanent part of its everyday operation, whether as virus or as vitamin.

This is a difficult task, not exactly what the age is clamoring for.[32] But Climacus is always ready to distinguish what the age demands from what it needs. So he concludes with a parable: "When at a banquet where the guests have already gorged themselves, someone is intent on having more courses served and someone else on having an emetic ready, it is certainly true that only the former has understood what the guests demand, but I wonder if the latter might not also claim to have considered what they might require" (187).

Climacus sees the call to becoming subjective as a purgative badly needed by an age that has seriously overindulged in a debilitating diet of world-historical objectivity. But he is not "objectively sure . . . of the usefulness of [his] medicine," not because he has doubts about the diagnosis but because he suspects that with this kind of medicine everything depends "simply and solely on the way it is used" (188). Subjectivity is not the kind of therapy that heals objectively. Its *what* is inseparable from its *how*. But that is the theme of the next chapter.

| N O T E S

1.   See *Lectures on the Philosophy of World History: Introduction* and *The Philosophy of History.*

2.   *Phenomenology,* 3–7. See note 42 in chapter 6 above.

3.   *Science of Logic,* 50, 26.

4.   *Science of Logic,* 42.

5.   *Science of Logic,* 51. Cf. Kant's *Critique of Pure Reason,* B viii.

6.   See Judge William's admonitions to the aesthete to choose himself absolutely and in his eternal validity. This is the central theme of his second letter (in EO, vol. 2), "The Balance between the Esthetic and the Ethical in the Development of the Personality."

7.   It seems to me that the issue Climacus worries about here is very close to the one Levinas tries to get at in terms of the distinction between the saying and the said in *Otherwise than Being or Beyond Essence,* trans. Alphonso Lingis (Dordrecht: Kluwer, 1991). The prayer example is suggested by Henry Nouwen, especially in *A Cry for Mercy* (Garden City, N.Y.: Doubleday, 1983).

8.   See note 6 above. In his second letter, Judge William is pleading with the young aesthete to become subjective.

9.   Nietzsche, *On the Genealogy of Morals,* preface, sections 3 and 5.

10.   See note 6 above.

11.   An advantage of pseudonymous writing for Kierkegaard is that he can let different authors mean different things by such terms as "ethics" in order to explore a variety of different questions. But this means that the reader must be careful not to assume univocity.

12.   See the discussion of science and religion in chapter 5.

13.   The concluding words of the *Encyclopedia* are a quotation from Aristotle's *Metaphysics,* 12.7.1072b 18–30.

14.   That people have "equal access" to world-historical importance without regard to their moral characters stems from the fact that the consequences of their actions are not within their control. At first Climacus speaks of the role that luck plays in greatness (134), but he immediately changes to speak of God in the role of governance as the decisive factor (135–40, 147–48).

15. That the ethical is not antithetical to the religious here—as it was in *Fear and Trembling*—is due to fact that Climacus means by it something quite different from what Silentio means. See note 11 above.

16. Kant, *Religion Within the Limits of Reason Alone,* trans. Theodore M. Greene and Hoyt H. Hudson (New York: Harper & Row, 1960), 142.

17. For the implicit discussion between Kierkegaard and Levinas on whether the ethical or the religious is prior, see Westphal, "Levinas's Teleological Suspension of the Religious," in *Ethics as First Philosophy,* ed. Adriaan T. Peperzak (New York: Routledge, 1995), 151–60.

18. The phrase comes from Schiller's poem "Resignation." Hegel cites it, without attribution, in his *Philosophy of Right* (§§340–41; cf. 339A), and in his *Encyclopedia* (§548 - *Philosophy of Mind*). For Hegel it clearly means that there is no court of appeal beyond history.

19. Having made his epistemological point, Climacus cannot resist adding a note for edification: "If he fancies himself a spectator there, he is simply forgetting that he himself is supposed to be the actor in that little theater and is to leave it to that royal spectator and poet how he wants to use him in that royal drama."

20. The target of this satire is Grundtvig. See chapter 5, note 3.

21. *Philosophy of Right,* remark to §153. Hegel had already told this story in *Natural Law,* trans. T. M. Knox ([Philadelphia, Pa.]: University of Pennsylvania Press, 1975), 115.

22. *Phenomenology,* 214.

23. On the theme of egalitarianism in Kierkegaard, see Gene Outka, "Equality and the Fate of Theism in Modern Culture," *Journal of Religion* 67, no. 3 (July 1987): 275–88; and "Equality and Individuality: Thoughts on Two Themes in Kierkegaard," *Journal of Religious Ethics* 10, no. 2 (Fall 1982): 171–203. In writings subsequent to *Postscript* this theme is strongly developed in "Purity of Heart," part 1 of *Upbuilding Discourses in Various Spirits* (1847), and in *Christian Discourses* (1848), especially the chapters entitled "The Anxiety of Lowliness" and "The Anxiety of Highness." Between these two texts, it plays an important role in *Works of Love* (1847), in which it begins to work its way out of hidden inwardness into worldly outwardness.

24. As usual, Climacus is not arguing for the abolition of the world-historical but for its teleological suspension in the ethical.

25. See chapter 5 above on approximation.

26. *Lectures on the History of Philosophy,* 3:257, 283.

27. Echoing Johannes de Silentio, for whom faith is the task of a lifetime, Climacus repeats this motif of subjectivity as such a task. See 161, 163–65, 171, 179, 181–82. He holds that "to finish too quickly is the greatest danger of all . . . when time itself is the task, it is a defect to finish ahead of time" (164).

28. This chapter begins and ends with Climacus presenting himself as the merchant of difficulty. See 130, 186–87.

29. These few pages deserve to be compared with Heidegger's analysis of being-toward-death in *Being and Time,* §§46–53, and Tolstoy's "The Death of Ivan Ilych," another source on which Heidegger is deeply dependent.

30. On the limits to what can be thematized, see Levinas's critique of Husserlian intentionality in *Totality and Infinity,* trans. Alphonso

Lingis (Pittsburgh, Pa.: Duquesne University Press, 1969), his distinction between the saying and the said in *Otherwise than Being,* and Marcel's distinction between a problem and a mystery in *The Mystery of Being,* trans. G. S. Fraser (Chicago, Ill.: Regnery, 1960) and throughout his writings.

31. "The Prereflective *Cogito* and the Being of the *Percipere*" is the title of section 3 of the introduction to Sartre's *Being and Nothingness.* Sartre's treatment can be construed as a commentary on Kant's analysis of "pure" or "transcendental" apperception, the "I think" that must be able "to accompany all my representations" (*Critique of Pure Reason,* B 131).

32. This entire chapter is fruitfully read in relation to *Two Ages,* a literary review that Kierkegaard wrote almost simultaneously with *Postscript* and published, under his own name, just a month later. Its subtitle is *The Age of Revolution and the Present Age,* and it contains a critique of "the present age" (the title of the portion of this text published in 1962 by Alexander Dru) focused on its loss of ethical-religious responsibility by viewing itself as "the public," by deifying the "positive principle of sociality," and by disregarding "the separation of the religious individual before God in the responsibility of eternity" (TA 90–96, 86). "The public" might be viewed as the synchronic equivalent of what, diachronically viewed, is "the world-historical."

| The Subjective Issue—
Truth Is Subjectivity
(Pages 189–300)

> But to become involved with God in any way other than be-
> ing wounded is impossible, for God himself is this: *how* one
> involves himself with Him. As far as physical and external
> objects are concerned, the object is something else than the
> mode. . . . In respect to God, the *how* is *what*. He who does
> not involve himself with God in the mode of absolute devo-
> tion does not become involved with God. (JP 2.1405)

Objectively put, the question of truth focuses on *what* I believe; subjectively put, on *how* I believe. Put more specifically in
terms of the religious question, objectively the question is
whether what I am related to is "the true God," while subjectively
the question is whether my relation "is in truth a God-relation"
(199). *"Objectively the emphasis is on* what *is said; subjectively
the emphasis is on* how *it is said"* (202). What was called the adverbial-ethical in the previous chapter here becomes an adverbial
theory of truth as subjectivity. Attention is shifted from the said
to the saying.[1]

Nothing in *Postscript* is as notorious as the suggestion that
truth is subjectivity. Is this not, for better or for worse, the skeptical subjectivism that means first relativism, then nihilism, and
finally cynicism? Is it not (for better) the liberation from all re-
straints? or (for worse) the destruction of all order and decency?
Is it not the epistemological version of the famous slogan "If God
did not exist, everything would be permitted"?[2]

But Climacus is no atheist, and God plays an important role
in his epistemology, as we have already seen. Like Kant, he regularly contrasts human with divine knowledge. First, reality is a
system for God but not for any human knower (118); then God is
the only proper observer of world history, the only one for whom
die Weltgeschichte ist das Weltgericht, since human observers are

responsible actors who are located within, not beyond, its becoming (158, 141). Thus he denies neither the system nor the world-historical perspective, only the availability of these modes of knowledge to humans, who in his technical, temporal sense of the term, exist.

In the present context, Climacus returns patiently to the same distinction. Truth, as the agreement of thought and being, obtains for God but not for any existing spirit, "because this spirit, itself existing, is in the process of becoming" (190). The identity of thought and being is a "chimera" for us, "not because truth is not an identity, but because the knower is an existing person, and thus truth cannot be an identity for him as long as he exists" (196). The human knower is "*situated* in existence" (213), which means that both the subject and often the object of knowledge are in process (189).

"Existence," as Climacus uses the term, is the denial of idealism's claim to have transcended the human condition in order to see the world *sub specie aeterni,* whether in the transcendental immediacy of the pure I-I or in the dialectical mediation of the subject-object, that is, the unity of subject and object in spirit's final self-consciousness (189–92; cf. 197–99). But just as he did not deny either system or the world-historical perspective earlier, so here he does not deny eternal truth as the identity of thought and being, only the presence (presentness) of such truth to human subjects, whose present is always on the move. As with Kant before him and Derrida after him, Climacus finds the radical temporality of the human condition to be the barrier to absolute knowledge.[3]

While denying human access to the divine objectivity, Climacus, like Kant, affirms a certain human objectivity. By abstracting from everything subjective, human thought attains objective knowledge in such areas as mathematics and history.[4] Climacus may have selected these examples to include two different modes of human objectivity, one formal and tautological, the other tied to approximation and the leap.[5] But in either case, objectivity is purchased by abstracting from everything subjective—which is to say from just that first-person dimension of human life without which the ethical and religious become meaningless. This renders the objectivity that is available to us inappropriate when it comes to understanding ourselves ethically and religiously. To try to impose the objectivity of the disciplines on the ethical and religious aspects of my existence is to adopt a methodological prejudice that will guarantee misunderstanding.[6]

At this point Climacus makes it clear that his affirmation of truth as subjectivity is not a general theory of truth but a theory of human truth in what he calls "essential" knowing, the knowing "that pertains to existence . . . whose relation to existence is essential." Knowing "that does not inwardly in the reflection of inwardness pertain to existence is accidental knowing, and its degree and scope, essentially viewed, are a matter of indifference." Because the link between knowing and existing is essential, or constitutive, for essential knowing, "only ethical and ethical-religious knowing is essential knowing" (198; cf. 202). Once again Climacus dismisses the strategies of idealism, the pure I-I and the dialectically mediated unity of subject and object (198–99). This time the reason is not that we cannot attain these standpoints but rather that every step we take in their direction is a step away, by abstraction, from what is essential to essential knowing, my responsibility for my own becoming.

There is another reason why objectivity is not the right tool for the task that Climacus has in mind, whether this means the divine objectivity that we cannot attain or the human objectivity that we can: "The existing person who chooses the objective way now enters upon all approximating deliberation intended to bring forth God objectively, which is not achieved in all eternity, because God is a subject and hence only for subjectivity in inwardness" (199–200). In other words, objectivity is a misrelation to God as well as to myself when the question is one of decisively choosing myself.

This is the setting for Climacus's theory of truth as subjectivity. We can summarize this setting as follows:

1. There is objective truth of two kinds.
2. One kind is unavailable to us.
3. Another kind is available to us, but it is inappropriate as the cognitive correlate to self-understanding and self-choice before the ethical and before God.
4. It is to this utterly important dimension of human life, and to it alone, that the theory of truth as subjectivity applies.

Taking these qualifications into account does not guarantee that we will find Climacus's theory either plausible or palatable, but it does assure that the theory to which we respond will be his own, not some construction of our own or of the careless reading of others. As we turn to that theory, we find it presented in four moments: as a satire, as a parable, as a definition, and as a portrait.

The satire is about madness. Those who wish to extend the objectivity of the sciences to the whole of life think that by so doing they secure themselves against the dangers of subjectivity, whose ultimate form is madness. But, Climacus suggests, the absence of inwardness is also madness, and the affirmation of objective truth may be a sign, not of sanity but of madness (194).

Suppose a patient escapes from a madhouse and, wanting to appear sane so as not to be discovered and returned, decides to convince everyone of his sanity by the objective truth of what he says. To this end he puts a skittle ball in the tail of his coat, so that with each step he takes it will bump him on the behind and remind him to say, "Boom! The earth is round." Is he not insane, this man "who hopes to prove that he is not lunatic by stating a truth universally accepted and universally regarded as objective?" His madness shows itself, not in the failure to find objective truth but in the inappropriateness of his objective posture to his real-life situation. Could it be the same with the assistant professor who, "every time his coattail reminds him to say something, says *de omnibus dubitandum est*" (195), presumably the first and essential step for modern philosophy from Descartes to Hegel on its path to objective certainty?[7]

In this satire, Climacus takes the Hegelian distinction between the merely correct and the true and gives it a decidedly anti-Hegelian twist, since the truth that surpasses mere correctness is the subjective rather than the speculative.[8] At the same time, he is able to distinguish two forms of madness, the kind that objectivity fears and the kind that it all too easily exhibits.[9] There is the madness of Don Quixote, "in which the passion of inwardness grasps a particular fixed finite idea." The madness consists, we might say, in the incongruity between the *what,* the object of concern, and the *how,* the quality of the concern. "But when inwardness is absent, parroting lunacy sets in, which is just as comic . . . when the insanity is the absence of inwardness, the comic is that the something known by the blissful person is the truth, truth that pertains to the whole human race but does not in the least pertain to the highly honored parroter. This kind of insanity is more inhuman than the other . . . one listens to [it] in cold horror" (195–96).[10]

The satire formulates the theory in this way: truth is subjectivity in just those contexts where the *what,* the said, be it ever so correct, objectively speaking, is rendered at once comic and tragic by a *how,* a saying that is devoid of the inwardness that makes the speaker human. But what about the converse? Suppose I get the *how* right and the *what* wrong (whether by the ultimate standards of divine objectivity or the distinctly penultimate standards of human objectivity)?

At this point Climacus introduces the parable that may be the most famous part of his entire authorship: "If someone who lives in the midst of Christianity enters, with knowledge of the true idea of God, the house of God, the house of the true God, and prays, but prays in untruth, and if someone lives in an idolatrous land but prays with all the passion of infinity, although his eyes are resting upon the image of an idol—*where, then, is there more truth?* The one prays in truth to God although he is worshipping an idol; the other prays in untruth to the true God and is therefore in truth worshipping an idol" (201, my emphasis).[11]

This is not, of course, an argument for the truth of Christianity. That is not the issue. It is important to recognize the *ad hominem* dimension of the story. Climacus is writing to an audience that does not doubt that the Christian conception of God is the right one and is proud to be in possession of this truth. Neither challenging nor defending that assumption, Climacus uses it as an assumption in order to pose his question.

It is also important to recognize what the question is. Although when he first distinguishes objectivity from subjectivity, Climacus asks, "Now, on which side is the truth?" (199), as if it were a simple either/or, he now asks a more nuanced question, "where, then, is there *more* truth?" (my emphasis). In fact, by posing the question that way just before the parable, in the middle of the parable, and immediately after the parable, he underscores the comparative character of his question. On the assumption that neither party is in a very good situation, since both are said to be "worshipping an idol," the question is whether one form of idolatry is worse than the other, whether one kind of error is closer to the truth than the other kind. Who is more to be pitied, Don Quixote, with his misdirected subjectivity, or the parroting assistant professor who lacks subjectivity altogether? Here we might formulate the (hypo)thesis that truth is subjectivity in this manner: truth is subjectivity in just those contexts where the inner integrity of the saying is more important than the outer correctness of the said.

To suggest, as Climacus does here, that prayer—or, more generally speaking, the God-relation—is just such a situation is to challenge the assumption that orthodoxy is more important than integrity. To put the point in an extreme manner, as is suggested by the parrot image employed twice in the satire, the parrot who can recite the Apostles' Creed is not a very good paradigm of piety. One might object that the parrot does not sincerely believe what it says. But Climacus asks whether the human who differs from the parrot only by sincerely believing the creed is not more like the parrot than like a truly pious person. What he means by inner integrity—his own words are "all the passion of infinity"—may include sincere belief but clearly points to a *how* that is not only or even primarily specified in those terms.

That is one reason why the (hypo)thesis he is exploring is not happily paraphrased as *it does not matter what you believe, as long as you are sincere.* The other reason is that nothing Climacus says suggests that it does not matter what one believes. To say that it is better to have a transmission that slips than to have a broken fuel pump is not to say that it does not matter whether or not your transmission slips. It is only to say that one problem is more serious than the other.

For all their rhetorical force, neither the satire nor the parable captures what we might call the epistemological Stoicism of Climacus. That task falls to the definition in which his (hypo)thesis is expressed a third way: "*An objective uncertainty, held fast through appropriation with the most passionate inwardness, is the truth,* the highest truth there is for an *existing* person" (203, his emphasis). This definition, he tells us, is "a paraphrasing of faith. Without risk, no faith" (204).

Stoic ethics rests on the observation that some things are within our power, while others are not, and on the admonition to direct our energies to the former. The phrase "objective uncertainty" points to the fact that in Climacus's ethics of belief, objective truth is not within our power. As early as his discussion of Lessing, he says, "The perpetual process of becoming is the uncertainty of earthly life, in which everything is uncertain" (86). Situated within existence as becoming, we cannot attain the certainty that belongs to the divine objectivity; and the human objectivity that is available to us is always a matter of approximation and thus a task never finished.[12] Climacus has, as it were, read his Peirce and is a fallibilist. The objectivity of the sciences leaves our best-established beliefs and theories subject to refutation and revision, or, in a word, uncertain.[13]

Climacus specifies this with relation to our knowledge of God: "I observe nature in order to find God, and I do indeed see omnipotence and wisdom, but I also see much that troubles and disturbs. The *summa summarum* [sum total] of this is an objective uncertainty" (203–4).

At this point epistemological Stoicism is a protest against giving primary attention to achieving objective certainty, both because it is not within our reach and because the pursuit of this chimera distracts us from what *is* within our power, the personal appropriation of our best moral and religious insights, fallible as they are. This does not entail that we abandon the critical examination of our beliefs; Climacus never praises subjectiv*ism*. It only forbids that the cognitive task of critique- and system-building, defined by an impossible goal, become so all-consuming that we not only neglect the more important tasks of subjectivity but also come to think of ourselves as a fantastical I-I or subject-object for whom such tasks are at best incidental, the kind children put aside in order to pursue the serious work of adulthood.

Implicit in this account are the two reasons that Climacus has for calling truth as presented in his definition "the highest truth there is for an *existing* person" (203). According to the Hegelian account, philosophy is higher than both ethical life (*Sittlichkeit*) and religion because it is the systematic, scientific certainty of the true meaning of everything. But for Climacus, philosophy, so construed, does not represent a higher truth because it is not attainable and because even if it were, it would be a step down rather than a step up.

It would be a movement in the wrong direction because the tasks of subjectivity are the highest tasks of all. They are closer to the core of what makes us human than are the tasks of objectivity. This is why the madness of "the highly honored parroter," in whom inwardness is absent, is "more inhuman" than the madness of Don Quixote (which involves the misdirection of inwardness) and can only be apprehended "in cold horror" (195–96). These tasks are to be pursued "with all the passion of infinity" (201)—with passion because they are self-involving rather than disinterested, and with the passion of infinity because—unlike the passion, say, for stamp collecting or bodybuilding—this passion about the very meaning and destiny of my existence is and deserves to be my ultimate concern.[14]

The fourth presentation of the idea of truth as subjectivity is a portrait of Socrates, intended to give flesh and blood to the abstract definition just presented. "He poses the question [of immortality] objectively, problematically: if there is an immortality. . . . He stakes his whole life on this 'if'; he dares to die, and with the passion of the infinite he has so ordered his whole life that it might be acceptable—*if* there is an immortality" (201). This passionate, inward appropriation of what is objectively uncertain makes the Socratic wisdom—or, more specifically, the Socratic ignorance—the embodiment of truth as subjectivity (204, 202).

The presentation of Socrates as a model confirms the earlier suggestion that truth as subjectivity is not a form of subjectiv*ism* in that it does not subscribe to any of subjectiv*ism*'s tenets: It does not matter what you believe as long as you are sincere;

Truth is, in the final analysis, a matter of personal taste; Since
we are not able to possess objective and final truth, it follows that
there is no such thing; So there is no point to critique and argument in the search for truth.

The introduction of Socrates permits Climacus to return to
the problematic of *Fragments*. But Socrates has changed from villain to hero. To call him the villain in *Fragments* is simply to note
his identification with the principle that knowledge is recollection, which Climacus takes to lie at the heart of the speculative
point of view. In his dissertation, Kierkegaard had described how
Socrates "so beautifully binds men firmly to the divine by showing
that all knowledge is recollection" (CI 30). Here, as in *Fragments,*
Climacus treats the recollection thesis as the heart of the speculative collapsing of the difference between the divine and the human; but now he portrays Socrates as shying away from it and
leaving it to Plato. Instead of being the embodiment of the speculative, he is the hero who challenges it: "Socrates essentially emphasizes existing, whereas Plato, forgetting this, loses himself in
speculative thought. . . . The thesis that all knowing is recollecting
belongs to speculative thought, and recollecting is immanence. . . .
To emphasize existence, which contains within it the qualification
of inwardness, is the Socratic, whereas the Platonic is to pursue
recollection and immanence" (205, 206n).[15]

Here Climacus adopts the sharp distinction, developed by
Kierkegaard in *The Concept of Irony,* between Plato as the paradigm of a speculative thinker and the "historical" Socrates, who
represents not the positivity of the idea and of myth but the negativity of irony and ignorance, the primacy of question over answer (CI 29–156).[16] He calls our attention to this change of
perspective, noting that in *Fragments* he had no need to distinguish Socrates from Plato (206n). This naturally raises the question, What is the need to do so now?

The answer is clear: to present Socrates as an analogue to
faith (205, 206n). This answer, in turn generates two further
questions: In what sense is Socrates an analogue to faith, and
what is the point of drawing this analogy?

With regard to the first of these, we need to recall that
Socrates is presented here as the embodiment of Climacus's definition of truth as subjectivity, a definition he describes as "a
paraphrasing of faith," emphasizing the element of risk in faith,
the uncertainty that finds itself "out on 70,000 fathoms of water"
rather than on the terra firma of pure (in)sight. Now the question
in *Fragments* about the possibility of going beyond Socrates takes
on a new meaning. It is no longer the stark antithesis between

the speculative standpoint and Christian faith as Climacus understands it but rather the subtler distinction between Socratic faith and Christian faith. In other words, it is no longer a matter of recollection versus revelation but a comparison of two modes of truth as subjectivity.

Already in the person of Socrates we encounter paradox.[17] "The paradox is the objective uncertainty that is the expression for the passion of inwardness that is truth. . . .The eternal, essential truth, that is, the truth that is related essentially to the existing person by pertaining essentially to what it means to exist . . . is a paradox" (205). This is not the paradox of *Fragments*. The objectivity that uncertainty perceived as the eternal, essential truth is not the incarnation of God but the immortality of the human person. That this truth is related to an existing person seems to mean that this truth, which is about the eternal, is essential to the meaning of a person's present existence in time; and that it is proposed for belief to an existing person, who is thereby asked to apprehend eternity from a radically temporal standpoint. In either the ethical or the epistemological case, the paradox is the tension between my immersion in time, on the one hand, and my transcendence of time, my belonging to eternity, on the other. It is this tension that Anti-Climacus refers to when describing the human self as a synthesis of the temporal and the eternal (SUD 13).

Immortality is objectively uncertain for Socratic ignorance by virtue of the paradoxical character of the human self, a duality that refuses to resolve itself into a dualism. This is what makes Socratic ignorance "an analogue to faith," or, more specifically, "an analogue to the category of the absurd" (205, 206n). In *Fear and Trembling,* another Johannes had used the terms "paradox" and "absurd" quite interchangeably (FT 33–67). Here, by contrast, the paradox to be found in Socrates is but an analogue to the absurd, to "the paradox *sensu eminentiori*" and to "faith *sensu eminentiori*" (206n). In relation to the Socratic paradox, the specifically Christian paradox, here designated as the absurd, contains "even less objective certainty" and generates an "infinitely deeper" inwardness (205). In either case "the unthinkable enters into the field of our thought only by rendering itself unthinkable there by excess, that is, by criticizing our thought."[18]

It will come as no surprise to readers of *Fragments* that Climacus identifies the specifically Christian paradox (the absurd) in terms of two notions: incarnation and sin. To complete our answer to the question of how Socrates is an analogue to Christian faith, it will be necessary to see how Climacus treats these two themes in relation to the problematic of going beyond Socrates.

In keeping with Kierkegaard's sense that Christianity makes no sense at all apart from its understanding of human sinfulness, Climacus introduces sin first. Consider the claim "Subjectivity is untruth" (207). Speculation affirms it, meaning that we must concentrate our efforts on becoming objective. But Socrates and Christianity, both teaching that truth is subjectivity, also begin with this affirmation. For Socrates, the untruth of subjectivity is precisely the desire to become objective, the flight from subjectivity itself. Thus the Sophists aesthetically flee the eternal and Plato speculatively flees the temporal in order to avoid living the tension—whose name is subjectivity—of being both. Christianity also sees the untruth of subjectivity as the unwillingness to be oneself,[19] but it interprets being in untruth as having passed into untruth in time and calls this passing sin. This has an important bearing on the possibility of returning to the truth, since "a change so essential has taken place in him that he in no way can take himself back into eternity by Socratically recollecting. . . . If even Socrates comprehended the dubiousness of taking himself speculatively out of existence back into eternity, when there was no dubiousness for the existing person except that he existed and, of course, that existing was the essential—now [that the existing person is understood as a sinner] it is impossible. He must go forward; to go backward is impossible" (207–9).

Twice in the passage just cited, Climacus speaks of backing out of time into eternity, a locution he will repeat by speaking of "the retreat out of existence into eternity by way of recollection" (209–10), "recollection's removal of itself from existence" (217), and "taking oneself out of existence back into the eternal through recollection" (226).[20] This is his graphic way of describing the Platonic strategy for escaping the tasks of subjectivity by becoming objective. The metaphysics of presence promises to put the subject in the direct and unmediated presence of the eternal, ultimate truth. In the *Phaedo,* Plato puts it this way: "we must get rid of the body and contemplate things by themselves with the soul by itself" (66e).

Climacus's point is quite simple. Socrates, whose only defense against this move is his awareness of human finitude in the mode of temporality, flirts with this possibility before recognizing its "dubiousness" and taking his stand with irony and ignorance. Christianity, with its employment of sin as an epistemological category, provides a stronger defense against this temptation. If it is not just my temporal situatedness that stands between me and a divine perspective on the real but also my having broken my properly human links to the eternal by my insistence on

moral and cognitive autonomy, then there is a double moat sepa-
rating me from objectivity: my finitude and my sinfulness. The
one limits my capacity, the other my willingness, to let eternal
truth come to light in the clearing of my understanding.

Socratic faith is an analogue of Christian faith by virtue of
recognizing the problematic character of the speculative project.
Christianity goes beyond Socrates by giving a more radical diagnosis of the problem on the side of the knowing subject.

Turning to the "object" of faith, that which is objectively uncertain, we find ourselves comparing immortality and incarnation as paradoxical. Climacus says, "Viewed Socratically, the
eternal essential truth is not at all paradoxical in itself, but only
by being related to an existing person" (205). To put it in the language of propositions, there is nothing paradoxical about the
proposition "the soul is immortal"; the objective uncertainty, here
called paradox to distinguish it from the objective uncertainty of
empirical knowledge and its approximation process, arises from
the assumption that this truth about eternity is to be grasped
from within time.

If we move from the Socratic situation, where "the paradox is
not in itself the paradox," to the Christian situation, where "the
paradox itself is the paradox," we can introduce the category of the
absurd to signify the difference (209). "What, then, is the absurd?
The absurd is that the eternal truth has come into existence in time,
that God has come into existence in time, that God . . . has been born
. . . as an individual human being" (210). In other words, there is
something problematic about the proposition "Jesus of Nazareth is
God incarnate" that is not found in the proposition "the soul is immortal." Since Climacus almost immediately begins to speak about
contradiction, it is tempting to read Climacus as saying that what
makes the Christian paradox absurd is the need to affirm a proposition that is formally self-contradictory.

But that is not what he says. In the first place, his claim that
with regard to the incarnation "the paradox itself is the paradox"
(by contrast to the Socratic situation, where "the paradox is not
in itself the paradox"), does not keep him from describing it as the
claim "that something that can become historical only in direct
opposition to all human understanding has become historical"
(211). In other words, for Climacus as for Silentio, the absurdity
of the Christian paradox is relative to the human point of view,
whose ultimacy they are both more than ready to question. Just
as stories about snow will be absurd to someone who knows only
the tropical rain forest, so the story of the incarnation will be absurd to those who have only the human understanding to go on.

But why, then, does Climacus suggest that the incarnation is itself or in itself the paradox? How can we reconcile the "in itself" language, which suggests that the incarnation is inherently absurd, with the language of relativity, which suggests that it is only absurd to those in a particular, non-normative situation? It looks as if Climacus wants to say that the "object" of Christian faith is problematic in a way that the "object" of Socratic faith is not; that is, apart from whatever problems arise from trying to recognize the truth of "the soul is immortal" and "Jesus of Nazareth is God incarnate" from within the temporal parameters of human experience, the latter proposition has a special problem of its own.

Is that problem one of self-contradiction? Does the first proposition parse as "A is B," the latter as "A is not-A"? While speaking of the absurdity of the incarnation, Climacus speaks twice of contradiction. Here is the first passage: "When Socrates believed that God is, he held fast the objective uncertainty with the entire passion of inwardness, and faith is precisely in this contradiction, in this risk. Now it is otherwise. Instead of the objective uncertainty, there is the certainty that, viewed objectively, it is the absurd" (210). Here the contradiction is already in the Socratic position, and it does not concern the logical form of the proposition but the experienced tension between the persuasion that God's existence is objectively uncertain and the practice of basing one's whole life on it. Climacus is using the term "contradiction" in good Hegelian fashion to designate situations of opposition, otherness, difference, and tension rather than in the narrower sense of formal logic.

Moreover, this passage suggests the relativity of the absurd. The "object" of Christian faith is said to be the absurd only under the qualifier "viewed objectively," and it is precisely against the normative ultimacy of the objective point of view that Climacus directs the best arguments and satires he can muster.

The second passage speaks of the object of faith as absurd "precisely because it contains the contradiction that something that can become historical only in direct opposition to all human understanding has become historical. This contradiction is the absurd, which can only be believed" (211). Here again the contradiction is not within the proposition but between the proposition and the human understanding. In other words, the absurdity in question is not the formal contradiction of a self-contradictory proposition; rather, it is the contradiction between a proposition and a particular point of view opposed to it.

Climacus seems to think that *from the human point of view* the idea of human immortality is inherently unproblematic (though it may be difficult to justify any knowledge claims on the topic), while the idea of a divine incarnation is inherently problematic. This way of speaking shows how the language of the "in itself" paradoxical and the language of the relativity of the paradox to a particular point of view can be combined. It is *for us* that the notion of incarnation is inherently (and not just epistemically) problematic. This might make sense as follows: viewed Platonically, the thesis of immortality is a claim about the eternity of the eternal, while viewed Christianly, the thesis of the incarnation is a claim about the eternal and infinite becoming a temporal and finite being. Any claim about the eternal will raise epistemological problems for knowers situated in time, but beyond this, claims about the eternal entering time introduce problems not found in claims about the eternity of the eternal. Hence the distinction between the paradox and the paradox *sensu eminentiori*.

One final piece of evidence confirms the interpretation of the paradox as being absurd only relative to a particular point of view. Climacus represents speculative philosophy as saying, "From the point of view of the eternal, the divine, the theocentric, there is no paradox," to which he replies, "I shall not be able to decide whether the speculative thinker is right, because I am only a poor existing human being who neither eternally nor divinely nor theocentrically is able to observe the eternal but must be content with existing" (212). If the paradox in question were inherently absurd, period, rather than inherently absurd for us (poor existing human beings), he would not be able to entertain the claim that there is a divine point of view, from which it is not paradoxical at all. But his response to this suggestion is not to deny its possibility, insisting on the absolute absurdity of incarnation; rather it is simply to insist that he cannot occupy the point of view in question.[21]

We can now complete our answer to the question of in what sense Socrates is an analogue of Christian faith. Socratic faith is an analogue of Christian faith by virtue of recognizing the problematic character of the speculative project. Christianity goes beyond Socrates by giving a more radical diagnosis of the problem on the side of the truth to be known.

But what is the point of making this comparison? The two-way contrast of *Fragments* has become a three-way contrast. On the one hand, Socratic subjectivity is compared with Christian subjectivity as its analogue; but the sharper contrast is between both modes of subjectivity and speculative objectivity, here represented by Platonic recollection. The basic contrast in *Fragments* between speculative thinking and Christianity is still a central theme, but moving Socrates to the role of ally rather than of antithesis to Christian subjectivity gives the analysis a new dimension.

In order to understand the significance of this new dimension, we need to keep *Postscript*'s table of contents in mind. Climacus is interested in comparing speculative philosophy (in such major representatives as Plato and Hegel) with Christian faith. To put the point in a contemporary parlance, Climacus is interested in freeing Christian faith, which he does not himself profess (617), from its Babylonian captivity to the onto-theological objectivity of the metaphysics of presence. He does not proceed as philosophers often do, by asking which propositions these standpoints hold in common, which are held by one but denied by the other, and which, of all these propositions, are true. He takes a phenomenological (subjective) rather than a propositional (objective) approach to the matter, asking what it means to become a Christian. Perhaps in some future life he has already read Thomas Nagel's essay "What Is It Like To Be a Bat?"[22] and was helped thereby to formulate his questions, What is it like to be a Christian? and how does that compare with being a speculative philosopher?

The present chapter belongs to a section entitled "The Subjective Issue, or How Subjectivity Must Be Constituted in Order That the Issue Can Be Manifest to It." The issue, of course, is becoming a Christian, and the question is a transcendental one about the conditions of the possibility of that activity. Where must I be in experiential or phenomenological space in order for Christian faith even to be a possibility for me? The answer, in a word, is subjectivity, and the point of the Socrates analogy is to present in concrete form the generic subjectivity that is the condition of the possibility of the specifically Christian mode of subjectivity. Socratic faith is presented neither as the antithesis of, nor even as an alternative to, Christian faith but rather as an analogue because the two are not species of the same genus. The one is the generic condition of the possibility of the other's specificity.[23]

This has an immediate consequence that Climacus is not hesitant to point out. He is willing to concede that, objectively speaking, Christianity may be true (231–32, 234, 369, 379); but on the other hand, speculative philosophy may be in the right (224, 271, 273). He remains noncommittal (619): "But if Christianity is perhaps in the wrong, this much is certain: speculative thought is definitely in the wrong" (226), not per se but in its claim to have explained Christian faith in such a way as to be its highest form.[24] In a later discussion of humor, Climacus will say, "Whether humor and speculative thought are in the right is something else, but they are never in the right in declaring themselves to be Christianity" (271n). The question is "how the speculative explanation is related to the Christianity that it explains" (226).

For Climacus the answer is clear: "And when Christianity declares itself to be the paradox,[25] the speculative explanation is not an explanation but a correction, a polite and indirect correction, such as befits a superior intellect in relation to the more limited" (220). In its modern form speculative thought is but a replay of "pagan reminiscence," the immanence that is "recollection's removal of itself from existence . . . to which there is nothing to object if it breaks directly with Christianity but much to object if it is supposed to be Christianity" (217). In other words, far better to be Lessing, who repudiates Christianity, than Hegel, who seeks to improve it.

The above contrast between a superior and a limited intellect introduces a second consequence that Climacus draws from the Socrates analogy and the truth-is-subjectivity hypo(thesis) to which it belongs. He sees a cultural elitism in speculative thought, for which the difference between "the best brain" and "the most obtuse" (217) or between "more and less gifted and educated people" (220) becomes important: "the speculator and the simple person in no way know the same thing when the simple person believes the paradox and the speculator knows that it is annulled" (227), but the latter knowledge requires a level of intellect and culture not available to everyone. In this way "humankind is vexed because there is not an equal relationship with God for all human beings. . . . Nor does [speculative thought] respect the equality implicit in the difference between the wise person and the simple person—that they know the same thing" (227). Both know "the paradox as paradox," and neither can "comprehend the divine mercy that can forgive sins" (228). The only difference between them—and it is "a meaningless trifle" (227)—is that the wise person will have a more learned understanding of the incomprehensibility; but, the wise one says to the simple believer, "Look, this difference certainly cannot disturb you . . . as if I had some advantage over you" (228).[26]

Climacus develops this egalitarian motif with reference to the distinctively Christian paradox. But he does so in such a way as to make it clear that this equality belongs to the sphere of subjectivity as such. Did not Socrates insist that he was wiser than others, not by having attained the idea but by seeing so clearly that he had not?

After telling the story of his "call" to the task of distinguishing speculation from subjectivity (a story that speaks for itself and needs no commentary), Climacus ends the present chapter with an appendix entitled "A Glance at a Contemporary Effort in Danish Literature." This is an extended review of Kierkegaard's pseudonymous writings to date[27] and the various volumes of "edifying" or "upbuilding" discourses that Kierkegaard published during the same period under his own name. Climacus identifies the pseudonymous writings as pseudonymous, with the exception of his own *Fragments,* which he includes in the review.

There are three reasons to read this appendix. First, it contains important reflections on authorship, readership, and indirect communication and, as in chapter 2 above, should be consulted whenever these issues in the Kierkegaardian corpus are under discussion. Second, it makes a stimulating accompaniment to the reading of each of the texts it reviews.

But neither of these functions of the appendix can account for its being placed at this point of *Postscript.* Why not, for example, include it with "A First and Last Explanation," appended to *Postscript* as a whole, in which Kierkegaard acknowledges being the "author" of all the pseudonymous works? Why put it in Climacus's voice, and why at just this point?

The answer to these questions gives us the third occasion for reading "A Glance." Climacus proposes a twofold relation between his truth-is-subjectivity (hypo)thesis and Kierkegaard's other writings, suggesting—as Kierkegaard himself will in *Point of View*—that these writings have a deep inner coherence that makes them best read in relation to each other and not in isolation. In the first place, Climacus reads the prior authorship as focusing on existing as a task, understood in terms of subjectivity and inwardness. As such, they contain an "indirect polemic against speculative thought, which is indifferent to existence" (252; cf. 264, 273).

Second, since several of the works reviewed directly develop the theory of the stages, placing their review at this point is an invitation to incorporate the theory of subjectivity into the theory of the stages. We have already seen that this involves recognizing a special affinity between the aesthetic and the speculative on the side of objectivity, and between the ethical and the religious on the side of subjectivity. Thus Climacus introduces his review by saying that his reflections on truth as subjectivity had led him to explore the relation between the aesthetic and the ethical, when, lo and behold, what should appear but *Either/Or* (251)?

But this makes sense only if there is some important link between the aesthetic and the speculative.

He is even more explicit about the other linkage. He notes that *Stages* is different from *Either / Or* by having a tripartite structure: the aesthetic as the realm of pleasure-perdition, the ethical as the realm of action-victory, and the religious as the realm of suffering.[28] "But despite this tripartition, the book is nevertheless an either/or. That is, the ethical and the religious stages have an essential relation to each other" (294).

In these two ways the reviews are not an interruption of his argument but an important supplement to it.

▌ N O T E S

1. The suggestion here is that the distinction between the saying and the said developed by Levinas in *Otherwise Than Being* and in such essays as "Phenomenon and Enigma" and the distinction between the what and the how developed by Climacus can be read as reciprocal commentaries. Something similar may well be going on when Derrida complains that "the dream or the ideal of philosophical discourse . . . isn't it to make tonal difference inaudible . . .?" ("Of an Apocalyptic Tone Newly Adopted in Philosophy," trans. John P. Leavey, Jr., in *Derrida and Negative Theology*, ed. Harold Coward and Toby Foshay [Albany: SUNY Press, 1992], 29).

2. Sartre misleadingly attributes these words of Ivan Karamazov to Dostoyevski in "Existentialism Is a Humanism."

3. Here again we encounter Climacus's critique of the metaphysics of presence. He is closer to Kant than to Derrida on this matter, since the latter finds no use for the contrast between human and divine knowledge. If system, totality, timeless knowledge, and so forth are not available to us as human knowers, then they have no meaning at all. Ironically, by taking this position, Derrida shows how deeply Hegelian he is, since for Hegel, too, there is ultimately no difference between the human and the divine mind.

Like Climacus, Nietzsche protests against the "reason" that purports to operate "*sub specie aeterni*" and the "idolaters of concepts" who worship it. He sees this notion as "a revolt against life" that "would require a position *outside* life" (*Twilight of the Idols*, in Walter Kaufmann, ed., *The Portable Nietzsche* [New York: The Viking Press, 1954], 479, 490). He speaks of life where Climacus speaks of existence. But the deeper difference lies in the fact that while Nietzsche identifies Christianity with this Platonizing tendency, Climacus seeks to distinguish it as sharply as possible from both Platonic and Hegelian claims to think *sub specie aeterni*.

4. Kant makes this distinction both as that between empirical realism and transcendental idealism and as that between phenomena and noumena. His examples of objectivity in the world of appearances would have been mathematics and physics.

5. Climacus says nothing to suggest that he holds a view different from that of Kierkegaard, as discussed above in chapter 6.

6.   Like Gadamer in *Truth and Method,* Climacus sees the achievement of objectivity through method not only as a historical achievement but also as a limitation of vision. Through such lenses some features of the world are seen much better, but others disappear altogether. The sciences represent, in the words of Houston Smith, a "restricted viewfinder." See his preface to *Meister Eckhart: The Essential Sermons, Commentaries, Treatises, and Defense,* trans. Edmund Colledge and Bernard McGinn (New York: Paulist Press, 1981), xii.

7.   Kierkegaard wrote, but did not publish, a book entitled *Johannes Climacus, or De Omnibus Dubitandum Est,* a satirical description of the attempt by the youthful Johannes to take seriously the claims of modern philosophy to begin with doubt but to go beyond doubt to certainty. It now accompanies *Philosophical Fragments.* For Hegel's account of the role of doubt in achieving philosophical science, see the introduction to the *Phenomenology;* section 1B of my *History and Truth in Hegel's Phenomenology;* and *The Encyclopedia Logic,* §§24A2, 39, 78, and 81 with the *Zusätze.*

8.   For Hegel's version, see *The Encyclopedia Logic,* §§172A, 213, and 213A; cf. 24A2. It corresponds rather closely to Hegel's distinctions between understanding and reason and between *Vorstellung* and *Begriff.*

9.   This can be read as Climacus's variation—a strong misreading, if you like—of the Hegelian theme that the fear of error, in this case the errors of subjectivity, can itself be a dangerous error. See *Phenomenology,* 47.

10.   For a splendid discussion of Kierkegaard's relation to Don Quixote, see Eric J. Ziolkowski, "Don Quixote and Kierkegaard's Understanding of the Single Individual in Society," in Connell and Evans, *Foundations of Kierkegaard's Vision of Community,* 130–43.

11.   Jean-Luc Marion develops a strong link between idolatry and the *how* in *God without Being,* trans. Thomas A. Carlson (Chicago, Ill.: University of Chicago Press, 1991), 7, 13.

12.   If Climacus shares the "empiricist" view of Kierkegaard, cited above, we would have to make an exception for tautologies, but this changes nothing in the present context.

13.   Although it is a theory of meaning more than a theory of truth, the Derridean account of undecidability is another analogue to what Climacus is saying. In a context where meaning has a kind of Gödelian indeterminacy, truth can hardly be fixed and final. The linkage is all the closer by virtue of the central role that temporality plays in Derrida's account.

14.   For a philosophy of religion developed in a different, Austinian vocabulary around the notion of self-involvement, see Donald Evans, *The Logic of Self-involvement* (London: SCM Press, 1963). There is an obvious affinity between the present account and Tillich's account of faith as ultimate concern in *Dynamics of Faith* (New York: Harper & Row, 1958). Climacus's account keeps the cognitive dimension of faith more sharply in view through his emphasis on the objective uncertainty that is being appropriated in passionate inwardness. The *what* does not disappear before the *how.*

15.   On the link between recollection and immanence, see also 217, 270–72, 291. For an interpretation linking immanence and idolatry, see Marion, *God without Being,* 28, 52, 67.

16. A similar primacy of question over answer occurs in Gadamer's *Truth and Method.* For an argument pointing to the convergence of Gadamer's hermeneutics and Kierkegaard's "epistemology of the cross," see Stephen N. N. Dunning, "Paradoxes in Interpretation: Kierkegaard and Gadamer," in *Kierkegaard in Post/Modernity,* ed. Matustik and Westphal, 125–41.

17. Climacus regularly relates the passion of subjectivity to paradox (199, 230, 233), making it possible to rephrase his definition of the highest truth for an existing person as the passionate appropriation of a paradox.

18. Marion, *God without Being,* 46. This is directly opposed to Heidegger's claim that "God can come into philosophy only insofar as philosophy, of its own accord and by its own nature, requires and determines that and how God enters into it" (quoted by Marion on p. 34). The possibility that Heidegger is closer to Hegel than to Climacus on the issues raised in *Postscript* is developed by Patricia Huntington in "Heidegger's Reading of Kierkegaard Revisited: From Ontological Abstraction to Ethical Concretion," in *Kierkegaard in Post/Modernity,* 43–65.

19. It is in these terms that Anti-Climacus analyzes despair in *Sickness unto Death.*

20. The same theme comes up in *Repetition,* where Constantin Constantius says that *"repetition* is a crucial expression for what 'recollection' was to the Greeks. Just as they taught that all knowing is a recollecting, modern philosophy will teach that all life is a repetition. . . . Repetition and recollection are the same movement, except in opposite directions, for what is recollected has been, is repeated backward, whereas genuine repetition is recollected forward" (R 131). For a very illuminating interpretation of this theme as a critique of the metaphysics of presence, see Caputo, *Radical Hermeneutics,* chapter 1.

21. For helpful discussions of this question of formal contradiction, see C. Stephen Evans, *Kierkegaard's "Fragments" and "Postscript": The Religious Philosophy of Johannes Climacus* (Atlantic Highlands, N.J.: Humanities Press, 1983), chapters 11–12, and *Passionate Reason,* chapter 7.

22. Thomas Nagel, "What Is It Like to Be a Bat?" in *Mortal Questions* (Cambridge: Cambridge University Press, 1979).

23. This same structure occurs later with respect to the category of "the upbuilding." Kierkegaard had already insisted that his "upbuilding discourses" (EUD) were not sermons. Climacus interprets this to mean that the category applies to subjectivity in general and not to specifically Christian faith: "The Christian truth as inwardness is also upbuilding, but this by no means implies that every upbuilding truth is Christian: the upbuilding is a wider category." In these discourses, which "use only ethical categories of immanence," Kierkegaard apparently wanted to see "how far one can go, purely philosophically" (256). But since the discourses "are indirectly a polemic against speculative thought" (273), this cannot be Platonic or Hegelian philosophy, but only Socratic.

24. This claim is central to Hegelian thought. See, for example, *Phenomenology,* chapters 7 and 8; *The Encyclopedia Logic,* §§1–5; and "Hegel's Theory of Religious Knowledge," chap. 11 of my *Hegel, Freedom, and Modernity.*

25. At the beginning of the paragraph in which this passage appears, Climacus makes explicit reference to a text that plays an important role throughout the Kierkegaardian corpus, 1 Cor. 1:21–25: "For since, in the wisdom of God, the world did not know God through wisdom, God decided, through the foolishness of our proclamation, to save those who believe. For Jews demand signs and Greeks desire wisdom, but we proclaim Christ crucified, a stumbling block to Jews and foolishness to Gentiles, but to those who are called, both Jews and Greeks, Christ the power of God and the wisdom of God. For God's foolishness is wiser than human wisdom, and God's weakness is stronger than human strength." It is this passage above all that he has in mind when he says things like "[Christianity] has proclaimed itself as *the paradox* and has required the inwardness of faith with regard to what is an offense to the Jews, foolishness to the Greeks—and an absurdity to the understanding. . . . Suppose that Christianity was and wants to be a mystery, an utter mystery, not a theatrical mystery that is revealed in the fifth act" (213).

26. This epistemological equality of the simple and the wise vis-à-vis the paradox reinforces the epistemological equality of the eyewitness believers and believers of subsequent generations, as developed in *Fragments*. See also Outka's essays cited in chapter 7, note 23, above. In *Two Ages* Kierkegaard distinguishes this kind of religious equality from the equality for which the present age congratulates itself, which he interprets as originating in envy, taking the form of leveling and resulting in a spiritually vapid collectivism. Modernity's break with antiquity, where "the man of distinction was what *others could not be*" will represent progress only for those who are educated by it to a religious aspiration for "what *all can be*" (TA 81–92, his emphasis).

27. These are listed in chapter 1.

28. This last linkage is developed at length in his chapter 4, division 2, A (Pathos), §2.

The Subjective Issue—
The Subjective Thinker
(Pages 301–60)

In no section of *Postscript* was Climacus in greater need of a tough editor. He becomes so repetitious that the recurrence of his central theme is less likely to evoke the musical analogy of a theme developed through reiteration in varied contexts (see chapter 5 above) than to evoke his own satire of the madman who sought to prove his sanity by incessantly repeating "Boom! The earth is round" (see chapter 8). He seems to have a skittle ball in his coat, and every time it bumps his behind, he says, "Abstract thinking abstracts from existence."

His central theme is indeed the claim that the kind of thinking that can produce a philosophical system needs to see the world *sub specie aeterni,* since time is disruptive of totality; therefore system-building can only occur in the pure or abstract thinking that abstracts from existence. His point is not that there is no place for abstract thinking but only that the abstract thinkers of the world owe it to themselves not to forget, absentmindedly, that they are existing human beings; and that they owe it to the rest of us to give an account of the relation of abstract thought to existence. This demand that the relation between the act and the agent of abstraction be thematized, or, in other words, that Hegelians spell out their version of Hume's "Be a philosopher; but amidst all your philosophy, be still a man," is a constant refrain (303, 306, 309, 313–15).[1]

That the issue is indeed "what it means to be human" (303) is perhaps best grasped with reference to the following excerpts from Kierkegaard's Gilleleie journal of 1835: "What I really lack is to be clear in my mind *what I am to do,* not what I am to know, except in so far as a certain understanding must precede every action. The thing is to understand myself, to see what God really wishes *me* to do; the thing is to find a truth which is true *for me,* to find *the idea for which I can live and die.* For what would be the use of discovering so-called objective truth . . . what good would it do me if truth stood before me, cold and naked, not caring whether I recognized her or not. . . . I certainly do not deny that I still recognize an *imperative of understanding* and that through it one can work upon men, *but it must be taken up into my life.* . . . That is what I lacked in order to be able *to lead a complete human life* and not merely one of the understanding. . . . For otherwise how near man is to madness, in spite of all his knowledge. What is truth but to live for an idea?" (JK 44–45).[2]

Climacus repeatedly expresses his admiration for the Greeks, who were not absentminded but kept their own existence clearly in mind. Not only Socrates and the Skeptics, whom we might expect Climacus to mention, but also Pythagoras, Plato, Aristotle, and Simonides are cited in this connection (303, 308–9, 311, 313, 318, 331, 333, 337, 352).[3] Finally, Christianity is also presented as seeing the task this way, though the difficulty in this case is greater because "existence is accentuated paradoxically as sin, and eternity paradoxically as the god [*Guden*] in time" (353–54). In keeping with his overall presentation of subjectivity, Climacus again insists that what he is talking about is not specifically Christian but a generic human possibility clearly recognized by the Greeks.[4] Thus the Greek philosophers become, as it were, the pagans who pray in passion to a false god, while the Hegelians become the dwellers in Christendom who pray to the true God falsely (201). The assault on Hegel continues to focus on the *how.*

Anticipating Anti-Climacus's dialectical definition of the self at the beginning of *Sickness unto Death* (SUD 13), Climacus defines existence as "composed of the eternal and the temporal" (301; cf. 309, 311–12), as "composed of the infinite and the finite" (302), and as the contemporaneity of thinking, imagination, and feeling (342–48). As such, "existing is a prodigious *contradiction* from which the subjective thinker is not to abstract" (350, my emphasis).[5]

If this is true, then abstract thinking cannot be the highest human task, the keystone of an authentic humanism. Like chapter 1 of section 2 (see chapter 7 above), whose subtitle reads in part "What Ethics Would Have to Judge If Becoming Subjective Were Not the Highest Task Assigned to a Human Being" (129), chapter 3 focuses on the question of the highest human task. To construe philosophical speculation as this task, as Climacus takes Hegelianism to do, would be to make a series of interrelated mistakes.

To begin with, it would be "the ignoring of the ethical and the misunderstanding of the religious" (307), since the ethical and religious tasks of human life involve action "in the eminent sense— I do not mean in terms of achievement but in terms of inwardness . . . and in full consciousness of an eternal responsibility" (304; cf. 338–41). In the pure thinking of Hegelian philosophy, the principle of contradiction is overcome and either/or is replaced with both/and (304–5). But existence does not occur *sub specie aeterni;* action always faces a future yet to be decided, an either/or that is inescapable.[6] In the most dramatic case, it is eternity that confronts the existing individual as the future, "whereas eternity is eternity only for the Eternal, who is not in a process of becoming . . . where the *eternal* relates itself as the *future* to the *person in a process of becoming*—there the absolute disjunction [either/or] belongs. . . . Certainly this is why Christianity has proclaimed the eternal as the future" (306–7).[7] By abstracting from the temporality of existing, pure thought removes itself from the domain of ethical and religious responsibility.

It might be countered that precisely what distinguishes Hegel from the Platonism of previous metaphysics is his sense of history, his interpretation of reality as becoming. This is true, but he is also the epitome of post-Kantian idealism's demand that philosophy be system.[8] If reality is history, one can grasp it as totality only at its conclusion, or, as Hegel himself puts it so vividly in the preface to *The Philosophy of Right,* "The owl of Minerva spreads its wings only with the falling of the dusk." Not only by shifting attention from the responsible individual to such macroentities as Chinese or modern European civilization but also by its relation to time, the system has no ethics. "To be able to explain the past, all of world history, is magnificent, but if the ability to understand only the past is supposed to be the highest for one still living," Climacus wonders if this is not "a dangerous skepticism" insofar as "no one can be led by this philosophy to understand himself, which is certainly an absolute condition for all other understanding" (310–11). Needless to say, Climacus's next word is "Socrates."

As usual, Climacus moves back and forth between the world-historical and the logical in Hegelian thought. On the latter point it is the thesis of the identity of thought and being that becomes his target. As with world history, this identity occurs for the observer, not the actor (319). Climacus's objection is crude, seemingly a deliberate caricature: Is thinking the same as creating? Do I produce a rose by thinking it? More importantly, do I become good merely by thinking the good? (329–30). "If what is thought were actuality, then what is thought out as perfectly as possible, when I as yet have not acted, would be the action. In this way there would be no action whatever, but the intellectual swallows the ethical. . . . To have thought something good that one wants to do, is that to have done it? Not at all" (338–39).

But Climacus knows full well that the idealist thesis of the identity of thought and being, whatever it means, never implies that to think a rose or an action is to create a rose or to perform an action. Climacus himself points out that this identity "must not be understood thus in relation to imperfect existences" (329). It holds, according to Hegel, only for the infinite totality, not the finite part.[9] But then, Climacus asks, what does it have to do with me? "If, then, an *existing person* asks about the relation between thinking and being, between thinking and existing [*existere*], and philosophy explains that this relation is one of identity, it does not answer the question, because it does not answer the questioner. . . . The philosophical thesis of the identity of thinking and being is just the opposite of what it seems to be; it expresses that thinking has completely abandoned existence, that it has emigrated and found a sixth continent where it is absolutely sufficient unto itself in the absolute identity of thinking and being" (330–31).

How could such an emigration be the highest human task? Perhaps it could if it were the path to actuality, which Hegel understands precisely as the coincidence of thought and being.[10] This is why he can claim that the actual is rational and vice versa and defend this as equivalent to the theological conception of divine providence.[11] This brings us back to the world-historical perspective, where we might seem closer to the actual than in the categoreal world of the Logic. But Climacus does not think so. For him, thinking takes place in the medium of abstraction, which means that all thinking and all knowing convert actuality to possibility (314–16). This is the Aristotelian thesis that knowledge is of the universal, restated by Hegel in the chapter entitled "Sense Certainty" in the *Phenomenology,* where he argues that however much we may mean the particular, we express the universal and that even such indexicals or token reflexive terms as "I" and "here" and "now" are universals inviting multiple instantiations. As such they signify possibilities.

All knowledge, all thinking, or perhaps we might say all representation, has its home in the world of universals, and thus of abstraction and possibility. There is but one exception: "All knowledge about actuality is possibility. The only actuality concerning which an existing person has *more than knowledge* is his own actuality, that he exists, and this actuality is his absolute interest. The demand of abstraction upon him is that he become disinterested in order to obtain something to know; the requirement of the ethical upon him is to be infinitely interested in existing" (316, my emphasis).

The contrast between interest (or passion) and objectivity (here abstraction) is familiar. What is new here is what we might call Climacus's ethical Cartesianism. Climacus is sharply critical of the Cartesian *cogito* (317–18), but he offers here his own version of the thesis that I am related to myself in a way dramatically different from the way I am related to anything else. The issue is not doubt and certainty but actuality and possibility,[12] for "genuine knowledge is a translation into possibility," and the "only actuality there is for an existing person is his own ethical actuality; concerning all other actuality he has *only knowledge*" (316, my emphasis). This is obviously not the skepticism that says we cannot know anything beyond our self-consciousness; the contrast is between "only knowledge" and "more than knowledge." But it is a claim that we have a unique relation to ourselves. The subject-object structure of representational knowledge is not the way I am given to myself as an ethically responsible subjectivity.[13] As a responsible agent, I am in touch with myself as actual in a way in which I am not in touch with any object of my knowledge as actual.[14]

The section of this chapter entitled, in part, "Poetic and Intellectual Ideality" is a further development of this analysis of actuality and possibility. The poetic or aesthetic is regularly linked to the intellectual or speculative both as the reduction of actuality to possibility and as the confused attempt to regain actuality in a medium whose essence is universality and thus possibility. Climacus reminds us of Aristotle's claim that poetry is "something more philosophic and of graver import than history, since its statements are of the nature rather of universals, whereas those of history are singulars" (318).[15] He does not share this view of the relative importance of the universal and the singular, but he does share this view of the relation between the poetic and the speculative. In other words, with help from Aristotle, he seeks to reinforce his revision of the theory of the stages, according to which the aesthetic and the speculative stand together over against the ethical and the religious.

The claim that abstract thinking is the highest human task implies that "thinking is superior to feeling and imagination" (304). Climacus finds this assumption to be doubly problematic. In the first place, it replaces spiritual equality with intellectual elitism: "With respect to existence, thinking is not at all superior

to imagination and feeling but is coordinate. In existence, the supremacy of thinking plays havoc. When, for example, someone
says: The expectancy of an eternal happiness *hereafter* is an idea
based upon the finite reflection of the understanding, a notion
that cannot maintain itself under the scrutiny of thinking—ergo,
one may very well talk about it in popular addresses to simple folk
who never outgrow the sphere of representative thought, but for the
thinking person this distinction must be canceled—then one must
answer: Quite right, under the scrutiny of thinking, of abstract
thinking, it cannot maintain itself; but then, in turn, abstract thinking cannot maintain itself against existence" (346–47).[16]

Just as serious is the way in which the supremacy of thinking to feeling and imagination would falsify the relation of the
individual to the species. World-historically speaking, abstract
thinking comes later than imagination and feeling. At a certain
point it becomes a new challenge for humanity. But this does not
make it a higher task, unless we "confuse the world-historical
development of the human spirit with the particular individuals
. . . as if development of spirit were something one generation
could dispose of by a will in favor of another." In the animal world
the individual "participates as a matter of course in the development of the species," but "the spiritually developed individual
takes his spiritual development along with him in death. If a succeeding individual is to attain it, it must occur through his self-
activity; therefore he must skip nothing. . . . Ethics focuses upon
the individual, and ethically understood it is every individual's
task to become a whole human being" (345–46). To tell me I
"must skip nothing" is to tell me that the relatively new tasks of
philosophical speculation do not absolve me from the age-old
moral and religious tasks involving feeling and imagination. I
cannot relax about them, as if historical development had put
them behind me as resolved. Today we might say that humanity's
new challenge in exploring outer space does not absolve any of us
individually from such ancient tasks as learning to live at peace
with the members of our family. Just as scientific-technological
thinking is not the highest task for an individual today, so, Climacus wants to claim, philosophical thinking (in the Hegelian,
but not in the Greek style) is not the highest task for himself and
his contemporaries.

On this point, as throughout the present chapter, Climacus's
individualism is conspicuous. What abstract thinking abstracts
from existence it abstracts from "this definite something . . . a
particular existing human being" (302). "The ethical immediately

embraces the single individual . . . [by] asking only ethically about actuality . . . every individual is ethically set apart by himself. . . . For existing ethically, it is an advantageous preliminary study to learn that the individual human being stands alone" (320, 323; cf. 324, 330, 343n, 346).

At the conclusion of the chapter, this affirmation of the individual as the locus of responsible subjectivity becomes a critique of the present age: "Every age has its own [specific immorality]; the immorality of our age is perhaps not lust and pleasure and sensuality, but rather a pantheistic, debauched contempt for individual human beings. In the midst of all the jubilation over our age and the nineteenth century there sounds a secret contempt for being a human being—in the midst of the importance of the generation there is a despair over being a human being. . . . And it is undeniable that if a person does not have ethical and religious enthusiasm he will despair over being an individual human being—otherwise not. . . . Just as in the desert individuals must travel in large caravans out of fear of robbers and wild animals, so individuals today have a horror of existence because it is godforsaken; they dare to live only in great herds and cling together *en masse* in order to be at least something" (355–56).[17]

It is important not to confuse what Climacus is up to with other kinds of individualism. It is not the Enlightenment's political liberalism, featuring the individual as the bearer of natural rights against the power of the state.[18] Nor is it romanticism's expressivism, featuring the individual as creative genius unconstrained by rigid rules, whether they be aesthetic, moral, political, or religious.[19] Nor is it existentialism's metaphysical rebellion, featuring the individual as a courageous but lonely protest against a Godless, meaningless world. It is ethical-religious subjectivity, featuring the individual as personally responsible for the choice of a certain kind of life and for the choices that stem from that choice.

It is especially important to notice that this latter individualism has nothing atomistic about it. On the contrary, it implies that precisely as one whose essence is to exist, in the sense of becoming subjective, I am essentially related both to God and to neighbor. Intersubjectivity is not an afterthought for this individualism, nor is it a contingent possibility for a substantial self that exists in itself and is conceived through itself. Because the self is intersubjectively constituted, it is as true for Climacus as it is for Hegel that I am who we are.[20] The difference is that Climacus is eager not to let excitement about who we are distract me from my personal responsibility in all those relationships that enable me to say "we."

There can be no doubt that throughout the Kierkegaardian corpus, pseudonymous and otherwise, there is a sustained effort to tempt or seduce me as the reader to reflect myself out of "Christendom," "the crowd," "the public," "the present age," and so forth in order to stand alone. But it is never to stand alone, period. It is always to stand alone before the ethical and the religious and thus alone before the claims made upon me by my neighbor and ultimately by God, claims that make it clear I could never be simply alone in the liberal, romantic, or existentialist senses except by flight.

▎ N O T E S

1. David Hume, *An Enquiry Concerning Human Understanding,* section 1.

2. Kierkegaard's final question here clearly anticipates the truth-as-subjectivity motif in *Postscript.*

3. In addition to a general reference to the Skeptics, Climacus cites Pyrrho, but misidentifies him as Zeno (see CUP 2:253n. 593). In a famous passage in the *Phenomenology,* Hegel also warns against abstract thinking and in doing so contrasts the Greeks and the moderns. But his concern is that the abstract universals of thought will lose contact with the content from which they have been abstracted rather than that they will lose contact with the thinkers who think them (cf. CUP 331). Thus the solution involves becoming more thoroughly objective, and Hegel can write in the same preface that "philosophy must beware of the wish to be edifying" (*Phenomenology,* 19–20, 5–6; cf. Gadamer, "Hegel and the Dialectic of the Ancient Philosophers," in *Hegel's Dialectic,* trans. P. Christopher Smith [New Haven, Conn.: Yale University Press, 1976], 5–34). By contrast, Kierkegaard has Judge William conclude volume 2 of *Either / Or* by including a sermon entitled "The Upbuilding [Edification] That Lies in the Thought That in Relation to God We Are Always in the Wrong." It concludes with the words: "for only the truth that builds up [edifies] is truth for you" (EO 2:339, 354; cf. JP 4.4847).

4. This evocation of the Greeks can be fruitfully contrasted with that to be found in the writings of Husserl and Heidegger.

5. Climacus has already described the human self as a "prodigious contradiction" (82; see chapter 6 above).

6. Cf. chapter 8, note 2. The open-future ingredient in every human experience is a theme that links Nietzsche, Heidegger, and Derrida to Climacus in opposition to Plato and Hegel.

7. Here Climacus reinforces the tension between existence and recollection, for which eternity is behind, rather than ahead of, one. See the discussion of pp. 207–26 in the previous chapter, and its note 20.

8. Read the preface to the *Phenomenology* against the background of Beiser, *The Fate of Reason.*

9. The principle of the identity of thought and being permeates the Hegelian system. It is especially important in Hegel's treatment of the ontological proof of God's existence. See *The Encyclopedia Logic,* §§51, 193; *Science of Logic,* 86–90, 442, 481–82, 705–8; *Lectures on the Philosophy of Religion,* 1:433–41, 3:65–73, 173–84, 351–58, 360–61; *Lectures on the History of Philosophy,* 3:54–56, 142–43, 239.

10. See, for example, *The Encyclopedia Logic,* §142.

11. Compare the preface of *The Philosophy of Right* with §6 of *The Encyclopedia Logic.* In his *Lectures on the Philosophy of World History,* Hegel makes a similar claim and gives a similar defense: *"But the only thought which philosophy brings with it is the simple idea of reason — the idea that reason governs the world, and that world history is therefore a rational process"* (see *Lectures,* ed. Nisbet, 27). Then Hegel assimilates this to *"the religious truth that the world is not a prey to chance and external, contingent causes, but is governed by providence"* (35). In both passages, the italics indicate that the passage in question is from Hegel's own manuscript rather than from student notes.

12. It will be remembered that *Johannes Climacus* is a satire on Cartesian doubt (cf. CUP 310). In the case of factual or empirical knowledge, we have already seen Climacus's fallibilist account in terms of "approximation."

13. I believe there is an important affinity between this argument and the claim found throughout the writings of Levinas that the structure of intentionality as developed by Husserl is not adequate to the way in which the Other is given as an ethical claim upon me. See *Totality and Infinity,* 28–29, 38, 44–46, 122–23; "Philosophy and the Idea of Infinity," "Meaning and Sense," and "Language and Proximity," in *Collected Philosophical Papers,* trans. Alphonso Lingis (Dordrecht: Martinus Nijhoff, 1987); "Ethics as First Philosophy," chap. 5 of *The Levinas Reader,* ed. Seán Hand (Oxford: Basil Blackwell, 1989); and Adriaan Peperzak, *To the Other: An Introduction to the Philosophy of Emmanuel Levinas* (West Lafayette, Ind.: Purdue University Press, 1993), 14–16, 58–59, 134, 213–14, 221–22.

14. This trans-representational presence to self is something like Sartre's pre-reflective *cogito* (see chapter 7, note 31), which means that absentmindedness for Climacus can be compared with Sartre's notion of bad faith. However, while the element of freedom is common to the notions of self-presence in Descartes, Sartre, and Climacus, only Climacus places the element of ethical-religious responsibility at its core. This radical presence to self is not, however, the total transparency for which the metaphysics of presence longs. As existing, I am given to myself as a responsible subjectivity with utter certainty. But far from this certainty being a foundation on which I can build a cognitive edifice or a home where I can rest, this certainty becomes the task of a lifetime, not just in terms of fulfilling this responsibility but also in terms of discovering its true meaning. On the nontransparency of the self to itself in Anti-Climacus, see my essay "Kierkegaard's Psychology of Unconscious Despair," in Perkins, *International Kierkegaard Commentary: The Sickness unto Death.*

15. Aristotle, *Poetics* 1451b6–7.

16. See the discussion of equality in chapter 8, including note 26. In the passage just cited, I have followed the Lowrie and Swenson translation in part in order to avoid the misleading implication of the Hongs' use of "conception" and "conceptual," both of which have overtones of the Hegelian *Begriff,* while what is at issue here is just the opposite, *Vorstellung.*

17. This use of the herd image invites comparison with Nietzsche's critique of the present age, as well as with *Two Ages,* the review that Kierkegaard published under his own name just a month after *Postscript.*

18. For the complicated question of Kierkegaard's relation to the emergent liberalism of Denmark in his time, see Kirmmse, *Kierkegaard in Golden Age Denmark.*

19. For a powerful analysis of expressivism, see Charles Taylor, *Hegel and Modern Society* (Cambridge: Cambridge University Press, 1979), and *Sources of the Self* (Cambridge, Mass.: Harvard University Press, 1989).

20. For Hegel's position, see my "Dialectic and Intersubjectivity," chap. 5 of *Hegel, Freedom, and Modernity.* The relational, intersubjective nature of the self in Kierkegaard's writings is especially central to *Sickness unto Death* and *Works of Love.*

The Subjective Issue—
For Orientation in
the Plan of *Fragments*
(Pages 361–84)

At the heart of Hegelian philosophy is the triple claim that philosophy has the same content as religion, differing only in form; that Christianity is the highest form of religion; and that by virtue of its conceptual form, Hegelian philosophy is the highest form of Christianity. Climacus wants to challenge the third claim by examining the first. If the form of speculative philosophy is objectivity rather than subjectivity, and if it therefore belongs to the aesthetic sphere rather than to the ethical-religious spheres, then has the content not been changed beyond recognition? Would it not be more honest to say that Hegelianism is not a form of Christianity at all, and, a fortiori, not the highest form?

The target of *Fragments* is Hegel and not Socrates. By spelling out the difference between recollection and revelation as two modes of access to the truth, Climacus seeks to show that Hegel falls in the former camp. Thus, what he presents as the movement from an inadequate form of Christianity (*Vorstellung*) to the adequate form (*Begriff*) is actually the movement beyond Christianity to paganism.

Climacus's quarrel with Hegel has the form, Is X or Y a more authentic expression of religion Z? In itself this is a theological dispute; but throughout the history of Christianity, as well as, for example, the history of Hinduism and Buddhism, such debates have often been the site of significant philosophical reflection. The central philosophical issue here is the meaning of human temporality. In his dissertation, Kierkegaard had commented on how Socrates "so beautifully binds men firmly to the divine by showing that all knowledge is recollection" (CI 30). In other words, he notes the linkage between the thesis of the divinity of the soul and the recollection thesis in the dialogues. Eternity is the natural home of the soul, and even when it is in time, it can attain direct access to the eternal, can see *sub specie aeterni*. In the tradition of the Orphics, Pythagoreans, and Empedocles, the Platonic dialogues employ the dualism of soul and body to undermine the duality between the human and divine.[1]

Hegelianism, whose tendency to collapse this latter difference has already been noted, goes one step further. Both as a logic and as a philosophy of history, its claim to embody an all-encompassing and all-culminating Logos is a claim to see the world *sub specie aeterni,* from the divine perspective. But the distinction between the here and the hereafter, between this life and the life to come, falls away (361–62). The momentary, mystical foretaste of divine glory of the dialogues is replaced by a realized eschatology in which the unhappy consciousness of living toward a beyond (*Jenseits*) is replaced by an ultimate human fulfillment here and now, totally present. In fulfillment of the truth of the Enlightenment, "The two worlds are reconciled and heaven is transplanted to earth below."[2]

Suddenly Climacus is talking about infant baptism. Without attacking the practice as such, he calls it "ludicrous" to see people take themselves to be Christians "solely by virtue of a baptismal certificate" (363), just as it is "ludicrous that a man for whom Christianity has meant nothing at all, not even so much that he cared to give it up, dies, and then at the graveside the pastor as a matter of course ushers him into the eternal happiness as it is understood in Christian terminology" (364). The problem with this is that it reduces Christianity to "custom and habit" (363–64), eliminates the need for decision and appropriation, and makes people Christians "as a matter of course" (365–68; cf. 373, 379).

In other words, infant baptism becomes ludicrous when it serves to eliminate the need *to become* a Christian.[3] "The parallel would be: just as one must be born, must have come into existence, in order *to become* a human being, inasmuch as an infant is not yet that, so one must be baptized in order *to become* a Christian" (366, my emphasis). These becomings, as the previous account of subjectivity is intended to make clear, are tasks of a lifetime. Just as one has not completed the task of becoming human by getting married and beginning a career,[4] so baptism and confirmation as rites of passage signify beginnings rather than completions of the task of becoming a Christian.

The abrupt shift from speculation to infant baptism is not an example of the style of undergraduate writing whose principle of organization is free association. Climacus sees these themes as two sides of the same coin, whose name is Christendom: "In other words, speculative thought makes paganism the outcome of Christianity, and to be Christian as a matter of course by being baptized changes Christendom into a baptized paganism" (368). That is, there is an elective affinity between Hegel and Christendom: the latter, whether it has heard of Hegel or not, is the everyday embodiment of Hegelian thought, while the former provides the ideological legitimation for Christendom's practices. The link is that both parties forget that "to exist does not mean to be *sub specie aeterni*" (362). The theoretical elevation of the human to the standpoint of the divine eliminates the need for becoming (decision, appropriation); it reflects and reinforces a network of social practices understood as living happily ever after, struggle and striving being completed. The present is sufficient to itself, needing no future fulfillment. Infant baptism does the same. It is the metaphysics of presence translated into daily life outside the academy.

This, Climacus tells us, is what *Fragments* is about. Its epistemological reflections are ideology critique. If he had thought that capitalism was the deepest pathology of modernity, he would have made political economy his theoretical target. But since his diagnosis points to a spiritual inertia as the Achilles heel of the modern world, he targets the Hegelian speculative project, which he sees as giving aid and comfort to practices that dehumanize. Ironically, according to his interpretation, it is precisely by compromising the difference between the human and the divine that Hegel legitimizes dehumanizing practices.

The second half of this section is entitled "The Importance of a Preliminary Agreement about What Christianity Is Before There Can Be Any Question of a Mediation of Christianity and Speculative Thought" (369). Here mediation is the name for the transformation of Christianity from its immediate, religious form (*Vorstellung*) to its mediated, philosophical form (*Begriff*). Another Hegelian name for such a mediation is *Aufhebung;* in the language of *Fear and Trembling,* we are talking about a teleological suspension. In both cases the process of recontextualization has negative and positive implications, cancellation and preservation. When X is *aufgehoben,* or teleologically suspended in Y, the immediate, self-sufficient form of X is canceled, and whatever belongs to that mode of its being is relativized as something insufficient by itself. But this has positive significance, for the claim is that Y is the truth, or *telos,* of X, and that in this process X realizes itself, or at least moves to a higher level of its normative development.

But such claims are not self-validating, and under certain circumstances they invite suspicion. Consider the claim that woman has her truth, or *telos,* in man, that she is nothing essential in herself but comes to self-realization only when properly related to man. Now suppose that it is man who makes this claim, that he keeps it asymmetrical, and that he reserves to himself the right to say who woman is and to define her proper relation to man. Is this insight or intimidation and imperialism?

Climacus is suspicious that the Hegelian mediation of Christianity and speculative philosophy has this form. First, the latter defines the former; then it becomes clear that the latter is the truth, or *telos,* of the former. As the prolegomenon to speculative philosophy for those who do not have words like "prolegomenon" in their vocabulary, Christianity is to be teleologically suspended in the system.

But no real mediation is possible. *Either* Christianity is defined as an inferior species of speculation, a lower stage on the divided line, in which case there is not enough otherness between it and speculation for mediation to be more than a tautology; *or* Christianity is allowed to define itself as the opposite of speculation, in which case mediation becomes quite impossible. Christianity will insist that it belongs to the realm of subjectivity, that speculation is objectivity, and that it is comical to suggest that objectivity is the truth, or *telos,* of subjectivity.

Climacus once again insists that he is not trying to show that Christianity is true. That question remains bracketed (369, 379; cf. 224–31). And yet he does take sides against Hegel by once again pointing to the intellectual elitism of the Hegelian position (377);[5] by refusing to allow speculative philosophy to define Christianity; and by rejecting the definition it sets forth.

As Climacus understands it, that definition represents Christianity as a kind of philosophical theory, or, to use theological language, as a doctrine. But "Christianity is not a doctrine. . . . If I were to say that Christianity is a doctrine about the Incarnation, about the Atonement, etc., misunderstanding would immediately be made easy" (379–81; cf. 370–71). The misunderstanding, of course, would be that the primary task in relation to Christianity is to understand it, that faith is first and foremost a matter of the intellect.

Unfortunately, in challenging this assumption so dramatically by saying that "Christianity is not a doctrine," Climacus opens the door for another misunderstanding, unless we read him carefully. He is not denying that Christianity has doctrinal content or that this content is essential to it. What he is denying is that Christianity is primarily to be understood as a metaphysical theory offered to our intellect for assent or denial. Belonging to subjectivity, it concerns how we live our lives and not just what propositions we believe. That Climacus does not exclude doctrinal content but only the reduction of Christianity to the theoretical sphere is clear from the fact that in the midst of denying that Christianity is a doctrine, he calls it a doctrine of a certain sort. "Surely a philosophical theory that is to be comprehended and speculatively understood is one thing, and a doctrine that is to be actualized in existence is something else. If there is to be any question of understanding with regard to this latter doctrine, then this understanding must be: to understand that it is to be existed in, to understand the difficulty of existing in it, what a prodigious existence-task [Existents-Opgave] this doctrine assigns to the learner. When with regard to a doctrine of this kind (an existence-communication [Existents-Meddelelse]) it at a given time becomes common to assume that to be what the doctrine enjoins is so very easy, but to understand the doctrine speculatively is very difficult, then a person can be in harmony with this doctrine (the existence-communication) when he tries to show how difficult it is, existing, to comply with the teaching. . . . Christianity is a doctrine of this kind" (379–80n). Here again Climacus is careful not to confuse subjectivity with subjectivism. The subjectivity of an existence-communication does not mean that the Christian makes up the world (and its rules) as s/he goes along but rather that s/he accepts the difficult task of complying with a teaching s/he did not invent and cannot recollect.

It is often suggested that Hegel refuted Kierkegaard proleptically when he presented the unhappy consciousness as a stage to be surpassed on the road to absolute knowledge in the *Phenomenology*. Climacus would reply that this view begs the question by assuming that faith or religious consciousness is to be understood as having a theoretical *telos*. To transfer it from the realm of subjectivity to that of objectivity is less to refute than to rape it. If unhappy consciousness were allowed to speak for itself it might say, "Yes, I long to see God face-to-face. But so far as the present life is concerned, my task is to learn to walk by faith and not by sight." In speaking thus, it would reveal the violence of the Hegelian *Aufhebung*.

Climacus anticipates an objection. If speculation cannot be trusted to give a disinterested definition of Christianity, it does not follow that Christianity's account of itself will be pure truth. The fact that man's definition of woman is tainted does not make woman's account of herself infallible and self-validating. Of course, the ethics of discourse forbids silencing the voices of those whose identities and interests are at stake, but it does not confer on those voices any absolute authority. On whose authority, then, must we accept the claim that Christianity belongs to subjectivity rather than to objectivity?

Climacus's response is that we can know what Christianity is without being a Christian, although we cannot know what it is to be a Christian without being one. Being a Christian is like being a bat, and you have to be on the inside to know what it is like.[6] But you do not have to be an insider to understand what Christianity is—in this case whether it belongs primarily to objectivity or to subjectivity. Part of the reason that Kierkegaard has both Johannes de Silentio and Johannes Climacus stand outside of the religious spheres they describe is to counter the suggestion that their accounts presuppose the bias of those spheres. Both of them claim that their insights about the religious life are attainable from outside that life, and they invite believer and unbeliever alike to judge for themselves. Although Climacus believes that Christianity defines itself as subjectivity, he appeals to no authority other than the reader's own honest investigation in deciding whether it should be understood as a philosophical theory or as an existence-communication.

He concludes by defining the overall task of his own authorship: "Although it may be beautiful and well intentioned, inasmuch as being a Christian is supposed to be the highest good, to want to help people to become Christians by making it easy, I venture according to my poor ability to take on the responsibility of making it difficult, as difficult as possible, yet without making it more difficult than it is" (381).

| NOTES

1. For this aspect of Greek thought, see Westphal, *God, Guilt, and Death: An Existential Phenomenology of Religion* (Bloomington: Indiana University Press, 1984), sections 9B and 9C.

2. *Phenomenology*, 355.

3. Note that the issue concerning infant baptism concerns the *how* rather than the *what*. The question of how ideas or practices function is at the heart of the hermeneutics of suspicion. See Westphal, *Suspicion and Faith: The Religious Uses of Modern Atheism* (Grand Rapids, Mich.: Eerdmans, 1993).

4. See the discussion in chapter 6 of the satire (CUP 85) in which these rites of passage are confused with the completion of spiritual striving.

5. Cf. the discussion of pp. 159–60, 217–28, and 346–47 in chapters 7, 8, and 9 respectively.

6. See chapter 8, note 22.

The Subjective Issue—Pathos (Pages 385–561)

Division 2 consists of a long section entitled "Pathos" and a short one entitled "The Dialectical," since "an existence-issue is pathos-filled and dialectical" (386). The distinction points backward to the difference between Socrates and Christianity in *Fragments* and forward to the difference between Religiousness A and Religiousness B, which Climacus will soon formulate, making it explicitly clear that we are dealing with subdivisions of the religious sphere.

But the two moments are not presented as species of a common genus. They relate more nearly as genus to species, for the dialectical is not an alternative to pathos but its intensification. "Religiousness A is not the *specifically* Christian religiousness. On the other hand, the dialectical is decisive only insofar as it is *joined together with* the pathos-filled and gives rise to a new pathos" (555, my emphasis). In other words, the "proper pathos" of the initial analysis is "made dialectical by *additional qualifications*" (385, my emphasis). What follows as the analysis of religious pathos and passion is offered as a phenomenology of religion as such.

The notions of pathos and passion continuously intertwine, but it is probably best not to treat them as quite synonymous. Because "we usually trace the pathos-filled to imagination and feeling," Climacus sees it as neglected in the logocentric nineteenth century (385). This double link to imagination and feeling is sufficient to link pathos to passion. In terms of aesthetic theory, pathos can refer both to the pity and fear aroused by a tragedy and to that aspect of the play that arouses them. While passion is a purely subjective concept, pathos has a dimension of the objective as well.

Climacus and his reader are phenomenological observers. Since they are not pure intellects but rather persons equipped with imagination and feeling, they can observe the pathos of the religious life, just as the readers of *Fear and Trembling* observe the pathos of the Abraham story. There will be a great deal of passion in what they observe, and it may arouse passion in them as well, possibly fear and trembling rather than pity and fear. The observer here is no mere spectator; what the text is ultimately about is neither Abraham nor Religiousness A but the meaning of his or her own life.[1] This is an existential phenomenology, not a phenomenology that would be a rigorous science. As such it directly implicates the observer.[2]

This is why, in spite of the fact that what follows is a phenomenology of the religious sphere, Climacus alludes several times at the beginning to the difference between the aesthetic and the ethical. He wants to highlight the difference between aesthetic and existential pathos (387). "With regard to the religious, the point is that this has passed through the ethical" (388). We are reminded that religion falls within the larger sphere of ethical-religious subjectivity so that we will not confuse the element of objectivity involved in being observers of religious pathos with a return to aesthetic-speculative objectivity.

The Initial Expression of Existential Pathos: Resignation

The analogy between observing the religious life and observing a tragic drama may seem strange. Climacus certainly does not identify the life of faith with tragedy; indeed, he is especially eager to resist the confusion of theater and church that he sees in Christendom.[3] Nor does he portray religion as devoid of joy. But he does see it as unhappy consciousness in the sense set forth in Hegel's *Phenomenology*. Stubbornly unseduced by the metaphysics of presence, religious consciousness knows that it does not now see God face-to-face, that its highest good is not a present possession. The pathos of the religious life lies in the fact that while it occurs in time, its goal, eternal happiness, lies in eternity. For Socratic as for Christian religiousness, the beyond (*Jenseits*)—to which Hegel was so deeply allergic—is essential to the religious life.

But this has consequences, both ontologically, for the structure of the self, and ontically, for its daily life. "Existence is composed of the infinite and the finite; the existing person is infinite and finite. Now, if to him an eternal happiness is his highest good, this means that in his acting the finite elements are once and for all reduced to what must be surrendered in relation to the eternal happiness" (391).

Here the self is seen as a dialectical tension whose poles are finite and infinite, temporal and eternal. Climacus anticipates the account that Anti-Climacus will give, which includes the following: "A human being is a synthesis of the infinite and the finite, of the temporal and the eternal, of freedom and necessity, in short, a synthesis" (SUD 13).[4] To be human is to live the tension of belonging at one time to two worlds.

But Climacus moves quickly from ontology to ethics, from theory to practice. If my highest good is an infinite good, namely, eternal happiness, then all finite goods, namely, all temporal happiness, will have to be "surrendered" for its sake. Climacus also calls this surrender "renunciation" (389n) but eventually settles on "resignation" as the term for the initial expression of existential pathos. Perhaps he recalls the discussion by another Johannes of the knight of infinite resignation in relation to the knight of faith (FT 27–53).

Resignation is not an isolated act but an all-inclusive form of being-in-the-world. "In relation to an eternal happiness as the absolute good, pathos does not mean words but that this idea transforms the whole existence of the existing person. . . . If the absolute τέλος [end, goal] does not absolutely transform the individual's existence by relating to it, then the individual does not relate himself with existential pathos but with esthetic pathos" (387; cf. 389, 393).[5] The immediate corollary is that "if there is something he is not willing to give up for its sake, then he is not relating himself to an eternal happiness" (393).[6]

Such a *telos* is "foolishness in the finite sense" (394), in part because it cannot be adequately described with the concepts of finitude. But to relate to such a goal, one need not have an adequate conception: "He needs only to allow resignation to inspect his entire immediacy with all its desires etc. If he finds a single fixed point, an obduracy, he is not relating himself to an eternal happiness" (394).

Climacus wishes to counter two misunderstandings of resignation: mediation and monasticism. Resignation counters immediacy: "When resignation makes a visitation to immediacy, it gives notice that the individual must not have his life in it" (395). It is the immediacy of desires rather than of thoughts that is before us, signifying a life oriented to the finite and temporal goods of this life. Evil or sinful desire is not at issue here. In the case of Abraham, immediacy would signify the desire to be a father to his beloved son and to share his life with Sarah, his wife.

Is Hegelian mediation then the required transcendence of this immediacy? Climacus thinks just the opposite. As he is wont to do, he represents his understanding of Hegel in terms of concrete, daily life. But by calling it mediation, he sustains the linkage between Hegelian theory and daily life.

> I do not know whether one should laugh or weep on hearing the enumeration: a good job, a beautiful wife, health, the rank of a councilor of justice—and in addition an eternal happiness, which is the same as assuming that the kingdom of *heaven* is a kingdom along with all the other kingdoms on *earth* and that one would look for information about it in a geography book (391; cf. 401).

> "Can't you describe [eternal happiness] to me 'while I shave,' just as one describes the loveliness of a woman, the royal purple, or distant regions?" (392)

> But someone who is situated with a wife and children in a good living, cozily indoors, and is a councilor of justice, a "serious man" who nevertheless wants to do something for his eternal happiness, provided the duties of his office and his wife and children permit it . . . (395)

Climacus takes these caricatures to represent the view of "mediation as something higher than resignation," whereas he thinks it is "in fact retrogression" (400).[7] But what have these vignettes to do with Hegel? The first quotation returns to the way in which the mediation of the human and divine collapses the difference between heaven and earth. When "heaven is transplanted to earth below,"[8] eternal happiness—even if that language were to be retained—would no longer signify a beyond but something here and now. The tension between finite goods that I can possess now and an infinite good that I cannot disappears.

The second quotation expresses the epistemological consequences (or presuppositions) of this realized eschatology. If heaven is already here, then the concepts that I already have should be adequate for describing it. The tension between finite goods that I can understand now and an infinite good conceptually incommensurable with them disappears.[9]

The third quotation expresses the ethical consequences (or presuppositions) of mediation. There is room in the life of successful and respectable people for religion, as long as it does not interfere with their success and respectability. No Abrahams, please. The tension between finite goods that I can legitimately seek and an infinite good that radically jeopardizes such pursuit disappears.

The tension disappears! Just as Christendom is a *Sittlichkeit* of relaxation, so the triumph of speculation over dialectic in Hegelian mediation means that all tensions, oppositions, and contradictions are overcome. Every dissonance is resolved, and we have reached the point in the story where "they lived happily ever after."

Vis-à-vis mediation, Socratic and Christian religiousness stand on common ground in two important respects. Both reject the metaphysics of presence. Both see the individual and his or her absolute *telos* as so related that "they cannot have each other in time" (397). For the individual, this means that life is the task of a lifetime, that epistemic and ethical striving are never finished this side of death.

But there is also a social implication: "It is true that the individual oriented toward the absolute τέλος is in the relative ends, but he is not in them in such a way that the absolute τέλος is exhausted in them" (400; cf. 460, 474). The relative goods cited above include, in Hegelian language, the goods of family, civil society, and the state. There is no quarrel with the Hegelian claim, "The institutions of ethical life (*Sittlichkeit*) are divine institutions." But when Hegel claims that "ethical life is the most genuine cultus," the implication seems to be that the highest tasks and fulfillments of human life are exhausted in them.[10]

If mediation is a both/and posture that seeks to have both the finite and the infinite without any tension between them, monasticism is an either/or posture that chooses between love of God and love of the world. Climacus has high praise for it. At least it has passion, and for this reason alone it is to be preferred to mediation (402, 414). It avoids the absurdity of applying the Delphic imperative *ne quid nimis* (avoid excess, everything in moderation) to the absolute τέλος (404). It thereby avoids the fatal flaw of mediation, the "revolt of the relative ends against the majesty of the absolute, which is to be drawn down to the level of everything else, and against the dignity of the human being, who is to be made a servant solely of the relative ends" (419), such as family, career, and country.

But Climacus bemoans the way in which the monastic movement "has been used" (401), or rather "misused" (417). Right from the outset monasticism mixed its respect for the majesty of the divine and the dignity of the human with two serious errors. One was that renunciation of the world is a meritorious act by means of which to earn God's favor. The other was that renunciation is an essentially outward affair, a matter of where one lives, what one wears, when one eats, and so forth (405; cf. 413–14).

But of course one lives somewhere, wears something, and eats sometimes, so the difference between the "religious" and "worldly" lives is made into a relative difference (405). What is worse, taking up the monastic life can all too easily be seen as something done once and for all, so that "now one is finished with it" (405). But since subjectivity is the task of a lifetime, this is to be finished far too early.

Far more serious is the misuse of the monastic ideal by Hegelian Christendom. Hegel's Protestantism—"We Lutherans (I am and will remain one)"[11]—consists very largely in the proud claim that modernity has replaced the vow of poverty with the responsibilities of civil society, the vow of chastity with the responsibilities of family life, and the vow of obedience with the responsibilities of citizenship.[12]

Climacus does not challenge the Protestant notion of daily life as vocation, of the religious significance of the institutions of ethical life. But just as he earlier resisted the Hegelian interpretation of the theme that "ethical life is the most genuine cultus," so now he resists the suggestion that the inadequacies of medieval monasticism guarantee the validity of modern mediation: "But even if the Middle Ages erred . . . it by no means follows that mediation is commendable" (402).

As usual, Climacus translates Hegelian theory into Copenhagen vignettes. He notes sardonically, "In our day there actually is no great reason to warn against the monastery" (415). Still, "we now and then still hear a pastor who, in a discourse urging his listeners to participate in life's innocent joys, warns against entering the monastery; one hears this and sees, behold, the pastor is so gripped by his subject that he perspires and wipes away the perspiration" (402; cf. 415, 417, 422).

If Climacus rejects both the Hegelian both/and and the monastic either/or, how does he understand resignation? His formula is direct enough. The task is "Simultaneously to Relate Oneself Absolutely to One's Absolute τέλος and Relatively to Relative Ends" (387; cf. 407, 414, 422, 431). This turns out to be a both/and and an either/or relation. It is a both/and because it clearly affirms, with mediation, the goodness of finite goods. If fortune takes them all away, one says "Oh, well," but this does not signify "indifference to the finite" (411–13). Perhaps Climacus is thinking of the knight of faith inspired by Silentio's Abraham: "He finds pleasure in everything, takes part in everything, and every time one sees him participating in something particular, he does it with an assiduousness that marks the worldly man who is attached to such things . . . his appetite is keener than Esau's . . . the finite tastes just as good to him as to one who never knew anything higher" (FT 39–40).

But it is also an either/or because in resignation we know that there is an infinite good so different from these goods that it radically relativizes our relation to them. Either we relate to it absolutely, in which case we view our pursuit of finite goods as only relatively important; or we do not relate to it at all: "if there is something [we are] not willing to give up for its sake, then [we are] not relating [ourselves] to an eternal happiness" (393).

Resignation knows that between "the absolute τέλος and relative ends" there is a "chasmic abyss" like that between heaven and hell (409). But it is not the difference between good and evil; one cannot simultaneously be or will both good and evil (420). The difference rests on the "absolute difference" between God and human beings (412). Because the lesser moment is the human and not the demonic—that is, good and not evil—it is to be relinquished but not repudiated.[13] That is why resignation requires, not that we give up everything finite, but that we be willing to do so for the sake of eternal happiness, should that prove necessary.

The individual who simultaneously relates absolutely to the absolute and relatively to the relative "does not cease to be a human being, does not take off the multitudinously compounded suit of finitude." But the clothes of finitude are like "a stranger's borrowed clothes. He is a stranger in the world of finitude, but he does not define his difference from *worldliness* by foreign dress . . . he is incognito, but his incognito consists in looking just like everyone else."[14] Climacus then switches metaphors in midpassage: "In immediacy, the individual is firmly rooted in the finite; . . . [with resignation] everything is changed, the roots are cut. He lives in the finite, but he does not have his life in it. . . . Just as the dentist loosens the gum tissue and cuts the nerve and lets the tooth remain, so also is his life in finitude loosened" (410).

But Climacus's best metaphor is neither sartorial nor dental: Resignation "does not necessarily mean that the existing person becomes indifferent to the finite. . . . An adult may very well join in children's play with total interest, may be the one who really makes the game lively, but he still does not play as a child. The person who understands it as his task to practice the absolute distinction relates himself to the finite in the same way" (413).

From the religious perspective that Climacus here portrays, resignation is authentic human temporality. Human being is neither being toward absolute knowledge nor being toward death but being toward eternal happiness. It is by leaving eternal happiness out of the picture that speculation triumphs over dialectic, identity over contradiction (421) in Hegelian mediation. The dialectical tension of a being who belongs both to time and to eternity is eliminated.[15]

Climacus constantly stresses the temporality of resignation. It is rooted in the fact that eternal happiness and the existing individual "cannot have each other in time" (397). This means that resignation must be practiced "every day" (396) "continually," and not just "once in a while" (408). Since existence moves forward toward eternity through daily life and not backward in recollection (411), the path is as long as life itself (428), and one must always be on guard against the danger of finishing too soon (406). This is what makes life "absolutely strenuous. . . . But there is nevertheless a tranquillity and a restfulness in all this strenuousness," at least in relation to "the agonizing self-contradiction of worldly passion [that] results from the individual's relating himself *absolutely* to a relative τέλος" (422).

A corollary to the temporality of resignation and a contributor to its strenuousness is its uncertainty. A "serious man," quite likely encouraged by a confused pastoral discourse, may say, "But is it certain and definite that there is such a good, is it certain and definite that there is an eternal happiness in store?—because in that case I surely would aspire to it; otherwise, I would be lunatic to risk everything for it" (422). This demand for certainty is the bourgeois Copenhagen version of philosophy as the demand for absolute knowledge. By bringing eternal happiness into the restricted economy of sound investment, where profit is guaranteed and risk eliminated (a conservative investment policy indeed!), this demand insists on walking by sight and not by faith (423–25).[16]

But this is either to finitize the eternal by making it wholly commensurate with time or to infinitize the human understanding by making it wholly adequate to the eternal. In either case it is a flight from existence. The existing individual can only pursue eternal happiness as "a daring venture" (423), for "it is actually too much to demand that something that is in store shall be definite and certain, because the future and the present do have a little moment between them, which makes it possible to expect the future but impossible *in praesenti* [at the present moment] to have certainty and definiteness . . . a present relation to a future is *eo ipso* one of uncertainty" (424). Once again the *what* is compatible only with a certain *how*: "Therefore eternal happiness, as the absolute good, has the remarkable quality that *it can be defined only by the mode in which it is acquired*" (427).[17] Like the earlier demand that eternal happiness be fully comprehensible, this demand that it be absolutely certain is rejected as a confusion about how a temporal being can relate to an eternal good.

This section concludes with a reminder that resignation belongs to a more generic religiousness than the specifically Christian: "A pagan can also do that, for example, venture everything upon the 'if' of immortality" (429). Climacus reminds himself and us that while he did not distinguish Socrates from Plato in *Fragments,* he is now distinguishing the "historical" Socrates of the *Apology,* for whom immortality is an uncertain possibility, from the "Platonic" Socrates of the *Phaedo,* who has a pocket full of proofs.

The Essential Expression of Existential Pathos: Suffering

This section is a fairly simple corollary to the previous one. The religious life is one of resignation. But resignation is suffering. So the religious life is essentially a life of suffering. To move beyond unhappy consciousness on the path to absolute knowledge, as Hegel does in the *Phenomenology,* is not to move to a higher form of religion but to leave the religious life entirely behind.

Before turning to the phenomenology of religious suffering, however, we should note two general features of this section. First, it brings to a new level of intensity the satire on the clergy, to which the reader has already been introduced. The form of this "attack upon Christendom" is not the least bit subtle, though the philosophical points on which it rests frequently are. This means that while *Postscript* should be required reading in every theological seminary for its sustained analysis of what distinguishes a genuine from a confused, even fraudulent, religious address (sermon), philosophers as well as pastors can explore these satires for insight into the religious life. It is worth slogging through even the interminable sections of this very long book if only for the brief but biting satire on the suggestion that the spiritual lethargy of the age would be cured if only we had a new hymnbook (478–80).

Second, in this section Climacus regularly identifies the confusions about the religious sphere, for which he holds the clergy especially responsible, as category mistakes. Just as space, time, substance, and causality are the conditions for the possibility of experience with Kant, so the teleological suspension of the ethical,

subjectivity, inwardness, passion, resignation, and now suffering
are conditions for the possibility of the religious life. If one has the
right content, "empirically" speaking, but expresses it in the categories of another sphere, the religious life is eliminated. Lacking
the conditions for its possibility, it becomes, quite literally, impossible. Nowhere is Hegel's argument for the inseparability of form
and content more to the point.[18] Ironically, of course.

When Anti-Climacus will later describe "The Calamity of
Christendom" by saying that "Christendom has abolished Christianity without really knowing it itself"—Climacus would say
that it did so by a series of category mistakes, and that he has
already anticipated his namesake in the attempt "to introduce
Christianity into Christendom" (PC 36). And he might well add
that it is not just a matter of Christianity but of the religious
sphere as such. The irony of a society that calls itself Christian
but is not even religious is too much to take in silence.

The authentically religious address "must always have its
totality-category present as a criterion, so that the experienced
person promptly perceives the total orientation in the life-view of
the address" (435). The spheres of existence have been differenti-
ated by the criteria they apply in asking about the good life. Here
Climacus assigns to their categorial structure that criteriological
role. When he talks about talking or living in this or that category, he is continuing the examination of the stages or spheres
of existence.

Often, as in this passage, he identifies the religious category
as a "totality-category." This term does not signify the totalizing
idea of speculative philosophy, which purports to render the
whole of reality completely intelligible. The religious category is
a totality-category because it calls for the reorientation of the
whole of life, Monday through Saturday as well as Sunday; and it
assigns this transformation as the task of one's entire lifetime.

Monasticism, it now turns out, was an "empirical" mistake,
not a category mistake. For all its problems, it understood that
the whole of life was to be lived before God. But Climacus distinguishes three forms of life possible in Christendom, which are,
religiously speaking, lower than monasticism by virtue of a category mistake that takes them out of the religious altogether.

Speaking of all three, Climacus says that "by going to church
once a week, all such religiousness emancipates itself from having the relationship with God present every day in everything
[the totality-category]. On Sunday, it obtains permission—not
quite like the child, to make merry all week long—but permission
not to think anymore about God all week long" (474). By seeking

to restrict the religious life to Sunday, each in its own way keeps even Sunday from being religious.

The first alternative is "when the individual returns home from the Sunday relationship with God to exist purely immediately in the dialectic of the pleasant and unpleasant" (474). In other words, weekdays are lived in aesthetic categories. The second alternative is "when the individual returns home from the Sunday relationship with God to exist in a finite ethic and is not aware of the persistent claim of the relationship with God while he does his job, earns money, etc." (474). For this person, weekdays are lived in an ethical sphere whose *Sittlichkeit* is thoroughly secular. The third alternative is "when the individual returns home from the Sunday relationship with God to have his life in a speculative-ethical view that as a matter of course lets the relationship with God exhaust itself in relative ends, a life-view with this formula: competence in one's occupation . . . is the highest expression of the relationship with God, and thus one does not actually need to go to church" (474; cf. 400, 460). In other words, weekdays are lived in an ethical sphere whose *Sittlichkeit* understands itself to be religious.

True, there is an irony in returning home from church on Sunday after having learned that "one does not actually need to go to church." But if, as Hegel says, "ethical life is the most genuine cultus,"[19] this would seem to be the conclusion that follows. And one might discover after the fact that one has gone to church for psychological, social, or business reasons rather than for worship, "the maximum for a being's relationship with God" (413). If the highest norms for my life are the practices of my society and the ideas of my culture, then the fact that I give a religious interpretation to these practices and ideas only means that they are all the divinity I need; but this should not disguise the fact that I have given God the door. Whether we embody the happy marriage of liberal politics with liberal religion or of conservative politics with conservative religion, if God's only function is to justify but never to challenge our beliefs and practices (though yours are quite another matter), then God has been reduced to the Wizard of Oz, whose ventriloquist we are.

Although Climacus describes himself as a humorist and not a religious person (483, 501), he thinks it a shame that God should be so degraded and humans so self-deceived. As a counter to the category mistakes that make this possible, he offers his analysis of religious suffering. His first corollary to the previous discussion of resignation is simple enough: as a life of resignation, the religious life is a life of suffering. In the first instance,

resignation is a kind of dying. It is the process of dying to immediacy. Formally speaking, immediacy signifies our natural condition; materially speaking, in this context, it designates life
without the otherness of the God relation. From the fact that "ab-
soluteness is not directly the element of finite existence" (483) it
does not follow that our natural life is one of relating relatively to
relative ends. On the contrary, we regularly find ourselves absolutely related to relative ends (431, 460–61), and this is what Climacus understands by immediacy. Although he views this
condition as an "agonizing self-contradiction" (422), he is under
no illusions that the process of dying to it is anything but painful.

There is a second dimension to the pain of resignation. If in
this process the world of finite ends is too much with us, the absolute τέλος always exceeds our grasp. To enter the religious life
and the painful process of dying to my immediate self is already
to have defined my highest joy as eternal happiness. But since I
am in time, this joy is ahead of me rather than present, and my
separation from it is also painful (453).

To suffer is not only to feel; it is also to undergo, to endure. It
refers to a certain passivity or impotence. One side of the concept
of suffering participates in the difference between pain and pleasure, the other side in the difference between acting and being
acted upon. Now immediacy shows itself as "the wish to be capable of everything" (461).

Climacus derives the third dimension of the suffering of resignation from this other side of its meaning. Perhaps because it is
less obvious than the first two, he devotes much more time to it.
To act religiously is to suffer in part because in such action the self
experiences not its ability but its inability. For example, the task
of dying to immediacy is the task of changing oneself. But "the action of inwardness is suffering, because the individual is unable to
transform himself" (432–33). Climacus, at any rate, is quite clear
that the strenuous task he describes is one that he is unable to perform, which is part of the reason he is suspicious of those who have
gone beyond the religious "by embracing speculative thought and
world history" (498–99).

Typically, he does not develop this point as a direct attack on
Hegelianism. He turns rather to everyday life in Copenhagen
and to the question of what it would take for Sunday sermons to
provide support for the religious life on weekdays: "The religious
speaker who does not know how the task appears in everyday life
and in the living room could just as well keep quiet. . . . It is in the
living room that the battle must be fought, lest the skirmishes of
religiousness become a changing-of-the-guard parade one day a

week. It is in the living room that the battle must be fought, not imaginatively in church, with the pastor shadowboxing and the listeners looking on. It is in the living room that the battle must be fought" (465; cf. 464).[20]

Or in the amusement park. If we are to flee the monastery, to which we were never tempted in the first place, presumably we might go out to Deer Park for some innocent recreation. But if the religious category is a totality-category, shaping the whole of life, we can ask what it would mean to do this religiously. How, for example, can I bring my trip to the park into relation to last Sunday's sermon, when the pastor said, "You must not put your trust in the world, and not in people, and not in yourself, but only in God, because a human being is himself capable of nothing. . . . We should always keep this in mind" (467)?

Here the pastor touched on the basis of this third dimension of suffering, the fact "that the individual is capable of doing nothing himself but is nothing before God, because here again the relationship with God is distinguishable by the negative, and self-annihilation [not merely self-transformation] is the essential form for the relationship with God" (461).[21] That was Sunday. What about Monday, Tuesday, and Wednesday? What would it mean to keep in mind that I am capable of nothing while I demonstrate my capacity to go to the park by doing so?

The triviality of this example is what makes it important. Questions about the relation between the human and divine are quite easy to understand in the abstract, much harder in the concrete (481). By avoiding the concreteness of daily life, the sermon, "although it preaches against the monastery . . . distances itself from actuality just as much as the monastery" (481). A parishioner, who likes that kind of preaching, finds Climacus's question annoying: "I am no heretic who wants to have the faith changed. Even if, according to what you say, it can be judged doubtful to what extent I actually am a believer, it is certain that I am an orthodox who abhors the Baptists. On the other hand, it never occurs to me to bring such trifles as going out to the amusement park into connection with the thought of God" (477). Nor does it occur to him that in this way he makes life easier for himself, since "the more unimportant something is, the more difficult it is to join the God-conception together with it" (487).

Just as human incapacity before God is easier to understand in the abstract than in the concrete, so it is easy to say "that a human being is nothing before God" but "difficult to express this in existence" (463; cf. 471, 494). At the level of abstract theory, the superior intellect may have an advantage, but at the level of concrete practice, it evaporates. Striking once more against intellectual elitism, Climacus insists that the task he is considering is "as difficult for the most eminent intellect" as for the most simple person (469). Just as important, the task of discourse is not to minimize the difficulty, as if to make religion attractive to the consumer by reducing it to bargain prices, but to present the difficulty as clearly as possible (465–66).[22] If the clergy will not accept this unpopular task, says Climacus, "then I will do it, I who am neither a religious speaker nor a religious person, but just a humorous, imaginatively constructing psychologist" (483).

But is it not the pastor's task to comfort? Yes, but "if it is a pastor's task to comfort, then he also ought to know how, when necessary, to make the religious so difficult that it brings every insubordinate to his knees" (482). Recalling his earlier reference to self-annihilation before God (461; cf. 489), Climacus adds, "We left the religious person in the crisis of sickness; but this sickness is not unto death. We shall now let him be strengthened by the very same conception that destroyed him, by the conception of God" (488).

These passages explain why Climacus accentuates the negative side of the religious life. It is not because he denies the positive, the element of comfort and strengthening, but because he suspects the triumph of the speculative over the dialectical in the discourse of both the Hegelians and the Danish clergy, discourses designed to relax the tension between negative and positive. Like Rudolf Otto, he finds the divine *mysterium* to be *tremendum* (terrifying, repelling) before it is *fascinans* (attractive, reassuring).[23] It is "no wonder then that the Jew assumed that the sight of God was death and the pagans that the God-relationship was the harbinger of madness! Even though the conception of God is the absolute help, it is also the one and only help that is absolutely able to show a person his own helplessness" (484).

There is a certain stubbornness to the religious sphere in relation to these three dimensions of religious suffering. It refuses to let its unhappy consciousness be assuaged by anything but the arrival of the eternal happiness for which it waits in hope. Without professing to give an adequate description of what that will be, the preceding analysis implies that somehow it will involve transformation into a new immediacy to which one will not need to die, the presence rather than the absence of a good sufficiently absolute to relativize all other goods, and an end to the fear and anxiety generated by the nothingness of the finite in relation to the infinite. By these criteria, the claim of Hegel's *Phenomenology of Spirit* to be the *Aufhebung* of unhappy consciousness and the subsequent claim that the *Phenomenology* refuted Kierke-gaard before he was even born might appear comical. Perhaps Climacus is the humorist he claims to be.

His second corollary linking suffering to resignation states that the suffering proper to the religious life is essential to it; it is the essential expression of existential pathos. Far from being either accidental or occasional, it is a sign in the absence of which the religious life itself is absent.

The first indication of this is the inwardness of religious suffering. It is to be sharply distinguished from the external suffering that belongs to the aesthetic categories of fortune and misfortune (438–40). This suffering is external not because it pertains to my body or my bank account; depression is a mental suffering that normally is to be understood as misfortune. Inwardness is "the individual's relation to himself before God" (436–37),[24] and psychic distress, such as depression, would be religious suffering only if it were an essential aspect of the God relation. The mark of the religious life is the category "before God" (469, 489, 497). To say that "action in inwardness is suffering" (433) is to say that to relate oneself to oneself before God in time is to suffer neither accidentally nor occasionally but essentially.

This means that when we read in the New Testament that "the apostles when they were flogged went away joyful, thanking God that it was granted them to suffer something for the sake of Christ" (452), we should not understand this to be religious suffering. That they considered themselves fortunate rather than unfortunate does not change the fact that this suffering came to them accidentally and occasionally. Whether each is a "knight of hidden inwardness" in this situation we cannot tell, for what distinguishes such a knight from others is precisely what we cannot see.[25] True, "a contradiction will appear as [such a knight] relates himself to the world around him . . . [but the] contradiction does not consist in his being different from everyone else . . . the contradiction is that he, with all this inwardness hidden within him, with this pregnancy of suffering and benediction in his inner being, looks just like all the others" (499).

The second sign that religious suffering is essential is specifically temporal. Already implicit in the analysis of inwardness, the fact that this suffering is not occasional is made fully explicit. Its "continuance" is as essential to it as it is to the religious life (443–47, 499): "When Scripture says that God dwells in a broken and contrite heart, this is not an expression for an accidental, transitory, momentary condition . . . but rather for the essential meaning of suffering for the relationship with God" (445). This is another way of saying that the task of renunciation "is ideal and perhaps is never accomplished by anyone; it is only on paper that one begins summarily and is promptly finished" (431).

If there is a multifaceted suffering that is essential to the religious life, does this mean that the religious person "wants suffering" (434)? Yes, but we must be careful here, for this suffering is "not flagellation and other such things; it is not *self-torment*" (463). Just as for Aristotle pleasure is not the goal of action but the natural accompaniment of actions that have some other goal, so pain and self-annihilation before God are not the goals of the religious life but the natural accompaniments of any God relationship that has not lapsed into aesthetic or ethical categories. To want this suffering is simply to want to live a life that is not such a lapse.

Transitional Reflections on Irony and Humor

What may easily appear to be a digression on irony and humor at this point is in fact an attempt to deepen the analysis of the religious person as a "knight of hidden inwardness." Climacus writes, "There are three existence-spheres: the esthetic, the ethical, the religious. To these there is a respectively corresponding *confinium* [border territory]: irony is the *confinium* between the esthetic and the ethical; humor is the *confinium* between the ethical and the religious" (501–2).

But it is not as boundary zones or as transitional stages that Climacus focuses on irony and humor; it is rather as the disguises in which the ethical and the religious, respectively, may manifest themselves. Irony is the incognito of the ethical, and humor is the incognito of the religious. Thus in their presence one can reasonably suspect the presence of an ethical or religious person. But the observer can be fooled. Just as it is not necessary that the ethical or the religious manifest themselves in this way, so it is not necessary that the practicing ironist is an ethical person or the practicing humorist a religious person (500–505; cf. 447). Climacus insists quite regularly that he is a humorist but not a religious person, let alone a Christian (451, 466, 483, 501, 511). We must see how this can be.

To begin with, irony and humor are modes of the comic, which means they concern themselves with contradiction, for "where there is life there is contradiction, and wherever there is contradiction, the comic is present" (514). There is nothing especially funny about the simultaneous assertion of *p* and not-*p,* and it is clear from the long footnote (514–19) in which Climacus illustrates contradiction as the key to the comic that formal, logical contradiction is not what he has in mind. It is rather *incongruity,* the *tension* that arises from perceiving elements that do not fit each other and that is released in laughter. Thus, to cite his first example, it is funny that Hamlet swears by the fire tongs because of the *discrepancy* between "the solemnity of the oath" and the triviality of the fire tongs (514).

We should not be surprised that it is not as literary devices that Climacus distinguishes these two species of the comic. He is interested in them, if not as modes of being-in-the-world, at least as outward expressions of such modes; accordingly, the contradiction that gives rise to them concerns the very structure of human existence.

Thus irony arises "by continually joining the particulars of the finite with the ethical infinite requirement and allowing the contradiction to come into existence" (502). The discrepancy is between the finite and the (ethically) infinite or between the relative and "the absolute requirement" (503). The infinite and absolute character of the ethical requirement stems both from the categorical nature of its obligation and the absolute origin from which it derives.

Accordingly, Climacus reiterates Kierkegaard's claim in his dissertation that it is the proper task of irony to deliver us from "the snares of relativity" (CI 77). The true ironist does not "let himself be caught in any relativity" but has the strength "to comprehend ironically" all the relativities of life (502, 502n). This means holding both my performance and our practices up against the infinite and absolute requirement of the ethical and recognizing them as approximations at best, or, in other words, as failures to satisfy the demands of the ethical.

When Climacus says that irony "is the unity of ethical passion, which in inwardness infinitely accentuates one's own *I* in relation to the ethical requirement—and culture" (503), this does not mean holding oneself up before the expectations of the ethical and of one's own culture but holding oneself and one's own culture up before the infinite and absolute expectations of the ethical. As Evans puts it, *"Irony represents the discovery of the self as distinct from a cultural ensemble."*[26] The correctness of this reading is confirmed when Climacus decries the "desperate attempt of the miscarried Hegelian ethics to make the state into the court of last resort of ethics" (503n).

Before we can see how humor relates to irony and then how it is possible for an observer to be fooled by an ironist who is not ethical and a humorist who is not religious, we must deal with an

obvious problem. As just presented, irony has the teleological suspension of the ethical built into it (see chapter 3 above). So how
can it be the incognito of the ethical? The answer is fairly simple.
Johannes Climacus is not Johannes de Silentio. Both want to emphasize the relativity of any culture, any state, any *Sittlichkeit,*
and to protest the tendency of Hegel and of Christendom to forget
this. To this end Silentio identifies the ethical with the historically concrete embodiments of the difference between good and
evil, right and wrong, which always tend to absolutize themselves, and distinguishes this ethical from the religious that always insists on the relativity of every *Sittlichkeit.*

By contrast, Climacus treats the ethical and the religious as
the closest of relatives by virtue of their commitment to subjectivity and inwardness. When he treats Hegel not as the embodiment
of the ethical sphere but as its disappearance, it is not because he
disagrees substantively with Silentio but because they use the
term "ethical" differently. Relative to Judge William's presentation of the ethical in *Either/Or,* we might say that Climacus appeals to the formal conception of ethics as concerning the eternal
validity of the self, while Silentio draws on the immediate tran-
scription of this into the concreteness of bourgeois marriage.[27]
When Climacus treats Socratic irony as belonging to the ethical,
he recognizes the apparent tension between this and his earlier
assimilation of Socrates to the religious (503, 504n). But this only
means that what Climacus understands by the ethical is hardly
to be distinguished from the religious. Both involve a hidden inwardness, of which the comic may or may not be the sign.

What, then, is the difference between irony as the incognito
of the ethical and humor as the incognito of the religious? If irony
arises through the juxtaposition of the "infinite" and "absolute"
requirement with the finitude of human existence, personal and
corporate, the humorist "joins the conception of God together
with everything and sees the contradiction" (505). The difference
is as little or as great as the difference between "infinite" and "absolute" on one side and "God" on the other.[28]

This difference does not help us to see why Climacus classi-
fies satire and caricature under humor rather than as species of
irony (though that classification helps us to understand why he
considers himself a humorist). As a theory of the comic, our interlude clearly has its limitations. But its purpose is to help us better
understand the hidden inwardness that we now can see as belonging to the ethical (in Climacus's sense) as well as to the religious.
And now we are in a position to see how it is possible for Climacus
himself to be a humorist without being a religious person.

As knights of hidden inwardness, the ethical and religious persons recognize the discrepancy between themselves (individually and collectively) and the infinite and absolute requirement, one the one hand, and God, on the other. This is the "contradiction" that enables them to see human existence as comic and to appear incognito in a publicly visible irony or humor. But the comedians who fool the observer into thinking that they are truly ethical and religious persons have the same insight as the foundation of their irony and humor that undergirds the ethical and religious life. The difference is not at the level of outward practice or of theoretical foundation but of inward practice.

The mere ironist, who is not also an ethical person, "is able to talk about himself as about a third person, to join himself as a vanishing particular together with the absolute requirement." But "it is still not certain that he is an ethicist. He is an ethicist only by relating himself within himself to the absolute requirement. Such an ethicist uses irony as his incognito" (502–3).[29] Similarly, the mere humorist "joins the conception of God together with something else and brings out the contradiction—but he does not relate himself to God in religious passion. . . . He changes himself into a jesting and yet profound transition area for all these transactions, but he does not relate himself to God" (505).

The mere ironist and the mere humorist have the same insights as the corresponding ethical and religious persons; they lack only the personal appropriation of the ethical and religious tasks implicit in these insights. This means that the mere humorist, while ever so close to the religious, is just as close to cynicism, just as the mere ironist, while ever so close to the ethical, is just as close to nihilism.[30] This ambiguity lies in the difference between the *what* and the *how*. *What* the mere ironist and mere humorist do is the same as what the truly ethical and religious persons do when comedy becomes their incognito—they point out the discrepancy between the ideal and the real in human life. But *how* they do it is radically different. And this difference is radically inward, not publicly visible.

This gives rise to another "contradiction," which in turn gives rise to more comedy. This time the discrepancy is between the inner and the outer, between behavior and the heart (499, 504, 508, 511). What is comical here is not the mere ironist or humorist as such but the mistake (whether made by themselves or by others) of confusing their comical practice with the hidden inwardness, of which it could have been the sign. In Lee Barrett's words, "humor attacks the identification of any finite experience, practice, or institution with true religiosity. Humor laughs at everything that masquerades as piety."[31] It is all right for piety to masquerade as humor; but it is not all right for humor to masquerade as piety, any more than it is all right for speculation or bourgeois marriage to masquerade as piety. In the former case the inner gives itself an appropriate (if not adequate) outer form; in the latter case, the outer inappropriately equates itself with, and substitutes itself for, the inner. In doing so, it makes existence much too easy.

In the midst of these discussions, Climacus writes, "It is a pious and in the strictest sense godly expression for the relationship with God to confess oneself to be a sinner" (512). We do not usually associate comedy and confession so closely, but according to Climacus's analysis, the same discrepancy between human performance and divine expectation that gives rise to humor will also, for the truly religious knight of hidden inwardness, give rise to the confession of sin. A few pages later Climacus broadens this comment to include the ethical: "Repentance is in the ethical-religious sphere and thus is qualified in such a way that it has only one higher sphere, namely, the religious in the strictest sense" (519).

It sounds as if he is equating the ethical-religious sphere with what he is about to call Religiousness A and the religious in the strictest sense with what he is about to call Religiousness B. If this reading is correct, it would complete the collapse of the distinction between the ethical and the religious, making the former a subdivision of the latter (but not in the sense of the ethical that was teleologically suspended by Silentio's Abraham).

We can now see why this interlude is placed where it is. While the discussion of suffering grew right out of the discussion of resignation, there is no direct transition from the analysis of suffering to the third moment, with which Climacus will conclude his long account of existential pathos. But his interpretation of irony and humor inevitably gives rise to thoughts of sin and repentance and thus serves to introduce that third moment.

❙ The Decisive Expression of Existential Pathos: Guilt

The opening paragraph of this section contains the word "task" no fewer than seven times. The task in question is the one described in §1: "Simultaneously to Relate Oneself Absolutely to One's Absolute τέλος and Relatively to Relative Ends" (387; cf.

407, 414, 422, 431). In the existentialism of *Postscript*, "existence" is the designation of the one to whom this task is assigned. We have already seen that it calls for a total transformation of the self (387) that can be described in terms of renunciation (389n), surrender (391), and resignation (394). This means that we are located in the ethical sphere or in the religious sphere, which presupposes the ethical.

Against this background and taken together with the sustained polemic against the speculative, the world-historical, the system, and mediation, the sevenfold repetition of the word "task" points to a theme in Climacus that can be expressed in the language of Levinas: ethics as first philosophy.[32] Philosophical reflection must be in the service of human responsibility above all else. Reflection on being or the idea or the historical unfolding of spirit must be teleologically suspended in an appropriative reflection (double reflection) on the infinite task of being human. Accordingly, when Climacus discusses irony, the finite is not juxtaposed to the infinite or the absolute but to the infinite and absolute requirement; similarly, the discrepancy between the finite and God, which gives rise to humor, does not concern the latter as the onto-theo-logical ground of the unity of the all in the one but as the origin of the infinite and absolute requirement. This is why "It is a pious and in the strictest sense godly expression for the relationship with God to confess oneself to be a sinner" (512).

That guilt is the decisive expression of existential pathos stems from the facts that existential reflection refuses to retreat from the ethical into the aesthetic or the speculative and that existential reflection discovers our failure to fulfill the infinite and absolute task set for us, whether by the Platonic Good or the biblical God.[33] Resignation calls our attention to this task, and suffering and guilt underscore the pain and the failure involved in being essentially related to it. It is no wonder that Climacus finds himself surrounded by attempts to lower the price of successful existence by reducing the task or that he defines his own mission as preserving its full difficulty. A life lived in pursuit of eternal happiness is no easier than one lived in pursuit of the Holy Grail or the gold medal. It is just that in the former case the obstacles that have to be overcome are located in hidden inwardness; and just as it would be a tragedy (and comedy) of major proportions to declare victory too early by confusing some quite ordinary cup or medallion with the Holy Grail or the gold medal, so it would be tragicomic to confuse speculative insight or civil respectability with a relation in hidden inwardness to eternal happiness.

In the present section Climacus targets two such confusions, motivated (however subconsciously) by the desire to make existence easier than it actually is. The first is to eliminate guilt altogether by existing abstractly (or better, by abstracting oneself out of existence). For such "existence," life is easy because the task is finished as soon as it is set forth (526). But a task that is completed as soon as it is set forth is no task at all.

Climacus makes it clear that the project of avoiding guilt consciousness "by living abstractly" is a question of categories, of spheres (534). In the objectivity of the aesthetic and the speculative, guilt consciousness makes no sense, unless perhaps as a neurosis to be cured. Each in its own way practices what Anti-Climacus will call the "pantheistic" definition of sin as "something merely negative." According to this view human failure is simply "weakness, sensuousness, finitude, ignorance, etc." (SUD 96). The subjectivity of the ethical and religious spheres is the refusal of such "pantheism." Just as Levinas accuses philosophy's ontological preoccupation with reducing the other to the same,[34] so Climacus accuses objectivity of a pantheistic reduction of the all to the one, eliminating in the process the difference between human performance and the "absolute criterion" (547, 549) that permits guilt consciousness not only to arise but to be seen as the truth about my existence, and ours.

What makes objectivity abstract is not that it operates in some ethereal conceptual stratosphere. We are not dealing with a Humean equation of "abstract" with "abstruse." Objectivity is abstract because it abstracts the pre-ethical dimensions of human life from the ethical dimensions, which are their proper context.[35] The concerns of the aesthetic and the speculative are genuine human concerns; but they are not the highest human concerns. A posture that gives them primacy is subhuman because it has withdrawn from the essentially human.

While abstraction is the elimination of guilt altogether, childishness is its finitizing. Moral failure is allowed to appear, but in a context that might be described as guilt management. The first move here is a change of venue. Instead of allowing the evaluation to take place before God and "the absolute criterion," it is moved to "a human court," even though this is "unethical." The result is that everything becomes comparative, relative, and quantitative (530). The moral life is reduced to something like "the grades on a child's report card" (533). Relative to the expectations of this school system and this teacher, I did better than I did last marking period and better than most of my class, but still not as well as Suzy and Johnny. I did especially well in geography, though speling is still my Waterlou. But even there I only failed four of the tests outright.

Climacus is not hesitant to acknowledge that this "comparative, conventional, external, bourgeois conception of the ethical is useful enough in ordinary dealings." But if this were to exhaust a people's moral consciousness, they would be "essentially poverty-stricken ethically" and "essentially a bankrupt generation" (546). At the heart of this harsh judgment is the sense that the bourgeois-childish construal of the moral life is a "wretched contentment," as Nietzsche's Zarathustra would put it, that finitizes guilt so as to make it manageable (541–42, 550).

To make this point, Climacus recalls a nostalgic reference by a woman in considerable personal pain to "the happiness of a child"—to which another woman in the group replied, "Yes, and above all the happiness of childhood to be spanked" (551). Climacus resists the temptation of hearing this as an ironical reminder that childhood is not always happy and insists on asking wherein this particular happiness lies. "What is it that makes the child's life so easy? It is that so often 'quits' can be called and a new beginning is so frequently made" (551n and 550). The happiness lies not in the spanking but in the assurance that one can always pay off one's moral debts, however painfully, and begin again with a clean slate. The balance sheet always shows assets equal to liabilities, and one is never morally bankrupt.

Adult versions of this attempted happiness simply substitute another punisher for the paddling parent. Thus Climacus treats as childish any attempt to make fault commensurable (542, 554) with civil punishment, Nemesis and the Furies, or penance, including self-inflicted penance (525, 538, 540–42, 549–50).

For abstract thinking, guilt is to be treated therapeutically, as a neurosis to be cured; for childish thinking, it is to be treated commercially, as a debt to be paid. Climacus repudiates neither therapy nor punishment. But he insists that before the infinite and absolute requirement or before God, there is a guilt that resists reduction to these finite dimensions. He calls it total guilt (528–29, 536–38, 549, 554) or essential guilt (528–29, 531). We can call it transcendental guilt.

As transcendental, this guilt is prior to particular faults. I realize that my most fundamental task is dying to immediacy, and "just as the beginning is about to be made here, it is discovered that, since meanwhile time has been passing, a bad beginning has been made" (526). Whenever I set out to relate absolutely to the absolute and only relatively to the relative, I discover that I have already failed in this task. I never know myself in innocence.

As transcendental, this guilt is the condition of the possibility of particular faults. It is "this totality of guilt that ultimately makes it possible for someone to be guilty or not guilty in the particular" (529). This means that the "priority of the total guilt is no empirical qualification" (529).

As transcendental, this guilt is qualitative and not quantitative (529–30). "With regard to guilt-consciousness, childishness assumes that today, for example, he is guilty in this and that, then for eight days he is guiltless, but then on the ninth day everything goes wrong again" (531). By the same token, "to make oneself guilty fourteen times is child's play—this is also why childishness always keeps to the numerical" (536).

In all of these ways total guilt signifies the transcendental priority of sin to sins. I sin because I am a sinner, and not the other way around. Each particular fault is grounded in a fundamental project in which I commit myself absolutely to the relative and thus fail the most fundamental task of existence. I can never date the adoption of this fundamental project, but in every moment of ethical-religious seriousness, including the very first, I find it already operative.

But none of these ways of signifying the transcendental character of total guilt is quite adequate for Climacus. Not surprisingly, he turns to Plato for his decisive expression of guilt as the decisive expression of existential pathos. *As transcendental, this total guilt is recollected rather than remembered* (525, 530, 533–36, 538, 540, 550). My guilt goes deeper than any act I can remember, and recollection is the recognition of what is always already there, whether I recognize it or not. To call this recollection eternal, as Climacus regularly does, is not to suggest that in guilt consciousness I manage to do what I failed to do in speculative thought, back out of time into eternity, thereby easing the strenuousness of existence by ceasing to exist. It is rather to say that in my temporal relation to the eternal, I discover that every event I can remember is conditioned by a posture whose temporal origin I cannot discover.[36]

The Indian notion of karma and reincarnation, the Platonic myth of a preincarnate fall of the soul, and the Christian notion of original sin are all theories about the phenomenon to which Climacus points. But, in spite of Kierkegaard's well-known interest in the theology of original sin, Climacus presents no theological or metaphysical explanation of total guilt as transcendental fault. His "argument" is entirely phenomenological, and he points to this phenomenon as being of decisive importance for the religious sphere.

Total guilt is decisive because it signifies the relation of the self to its eternal happiness. It may be more obvious that such guilt signifies the distance of the self from its highest good, and indeed it does. The guilty self has not arrived at that place where "they live happily ever after." But without this guilt there is no relation to an eternal happiness (526–27, 534–35). This can be seen by asking where I would be without it. I would either be living in abstraction or in childishness, but these are just the places I end up if I do not allow my entire existence to be transformed by the idea of eternal happiness as my highest goal. To "exist" abstractly is to live in the aesthetic or the speculative; to "exist" childishly is to live in the ethical, as Silentio understands it. If I would live in the ethical-religious, as Climacus understands it, I must open myself to the experience of total guilt. That is why Climacus gives this startling definition: "The totality of guilt-consciousness in the single individual before God in relation to an eternal happiness is the religious" (554).

Another way of putting the same point relates it to the earlier discussion of truth as subjectivity. That eternal happiness is the *what* that orients my life is guaranteed, not by my theories about immortality in relation to God or the good, but by total guilt, as the *how* of my relation to what I take to be eternal happiness. Climacus seems to want to make total guilt not only the necessary but also the sufficient condition of the religious.

According to Climacus's account, the religious understanding of human existence is very sobering indeed. Resignation and suffering are bad enough; and now guilt. But he insists that "the eternal recollection of guilt in hidden inwardness is not despair" (554). He has tried to block the path to solving the problem of guilt by means of abstraction or childishness, but nothing in his analysis precludes the hope for grace and forgiveness (themes that will become increasingly important in Kierkegaard's authorship after *Postscript*). Far from seeing despair as the inevitable response to the recollection of guilt, Climacus sees it as only a certain kind of response, one characterized by "impatience" and "a kind of ill temper" (554).

The true knight of hidden inwardness will resist the temptation to such a tantrum, not only because it is not necessary but because it provides a powerful motivation toward abstraction and childishness in the hope of brightening one's spirits. But according to this analysis, which surely would be of interest to Anti-

Climacus as the author of *Sickness unto Death,* the aesthetic and the ethical spheres (the latter in Silentio's Hegelian sense as the ultimacy of bourgeois *Sittlichkeit*) would be the incognitos in which a despair in hidden inwardness masquerades.

The Intermediate Clause between A and B

Climacus's long chapter 4 was supposed to be about the issue of *Fragments,* namely, the problems raised by the possibility of basing one's eternal happiness on something in time that moreover could be in time only paradoxically or by virtue of the absurd. But the long discussion of existential pathos concludes with the reminder that it has not addressed that topic. The comic incongruity (contradiction) of prefacing the seventeen pages that finally address the topic with ten times that many that do not has two explanations. First, Climacus has already discussed this issue quite carefully in *Fragments* and discovers that he has little to add to it as such. Second, he is now primarily concerned with locating the existential space in which the problem can arise (and outside of which it simply disappears). The name of that space is subjectivity, and the entire book up to this point (555)—even the brief, opening discussion of objectivity—has been a sustained reflection on the nature of subjectivity.

We are given several important reminders in this transition from A to B, from what he now calls Religiousness A, the religion of pathos and immanence, to Religiousness B, the religion of the dialectical and of transcendence.

We are not looking at two species of one genus but at a species in relation to its genus. Religiousness B concerns itself with "the specifically Christian." The dialectical presupposes the pathos-filled and "gives rise to a new pathos. . . . Religiousness A must first be present in the individual before there can be any consideration of becoming aware of the dialectical B" (555–57; cf. 581).

Christianity's belief in the incarnation is dialectical. It involves an unresolved tension, the incongruity or contradiction of time receiving what does not belong to time. But this theme is not our introduction to dialectical contradiction. We have been encountering it all along in the dipolar structure of the human self as belonging to both time and eternity, to finitude and infinitude.[37] For this reason it is necessary to speak of "the dialectical in the second place" (556, 559, 581). This is in keeping with the interpretation of B as the intensification of A. It is only if we have resisted the speculative dissolution of the dialectical in the first place that the question of Christianity can meaningfully arise. And that resistance is what the long discussion of subjectivity as such has been all about.

Climacus reminds us that his task is "to make it difficult to become a Christian, yet not more difficult than it is" (557). Religiousness A, which is more strenuous than much that passes for Christianity in Christendom, helps both to highlight the difficulty and to make it clear that the problem is "not difficult for the obtuse and easy for the brainy" (557–58). This by now familiar egalitarian theme will be central to Climacus's account of Christian faith as dialectical.

Finally, while Religiousness A and Religiousness B are both dialectical, the former is the domain of immanence, since the self finds its God relation "within itself," while the latter is the domain of transcendence, since "the individual does not find the upbuilding by finding the relationship with God within himself but relates himself to something outside himself," namely, "God in time as an individual human being" (560–61n). This, too, will be an important theme in the chapter that follows.

❙ N O T E S

1. Cf. the opening of Heidegger's existential analytic of *Dasein:* "We are ourselves the entities to be analyzed. The Being of any such entity is *in each case mine.* . . . That Being which is an *issue* for this entity is in its very Being, is in each case mine" (*Being and Time,* 67).

2. On the theme of existential phenomenology, see the preface to Merleau-Ponty, *Phenomenology of Perception;* and chapter 8 of Paul Ricoeur, *Husserl: An Analysis of His Phenomenology,* trans. Edward G. Ballard and Lester E. Embree (Evanston, Ill.: Northwestern University Press, 1967).

3. Even A, the aesthete of *Either / Or,* satirizes this confusion: "One wishes to be edified in the theater, to be esthetically stimulated in church; one wishes to be converted by novels, to be entertained by devotional books" (EO 1:149).

4. Shifting the emphasis from time and eternity to necessity and freedom, Sartre will portray this structure in *Being and Nothingness* as the dialectical tension of facticity and transcendence.

5. Note again how the *what* is dependent on the *how,* and note the quotation with which this paragraph ends.

6. Although the God relation is not spelled out in terms of eternal happiness in the Abraham story, the relation of this account to *Fear and Trembling* will be obvious.

7. There is an irony here insofar as Hegel can be seen as a kind of Stoic. For such a reading, see my "Hegel, Tillich, and the Secular," chap. 13 of *Hegel, Freedom, and Modernity;* and "Hegel's *Angst vor dem Sollen,*" *The Owl of Minerva* 25, no. 2 (Spring 1994): 187–94.

8. *Phenomenology,* 355.

9. To be more precise, it is transformed into the difference between understanding and reason, two modes of human understanding. Not all, only some of my concepts are adequate to the infinite.

10. The two Hegelian quotations come, respectively, from *Lectures on the Philosophy of Religion*, 3:342 and 1:446.

11. *Hegel's Introduction to the Lectures on the History of Philosophy*, trans. T. M. Knox and A. V. Miller (Oxford: Clarendon Press, 1985), 133.

12. See my essay "Hegel and the Reformation," chap. 9 of *Hegel, Freedom, and Modernity*. It is worth noticing that Hegel does not challenge the economy of merit in monasticism, which is so troubling to Climacus, perhaps because the notion that we could be indebted to God (*schuldig*) makes so little sense in his system of thought.

13. See also the discussion of dialectic in chapter 4 above, especially in relation to *Either/Or* and *Fear and Trembling*.

14. See also FT 39–40, where the knight of faith "looks just like a tax collector" and is outwardly indistinguishable from a variety of ones' neighbors, from capitalist to merchant to clerk to postman to butcher.

15. From this perspective Heidegger's phenomenology of human temporality loses the "dignity of the human" by omitting the "majesty of the divine." The same would be true for Derrida's, for whom *différance* signifies not only spatial difference but also temporal deferral (see chapter 5, note 4 above). Compared with Hegel, they stress a finitude of temporality that undermines (total) presence. But compared with the religious, as Climacus presents it, they remain philosophers of identity. There is an otherness within time, but time itself has no other.

16. Cf. Derrida's interpretation of Hegelianism as a restricted economy in "From Restricted to General Economy: A Hegelianism without Reserve," in *Writing and Difference*.

17. Thus the uncertainty of eternal happiness is closely related to our difficulties in comprehending it, discussed earlier in this chapter. What I can fully comprehend and whose reality is beyond all possible doubt is not, if I am living in time, my eternal happiness.

18. In both versions of his Logic, Hegel argues that form and content do not vary independently. This is unintentionally ironic, of course, in relation to his claim that his philosophy has the same content as the Christian religion, but in a different form.

19. *Lectures on the Philosophy of Religion*, 1:446.

20. One could say that Climacus's task here is to show that this claim and the earlier claim that worship is "the maximum for a being's relationship with God" (413) are mutually implicative rather than contradictory. Of course, with his polemic against allowing the infinite to exhaust itself in finite ends, he cannot do this by simply identifying true worship with daily life.

21. For an extended analysis of this ontological inadequacy in the face of the sacred, see sections 2A and 2B in my *God, Guilt, Death*.

22. The "attack upon Christendom" in *Fear and Trembling* is framed with a satire on sales and bargain prices in the realm of the spirit. See the preface in relation to the epilogue.

23. See Rudolf Otto, *The Idea of the Holy*, trans. John W. Harvey (New York: Oxford University Press, 1958), especially chapters 4–6. This theme is central to *Fear and Trembling*.

24. Inwardness and subjectivity have often been seen as signs of an atomistic individualism in Kierkegaard's writings. Here we see the former as essentially involving a relational concept of the self. It should not come as a surprise that the religious sphere gives priority to the God relation over social relations.

25. The knight of hidden inwardness should be compared with *Fear and Trembling*'s knight of infinite resignation. In chapter 14 we will see Kierkegaard offer a later and different interpretation of the suffering of the apostles.

26. Evans, *Kierkegaard's "Fragments" and "Postscript,"* 195. The chapter from which this quotation comes is an illuminating analysis of the interlude on irony and humor. Another helpful treatment is found in chapter 7 of Sylvia Walsh, *Living Poetically: Kierkegaard's Existential Aesthetics* (University Park: Pennsylvania State University Press, 1994).

27. This accounts for the possibility of Climacus appealing to Judge William as a critic of Hegel's destruction of the ethical (503n). My own treatment of *Either/Or* in chapter 3 uses Silentio's vocabulary rather than Climacus's. Similarly, Jean-François Lyotard assimilates his theory of the comic to Silentio's teleological suspension of the ethical: "The law should always be respected with humor because it cannot be completely respected, except at the price of giving credence to the idea that it is the very mode of linking heterogeneities together, that it has the necessity of total Being. . . . The 'people' . . . is full of laughter. Politics is tragedy for the authorities, comedy for the people" (*The Differend,* trans. Georges Van Den Abbeele [Minneapolis: University of Minnesota Press, 1988], 144).

28. Kierkegaard gives a different account of the relation of humor to irony in his dissertation. See CI 329.

29. Clearly the term "ethicist" here does not mean "moral philosopher" but "person living in the ethical sphere."

30. Just this ambiguity hangs over contemporary postmodern philosophy. Whether its critiques of Enlightenment versions of self and society are headed in the direction of the ethical and religious or the cynical and nihilistic is not always easy to tell. What a given reader finds may be as much a function of his or her own inwardness as of the text. Thus Kierkegaard writes, "Irony is a healthiness insofar as it rescues the soul from relativity; it is a sickness insofar as it cannot bear the absolute except in the form of nothing" (CI 77).

31. Lee Barrett, "The Uses and Misuses of the Comic: Reflections on the *Corsair* Affair," in *International Kierkegaard Commentary: The Corsair Affair,* 133.

32. Levinas, "Ethics as First Philosophy."

33. Climacus is aware of the affinity of Platonism and Christianity even while seeking to highlight the deep divergence between them. See chapter 8, note 3 above.

34. See section 1 of *Totality and Infinity* and "Philosophy and the Idea of Infinity."

35. Although Hegel is one of the targets here, this use of the term "abstract" to signify the removal of something from its proper context is purely Hegelian.

36. We are very close to Levinas's notion of the trace as a past that was never present. See, for example, "Phenomena and Enigma" in *Collected Philosophical Papers.*

37. See the discussion of SLW 476, FT 98n, and CA 117 in chapter 3 above; the discussion of CUP 82 and 89 in chapter 6; the discussion of CUP 205, 206n, and 210 in chapter 8; the discussion of CUP 350 in chapter 9, and the discussion of irony and humor in the present chapter. For the Hegelian character of Climacus's account of the relation of the dialectical to the speculative, see chapter 4 above.

CHAPTER
T W E L V E | **The Subjective Issue—
The Dialectical
(Pages 561–86)**

Climacus finds human existence to be paradoxical and contradictory. Its dipolar structure makes it an incongruous inseparability of elements that do not easily unite. He might have done this with the classical definition of humans as rational animals, saying that rationality and animality contradict each other. Instead he does so in terms of the ways in which we belong both to finitude and to infinity, both to time and to eternity.

But in *Fragments* he had found the Christian affirmation that Jesus of Nazareth was God incarnate to be the absolute paradox, and as he now returns to this theme of "the absolute paradox, the absurd, the incomprehensible" (561), he has more than human dipolarity in mind. He sees Christianity as a move beyond Socrates to a new and intensified level of dialectical difficulty, which he has just called "the dialectical in the second place" (556, 559). Christianity is doubly dialectical because it superimposes on the universal dialectic of existence as such the particular dialectic of an eternal God who "comes into existence in time, is born, grows up, and dies" (579).

As if directly to challenge the Scholastic adage that the mysteries of Christian faith go beyond reason but not against it, Climacus repeatedly insists that Christian faith must be "against the understanding" (565–66, 568, 579n, 585). Twice he even describes faith as "the crucifixion of the understanding" (564). Christianity rests on a "dialectical contradiction" (570–81) of an unusually intense sort.

This means that Religiousness B, even more than Religiousness A, will be a challenge to the rationalist project of rendering the whole of reality intelligible to human understanding. In view of the widespread tendency to interpret any critique of reason (or of logocentrism) as an anything-goes irrationalism, it is important to be as clear as possible about what he is saying.

We found him dealing briefly with the dialectical contradiction of Christianity in chapter 8 above. Against the notion that the contradiction involved was the formal logical contradiction of asserting a proposition and its denial at the same time, a threefold argument was offered. First, Climacus uses the language of contradiction in a Hegelian sense, which signifies tension, incongruity, and opposition rather than formal, propositional contradiction. Second, the contradictions to which he points are often existential rather than epistemological—for example, the contradiction sometimes involved in wanting one's students to do well and feeling an obligation to give honest grades.

Third, where contradiction does have a clearly epistemic focus, it lies in the incongruity between the content of a particular belief and a larger frame of reference that excludes that belief but whose normative credentials are open to question. The issue becomes whether the belief in question signifies an anomaly that calls for a paradigm shift, or whether it should be rejected on the basis of the prevailing paradigm. In light of these factors, it would be a dramatic semantic shift if Climacus were suddenly to start using "contradiction" as formal logicians use the term.

In the present context the "contradiction" of the incarnation is closely related to the claim that it can only be believed "against the understanding." Does the contradiction lie within the belief itself or between it and the understanding? If the latter, whose understanding? Here, as in the earlier discussion, the contradiction turns out to be relational, and the paradigm that stands in contradiction to incarnation is human understanding. The passages that make this clear evoke memories of the earlier claim that existence "is a system—for God, but it cannot be a system for any existing spirit" (118). The contradiction is the incongruity of the divine and human standpoints.

Thus, for example, Christianity is paradoxical "as long as there is existing and only eternity has the explanation" (562). In other words, it is paradoxical for those who exist and whose understanding is temporal. If we could see things *sub specie aeterni*, the paradox would vanish. But to try to replace the paradox with an explanation is "to fancy that one is in eternity" and to flirt with that flight from concretion to abstraction that can make such a fancy seem fact (563). We know that Climacus thinks it impossible to back out of time into eternity, but here his critique is moral. This fancy is "impatience" (563). "The interpretation of the distinction 'here and hereafter' is decisive for every existence-communication. *Speculative thought* annuls it absolutely" (570), precisely in its assumption that reflection can take us out of time to where we can see things *sub specie aeterni*. But Climacus speaks of "the superorthodox" (562) and "revivalists" (566) as succumbing to the same temptation, finding the danger in the church as well as in the academy.[1]

It is arrogance as well as impatience to want to replace this contradiction with comprehension. To want to have "a higher understanding" and to be "a matchlessly brilliant seer" who can make everything divine commensurable with human understanding is worse than the monastic degeneration of wanting to be "honored as a holy person." It is the "sorry error" of wanting "to be like God" (564–65). That is why Climacus says that for the speculative project and, presumably, its ecclesiastical correlates, "all theology is anthropology" (579). The reference is to Ludwig Feuerbach, for whom this slogan signified, without apology and without disguise, the abolition of God and the deification of the human.[2]

Whether we speak of eternity having the explanation or of God as the one who understands what we find incomprehensible, the working assumption in these passages is that there is a point of view from which there is nothing contradictory about the incarnation. The problem is simply that by virtue of existence we are not able to occupy it and should not try to do so: "The paradox is connected essentially with being a human being" (566).

Since formal contradiction comes near the top of any list of nonsense, this reading is further strengthened by Climacus's insistence that the incomprehensible, which is believed against the understanding, is not nonsense (566). The context for this is a reminder that Socratic ignorance is an analogue of faith (566; cf. 205, 206n). But the root of Socratic ignorance (as Climacus understands it) was not an uncanny ability to detect formal contradictions where others failed to notice them but an uncanny ability to remember the limitations of existence when others tended to forget them (see 206n). The Socratic syllogism goes like this:

Knowledge is recollection, the reflection of the self out of time and into eternity.

But this is something I cannot do (at least in my present condition).

Therefore I do not have knowledge, and my wisdom consists in recognizing this.

Socrates is an analogue of faith because he teaches us that we can understand that there are things we cannot understand.

This is the context in which we must read what Climacus says about the dialectical contradiction that constitutes Christianity. According to his first formulation, the contradiction arises "because the eternal itself has come into existence at a moment of time" (570). Before developing this, he gets involved in a discussion of immanence and transcendence, to which we shall shortly return. According to his second formulation, the contradiction is *"That an Eternal Happiness Is Based on the Relation to Something Historical"* (574). There is nothing new here. We are simply reminded that historical knowledge is never more than an approximation, and the contradiction lies in basing one's eternal happiness on an approximation. Clearly this is an existential contradiction, not a propositional one. There is something deeply incongruous about the import of what is at issue and the level of cognitive certainty available to the one whose life is at stake.

In the third formulation, the contradiction arises from the fact *"That the Historical under Consideration Here Is Not Something Historical in the Ordinary Sense But Consists of That Which Can Become Historical Only against Its Nature, Consequently by Virtue of the Absurd"* (578). This is the point at which the formal logical interpretation of contradiction seems most attractive. But consider the account in 2 Kings 6, according to which the prophet Elisha made an ax head float after it had fallen into the Jordan River. It is surely against the nature of an ax head to float in water, and belief in the factual truth of this story is anything but unproblematic. But the problem concerns whether God enabled the prophet to perform a miracle, not whether the potential believer in this story is willing to assert both a proposition and its denial. Not even Hume thought the problem with miracle stories was one of formal contradiction. So it is not clear that in the case before us we should construe a claim about something acting contrary to its nature as involving formal contradiction.

Still less should we do so when we remember that Climacus has (once again) just given us an alternative understanding of contradiction, one that points to the conflict between a belief (an anomaly) and a framework of intelligibility (a paradigm), in this case human understanding, that it interrupts. The fact that this interruption is not a formal logical interruption should not lead us to take it lightly. Climacus is making the claim that Christianity stands in tension with all forms of human understanding, that it exceeds every human system of intelligibility, ancient, medieval, modern, and postmodern. According to the thought experiment of *Fragments,* the revelational alternative to recollection envisages the learner as lacking both the truth and the condition for recognizing the truth. Both must be given by the God who is teacher and savior. Here Climacus is simply repeating this analysis of human understanding and extending it to human systems of thought.

Thus, even if Hegelianism could show that it is the fulfillment of the Western Logos, that would not give it any ultimate authority in the eyes of Christianity. But, on the other hand, even if one denounces Hegel and all his works—perhaps in a postmodern tone of voice—it does not follow that the alternative account of human understanding that one gives will be any less vulnerable to interruption by Christian claims.

Two further themes occupy Climacus in this section, each in its own way a commentary on its central theme, "against the understanding." One is the return of the egalitarian motif that we have already encountered in chapters 2, 7, 8, and 9 above.[3] The issue concerns the difficulty of Christianity, a matter of no small importance to Climacus. For the "genius" who would gain "a higher understanding" by virtue of being a "matchlessly brilliant seer," the "difficulty and incomprehensibility are an obstacle to 'the dull,' [but] he is brilliant enough—to catch a glimpse into the dark saying" (564–65). This is a misunderstanding that "consists in the delusion that the incomprehensibility of the paradox is supposed to be connected with the difference of greater and lesser understanding, with the comparison between good and poor minds. The paradox is connected essentially with being a human being, and qualitatively with each human being in particular, whether he has much or little understanding" (566). The problem with the Hegelians, with the superorthodox, and even the revivalists is that they forget this and set themselves up as teachers of the human race on the basis of their superior understanding.[4]

The other supplemental theme in this section is that of immanence. Once again, this is not a new theme, and we are dealing with development and recapitulation rather than exposition. In his earlier critique of speculation, Climacus describes it as "remaining in immanence, which is recollection's removal of itself from existence" (217; cf. 270–73, 291), backing out of time into eternity.[5] Recollection can be described as immanence because its assumption is that the truth is within me and that I have the condition for recognizing it. In order to achieve knowledge, I need not go outside myself nor need anything to come to me from outside myself.

We have seen that in *Postscript* (as distinct from *Fragments*), Climacus distinguishes Socrates from Plato, emphasizing Socratic irony and Socratic ignorance. In his earlier discussion, he presents Socrates as departing from Plato's speculative pursuit of recollection as immanence by remembering and emphasizing existence. By being "beyond speculative thought" in this way, Socrates becomes an analogue of paradoxical, Christian faith (206n). Now Climacus adds a refinement to that claim designed to show that Religiousness A, of which Socrates has been the paradigm throughout *Postscript,* is as much a nostalgia for speculation as a break with it. "*Religiousness A,* which is not speculation but nevertheless is speculative, reflects upon [the distinction between 'here' and 'hereafter'] by reflecting upon existing, but even the decisive category of guilt-consciousness is still within immanence" (570). More generally speaking, the "contradiction" between time and eternity "is only within immanence" (573n).

Climacus provides his own commentary: "For speculation, existence has vanished and only pure being is; for Religiousness A, only the actuality of existence is, and yet *the eternal* is continually hidden by it and in hiddenness *is present.* The paradoxical-religious establishes absolutely the contradiction between existence and the eternal, because this, that the eternal is present at a specific moment of time, expresses that existence is *abandoned by the hidden immanence of the eternal* . . . and this is the break with immanence" (571, emphasis changed).[6]

For Socrates, the eternal is not simply present to one who exists. It is hidden. But in its hiddenness it is present. What does this mean? Most simply put, it means that Socrates knows no other knowledge than recollection, even when he insists on treating the verb "to know" as a task word rather than an achievement word. In the pursuit of knowledge he looks for no help from outside himself. In this way he is as much a continuation of the metaphysics of presence as he is a break with it. The decisive break comes when, in view of the paradox, we find ourselves "*abandoned by the hidden immanence of the eternal.*"

In light of this analysis, Climacus restates his theory of existence spheres: "*Immediacy, the esthetic,* finds no contradiction in existing; to exist is one thing, contradiction is something else that comes from without" (572). There is opposition when the world refuses to be my oyster and I experience boredom or misfortune. But this is not a conflict between myself and anything to which I am essentially related, such as the eternal. No divided self arises from this conflict.[7]

By contrast, the ethical self knows itself to be essentially related to the eternal. It has chosen itself in its eternal validity: "If the individual is dialectically turned inward in self-assertion in such a way that the ultimate foundation does not in itself become dialectical, since the underlying self is used to surmount and assert itself, then we have the *ethical interpretation. . . . The ethical* finds contradiction but within self-assertion" (572). This is simply a restatement of the earlier formula that "ethical existence is essentially struggle and victory" (288). The ethical self senses the incongruity between its actuality and its ideality, but in the absence of guilt consciousness, which is decisive for the religious sphere, it is confident that it can resolve the problem.

"If the individual is defined as dialectically turned inward in self-annihilation before God, then we have *Religiousness A. . . .* [It] comprehends contradiction as suffering in self-annihilation, yet within immanence" (572). Religious suffering has been presented as the pain of perpetually dying to immediacy. It gives rise to guilt consciousness as the realization that one has always failed in this task. This can be described as self-annihilation simply because it is the death of the self-assertive confidence that characterizes the ethical sphere. Yet it remains within immanence, since it is open to no help from outside itself. That is why Climacus can say that it "hinders the existing person in abstractly remaining in immanence or in becoming abstract by wanting to remain in immanence" (573).

This is startling language. Up to now the charge of abstraction has been reserved all but entirely for the speculative sphere, which abstracts from the concreteness of existence by its putative flight to eternity. Religiousness A has been the triumph of concrete existing over this abstraction. To call it abstract now is to suggest that it withdraws from something essential to itself. How can immanence as such be abstraction, even when it has made the Socratic break with speculation in order to preserve existence?

For Religiousness B, "every remnant of original immanence [is] annihilated, and all connection [is] cut away. . . . The *paradoxical-religious* breaks with immanence and makes existing the absolute contradiction—not within immanence but in opposition to immanence. There is no immanental underlying kinship between the temporal and the eternal, because the eternal itself has entered into time and wants to establish kinship there" (572–73).

What makes Religiousness A abstract is its withdrawal from that to which it is essentially related (but to which it has no immanent connection), namely, God in time. We can express this kind of abstraction more concretely. Immanence prevailed in the Garden of Eden, where it was possible for Adam and Eve to meet God face-to-face. The metaphysics of presence was not a theory but a daily experience. As the embodiment of Religiousness A, Socrates is the realization of paradise lost. It is no longer possible to meet God face-to-face, but hidden in the trees and underbrush, God is never very far away. It is even possible to converse, though the wind and other noises in the garden make it impossible to be sure one has heard the divine message correctly. This is the "immanental underlying kinship between the temporal and the eternal" spoken of above. The permanent, hidden presence of God makes an invasion like the incarnation quite unnecessary, even unwelcome. The garden is not what it used to be (guilt consciousness), but at least I am still there (immanence).

Religiousness B is existence east of Eden. Its decisive break with immanence is the realization of having been expelled from the garden, separated from the place of divine presence by a flaming sword. Without access to that place, even the hidden presence of God will be possible for me only if God comes to where I am. God in time (where I exist, even according to the Socratic assumption) has become essential to me, both as the teacher who can give me the truth and the condition for recognizing it and as the savior who can give me eternal happiness. From this perspective Religiousness A is abstract because, by virtue of the illusion of still being in the garden of hidden presence, it cuts itself off from the God to whom it is essentially related.

In the following formulation, Climacus once again collapses the distinction between the ethical and Religiousness A. The faith that constitutes Religiousness B "is a totally unique sphere, which, paradoxically from the esthetic and the metaphysical points of view, accentuates actuality [the concrete actuality of the existing self] and, paradoxically from the ethical point of view, accentuates the actuality of another person [God in time], not one's own" (580).[8] Here is the alterity that makes a decisive break with immanence (and with the metaphysics of presence). It is not the alterity of ideality to actuality or of eternity to time. It is the alterity of the divine person to the human person when the face-to-face friendship of creation has become the distant hostility of the fall. We must remember that all the way back in the thought experiment of *Fragments,* the possibility of going beyond Socrates presupposed that the absence of the eternal from temporal existence was the result of fault. Here Socrates, as distinct from Plato, is seen as recognizing fault but also as giving it a far less radical interpretation than Christianity.

A brief coda to this long chapter (our chapters 11 and 12), entitled "Appendix to B," sets forth "The Retroactive Effect of the

Dialectical on Pathos Leading to a Sharpened Pathos" (581). The dialectical problems associated with the incarnation are conceptual, but Climacus is not interested in them merely as such. If the whole of existence is to be transformed by the hope of an eternal happiness (387), the trans-cognitive dimensions must not be forgotten. If, as suggested in chapter 11, we think of religious pathos in terms of the fear and trembling of Silentio rather than the fear and pity of Aristotle, the point is simply that the doubly dialectical character of Christianity intensifies the fear and trembling that properly accompany Religiousness A. In terms of guilt consciousness, it changes my relation to myself; in terms of the possibility of offense,[9] it changes my relation to God; and in terms of human sympathy, it changes my relation to my neighbors. In each case it adds tension to the relationship rather than relaxing tension.

It may seem that Climacus is not a very good salesman of the religious life, accentuating, as he does, the difficulties that confront the believing soul. But we need to remember that he does not present himself as an exemplar even of Religiousness A, much less of B; that he is more interested in being faithful to his subject matter than in winning the approval of a public more interested in naturalizing and domesticating it (585); and that he would like to be able to say to Nietzsche that he knows something about possibilities in both Platonism and in Christianity for a religious life that could never be described as "wretched contentment."

I NOTES

1. One need not be a Hegelian to have a system. The "superorthodox" have theirs and the "revivalists" have theirs, though the latter often try desperately not to notice this by ridiculing the systems of the philosophers and the more learned theologians. One does not necessarily escape the danger that concerns Climacus by turning to confessional orthodoxy or to anticreedal pietism.

2. See especially Ludwig Feuerbach, *The Essence of Christianity,* trans. George Eliot (New York. Harper & Row, 1957).

3. For chapters 7, 8, and 9, see notes 23, 26, and 16, respectively. It should be noted that in chapter 8, as in the present chapter, the equality motif is presented as a corollary to the paradoxical character of Christian faith.

4. Wanda Warren Berry has argued that the equality motif in Kierkegaard's writings has a bearing on issues raised by feminists. See "The Heterosexual Imagination and Aesthetic Existence in Kierkegaard's *Either/Or,* Part One," in *International Kierkegaard Commentary: Either/Or 1,* 201–28; and "Judge William Judging Woman: Existentialism and Essentialism in Kierkegaard's *Either/Or,* Part Two," in *International Kierkegaard Commentary: Either/Or 2,* 33–57.

5. The discussion of the immanence of the world-historical point of view, according to which God is immanent in the world as "the moving spirit in a process" (156), involves a somewhat different issue. Whether God is to be found within the world is not quite the same question as whether God is to be found within the self.

6.   Compare this passage with Derrida's interpretation of Heidegger in "The Ends of Man," 123–36.

7.   As an aesthetic self I am already divided by the many stars to which I try to hitch my wagon, but this is true in success as well as in failure.

8.   Levinas, Marcel, Buber, and Sartre all have powerful versions of the thesis that the self is essentially related to the Other as another person. Even when they acknowledge a divine person, their phenomenologies focus on the other human person. But like Climacus, they refuse to reduce alterity to anything less concrete than another self.

9.   That faith must pass through the possibility of offense is a theme developed more fully by Climacus in *Fragments* and by Anti-Climacus in both *Sickness unto Death* and *Practice in Christianity*.

| **The Subjective Issue —
Conclusion Together
with Appendix
(Pages 587–630)**

In the conclusion to his *Postscript,* Climacus makes it clear that
his primary goal is to distinguish, and thus protect, Christianity
from two unreasonable facsimiles: Hegelian speculation and a
certain orthodoxy that he calls childish (603). Both present themselves as the highest form of Christianity, but both represent "the
cozy security with which people have managed to make being a
Christian and being a human being synonymous" (595). As a result, "very little is heard about the work of inwardness in becoming and continuing to be a Christian" (605).

But why is Climacus, the humorist who does not profess to be
religious at all, much less Christian, so passionate about keeping
Christianity unadulterated? He gives us a surprisingly Nietzschean answer: "Honesty is preferable to half measures" (588–89).
It is in the name of intellectual honesty that he insists on distinguishing true Christianity from both Hegelian speculation and
childish orthodoxy, thereby not too subtly indicting them both on
the charge of fraud. By putting the argument of *Postscript* in the
mouth of such a Climacus, Kierkegaard is able to make a strong
and important claim: It is not necessary to be a passionately com-
mitted Christian like me to see that much of what passes for
Christianity is a cheap imitation; it only takes a strong commitment to intellectual honesty. Whether one's interest in Christianity is positive (becoming a Christian) or negative (criticizing
Christianity), one would do well to engage the real thing.

The polemic against the speculative version of Christianity
is brief and familiar. Failing to see the true difficulty of faith,
speculation assumes that it represents a task easily and already
completed, freeing one to "go further" to understanding, to
"higher discoveries that transcend plain and simple Christianity"

(588; cf. 595–96). This is doubly problematic, as Climacus has been complaining all along. On the one hand, it involves an abstraction from existence, so that "little is heard about the work of inwardness" (605) that constitutes religious subjectivity. On the other hand, it involves an intellectual elitism, whereby the difficulty of Christianity is restricted to "lay people" (587), to "obtuse people" (595; cf. 609), and to "the simple person" with "less understanding" (607). Climacus insists that the difficulty is such that a high IQ and a few graduate degrees are no advantage: "Faith is properly made the most difficult of all, but qualitatively-dialectically, that is, equally difficult for all" (596).

Because of its difficulty, "Christianity in its decisive form is not suitable for every age in life" (590), and regardless of good intentions, "it is rape to coerce the child's existence into the decisive Christian categories." Moreover, it is "immense obtuseness" to mistake the religion appropriate to childhood for true Christianity (601–2). "Childlike Christianity, which in a little child is loveable, in an adult is the childish orthodoxy that, beatified in the fanciful, has managed to draw Christ's name into it. An orthodoxy such as that confuses everything" (595). In this childish Christianity, "from which the terror has been removed[1] . . . the *innocent* child is led to God or Christ. Is this Christianity, the point of which is that it is the sinner who takes refuge in the paradox?" Although the question is rhetorical, Climacus answers it anyway. No, this is "actually not Christianity but idyllic mythology" (591).

A key role in this mythology is played by the sacrament of baptism, which "is orthodoxly stressed to such an extreme" that it becomes heretical to speak of the need for rebirth, in spite of Jesus' conversation with Nicodemus in 3 John, "because hyperorthodoxly a little child is regarded as actually having become a Christian by being baptized" (595). Climacus does not object to infant baptism as such. But he only considers it "defensible as the anticipation of possibility" (601).[2]

This possibility is one of inward appropriation, of course. To be authentically Christian this appropriation must be "the paradoxical inwardness that is specifically different from all other inwardness. Being a Christian is defined not by the 'what' of Christianity but by the 'how' of the Christian" (610). Just as the earlier claim that Christianity is not a doctrine turned out to mean that it is not merely a doctrine, so this claim means that Christianity is not merely its *what*. There is no suggestion here that the *how* can replace the *what* or that it is compatible with any old *what*. "This 'how' can fit only one thing, the absolute paradox" (610–11). In other words, the orthodox doctrine of the incarnation is absolutely essential to Christianity. But it is only a necessary and not a sufficient condition. In order to give a specifically Christian definition of faith, Climacus now inserts reference to the paradox of God in time into his earlier definition: "Faith is the objective uncertainty with the repulsion of the absurd, held fast in the passion of inwardness, which is the relation of inwardness intensified to its highest" (611; cf. 203–4).

Climacus concludes his long and deliberately, if excessively, repetitive *Postscript* with two postscripts of its own, an appendix entitled "An Understanding with the Reader" and a few pages entitled "A First and Last Explanation." Both concern authorship and readership. We have discussed the latter of these postscripts in chapter 2 above. It is the announcement in which Kierkegaard acknowledges that he is the author of the pseudonymous works, albeit "not an author in the usual sense, but as one who has cooperated so that the pseudonyms could become authors" (628). As a pseudonymous publication that announces its own pseudonymity and identifies the writer who created its author, *Postscript* is surely a rare, if not unique, volume.

Speaking in his own voice, Kierkegaard asks that we remember him "as irrelevant to the books" (629). It is not just that we are not to make his biography the key to understanding them, but we are not even to attribute the ideas to him, since "in the pseudonymous books there is not a single word by me. I have no opinion about them except as a third party, no knowledge of their meaning except as a reader" (626). Hence "my wish, my prayer, that [the reader] will do me the kindness of citing the respective pseudonymous author's name, not mine" (627).

We are familiar with this Kierkegaardian stance, having peeked ahead at the outset of our journey through *Postscript* to its own concluding unscientific postscript. But we might be a bit surprised when we turn from Kierkegaard's "First and Last Declaration" to Climacus's "Understanding with the Reader" to find Climacus himself making three very Kierkegaardian gestures to distance himself from the text whose author he is. First, he insists that he writes without authority, that he is not one of those "great men who are able and willing to be the authority, from whom one has the benefit of accepting their opinion as a matter of course" (618–19). Like the Socrates he obviously admires, he insists that he is only a learner who cannot teach others (622–23).

Second, he insists that he writes as one without any opinions, except "that it must be the most difficult of all to become a Christian" (619). But this is no opinion in the standard sense, a point of view that can become a party line for public opinion by flattering those who hold it and insulting others.

Still, this opinion is something of an opinion, and since Climacus tells us that it is his only opinion (as a writer), we can assume that it is the central thesis of his book. But the idea of writing a book with a central thesis makes him nervous, makes him sound too much like a teacher. So, finally, he places his only opinion (as a writer) under erasure. Just before Kierkegaard tells us that what he writes is actually written by others, Climacus tell us that "what I write contains the notice that everything is to be understood in such a way that it is revoked" (619), expecting the reader to understand "that to write a book and to revoke it is not the same as refraining from writing it" (621).

If Climacus were an ironist, we might take this to mean that what he has said is undermined by how he has said it, as in "Brutus is an honorable man." But he would be a poor ironist who, having spoken ironically, has to tell us that we should hear him that way; and in any case, Climacus is a humorist and not an ironist. So what does it mean to write such a long book and then revoke it? By telling us that revoking is not the same as not writing, Climacus makes it clear that he wants to place the ideas of his book before the reader, and since we have no reason to think that he places them before us ironically, we can assume that he wants to place them before us at face value. What he means to withdraw by means of revocation is not the ideas but himself as author. Like Kierkegaard, he wants to leave the reader alone with the text.[3] By revoking his text he tells us that he will not wait around for our reaction or wait at home for our reviews. He has no wish to recruit us as disciples or to refute us as critics. Instead he tells us that his book is "simply and solely about myself" and presents himself as the kind of reader he hopes to find:

> I, Johannes Climacus, now thirty years old, born in Copenhagen, a plain, ordinary human being like most people, have heard it said that there is a highest good in store that is called an eternal happiness, and that Christianity conditions this upon a person's relation to it. I now ask: How do I become a Christian? (617)

| N O T E S

   1.   Climacus repeats this reference to the terror of Christianity on pp. 592, 598, and 600. These passages should be compared with the discussion of the *mysterium tremendum et fascinans* in chapter 11, note 23.

   2.   Compare this discussion of infant baptism with the very similar discussion in chapter 10 above.

   3.   See the latter part of chapter 2 above, especially note 24.

Beyond *Postscript:* The Teleological Suspension of Hidden Inwardness in Religiousness C

The writings of Johannes Climacus constitute a prophetic double challenge to Nietzsche. By distinguishing Christianity from Platonism, first without distinguishing Plato from Socrates (*Fragments*) and then in the context of a sharp distinction between them (*Postscript*), he protests Nietzsche's habit of lumping them together. In spite of affinities, there are essential differences between Christianity and both Platonic speculation and Socratic ignorance, based as they are on the universally human.

Then, by repudiating as "wretched contentment" several ideologies posing as Christianity, Climacus challenges the Nietzschean assumption that such a challenge is automatically secular and atheistic. True faith, as he sees it, has just as strong an interest as unbelief has in exposing spiritual complacency masquerading as spiritual seriousness. If we take Climacus seriously, we may find it necessary to restage the debate between Nietzsche and Christianity in ways that will not be entirely welcome to advocates of either side.

But what about Marx? Johannes de Silentio engages him in the theory of the teleological suspension of the ethical. According to that view religion is a form of ideology critique by virtue of its challenge to the self-absolutizing tendencies of every human *Sittlichkeit,* including the metanarratives by which each society tries to persuade itself that it is the ultimate embodiment of the right and the good. Silentio rudely interrupts the Marxian suggestion that religion always functions to legitimize the status quo.

But for Climacus the knight of faith becomes the knight of hidden inwardness, whose only outward manifestation is humor as incognito. Humor, like irony, can be a form of ideology critique, as those who live in totalitarian societies know. If religion teaches us to laugh at the powers that be (including ourselves, of course, which Marx might not entirely welcome), it functions as critique rather than ideology. But Marx will wonder whether such a critique is not entirely utopian and thus ideological, *malgré lui.* Marx will ask, Does the knight of hidden inwardness not live in the night, in which all cows are black, socially speaking? Is s/he not so totally devoted to private transactions with the eternal that what goes on in the *res publica* is a matter of indifference?

Climacus can answer that with reference to an eternal happiness, the welfare of the republic is only of relative importance (and Silentio might chime in that to absolutize the revolution, either before or after its success, is as problematic as to absolutize the established order). But even the most charitable Marxist will ask whether "relative importance" here is not just a cover for "indifference." Will those in power have anything to fear from the knight of hidden inwardness?

Having found (or been found by) our charitable Marxist, Climacus will not have much to say. His self is not the atomic, contractual self of bourgeois liberalism. It is essentially relational—to God or the eternal. He does not deny that it is also essentially related to other human selves in time, but that is because of his deafening silence on that question. His preoccupation with the eternal is so complete that our Marxist will have good reason to suspect that his knights of hidden inwardness will be unconcerned about social exploitation. It is as if in his presentation of Christianity he had heard the first half of Jesus' summary of the law, that we should love the Lord our God with all our heart, but had not heard or had forgotten the second half, that we should love our neighbor as ourselves (Matthew 22:34–40).

According to many readings this is the end of the line. It is assumed that Religiousness B is the culmination of the religious stage and the definitive expression of Christianity in Kierkegaard's writings.[1] But it is neither, and this assumption is possible only by ignoring or by reading carelessly the texts that make up Kierkegaard's "second" authorship. We have seen that the Climacus writings involve a revision or refinement of the theory of the stages, but a far more important revision, this time an extension, lies on the far side of Climacus.

One place we find such an extension is *Works of Love,* where Kierkegaard reflects precisely on the commandment, "You shall love your neighbor as yourself." This commandment is common to Judaism and Christianity, for which Abraham is the father of the faithful, since when Jesus uses it in his summary of the law, he is quoting Leviticus 19:18. Of the many things Kierkegaard says about love of one's neighbor, several are especially important in the present context.

First, love of one's neighbor is not just an inward feeling but an outward manifestation. Thus the first meditation is entitled "Love's Hidden Life and Its Recognizability by Its Fruits" (WL 5). Reflecting on the apostle's admonition, "Little children, let us not love in word or speech but in deed and in truth" (1 John 3:18), Kierkegaard's topic is not love or the words of love but the works of love, and he equates these works with the tree's fruit, its most unambiguous outward manifestation.

Second, love of one's neighbor is commanded rather than celebrated. Poets wax enthusiastic about friendship and erotic love, but these loves grow from preferences based on natural inclination and are actually a form of self-love. Lacking this natural foundation, love of one's neighbor can only be commanded (WL 17–43). In the language of *Fragments,* love of one's neighbor cannot be recollected but only revealed. In the language of *Postscript,* it cannot be grounded in speculation but only in ethical-religious subjectivity. In the language of Levinas, ethics is first philosophy.[2]

Third, since love of one's neighbor is presented as an essential part of the task of becoming a self, it is clear that the essentially relational self is essentially related to other human selves. When Kierkegaard writes, "'the neighbor' is what thinkers call 'the other,' that by which the selfishness in self-love is to be tested" (WL 21), it is clear that the radical alterity before which all self-assertion is put in question is no longer restricted to God as the divine other. The command generates an "unfathomable connectedness with all existence" (WL 9).

But finally, this human alterity is related to that divine alterity, and this in two ways. On the one hand, the command to love one's neighbor comes from God. Neither human nature nor human reason is appealed to here but a biblical command that comes from God in both the Jewish Torah and the Christian Gospel. On the other hand, the relation to God is the ground of the possibility of obeying this command:

> Just as the quiet lake originates deep down in the hidden springs no eye has seen, so also does a person's love originate even more deeply in God's love. If there were no gushing spring at the bottom, if God were not love, then there would be neither the little lake nor a human being's love. Just as the quiet lake originates darkly in the deep spring, so a human being's love originates mysteriously in God's love. Just as the quiet lake invites you to contemplate it but by the reflected image of darkness prevents you from seeing through

it, so also the mysterious origin of love in God's love prevents you from seeing its ground. (WL 9–10).

Hidden inwardness remains, but it is teleologically suspended in outwardly visible works of love. Here is an interpretation of biblical religion that goes beyond Climacus. I call it Religiousness C.[3]

Our Marxist observer might still ask whether the works of love are not still restricted to the private sphere, even if they are visible. The question would be, Do the perpetrators and beneficiaries of unjust social systems have anything to fear from works of love? Is not private charity more an asset than a threat to such systems?

An early sign that Kierkegaard is sensitive to this question comes from an interpretation of Acts 5 in which he takes issue with Climacus. The latter's *Postscript* commentary (452–54; cf. 507) reflects the restriction of the religious to hidden inwardness. The apostles were flogged by the authorities, and he insists that "the suffering spoken of in that passage is not religious suffering," merely external misfortune (452–53). Here is a confrontation between the apostles and the authorities, but he dismisses it as religiously insignificant because it is an outward conflict with the established order rather than an inner wrestling with God. A year after *Postscript* and six months before *Works of Love,* Kierkegaard sings a different tune. In *The Gospel of Sufferings,* he returns to the same flogging of the apostles. But unlike Climacus, he treats their suffering as religiously significant and interprets their joy as resting in the conviction *"that bold confidence is able in suffering to take power from the world and has the power to change scorn into honor, downfall into victory"* (UDVS 328). The conflict between the apostles and the worldly powers, far from being reduced to external misfortune, is presented as part of the meaning of following Christ.[4] In a journal entry the following year (1848) he repeats this position (JP 4.4617).

These passages from 1847 are the birth of Religiousness C. Just as Climacus's discussion of Religiousness B focused on the question of the specifically Christian form of inwardness, so Kierkegaard's discussion of what I call Religiousness C (which he shares with his final pseudonym, Anti-Climacus) asks about the specifically Christian form of outwardness. In *Works of Love* this outwardness involves an essential relation with my neighbor that challenges my self-love, while in *The Gospel of Suffering* it involves an essential relation to the established order that challenges that order's ultimacy. Even without having read *Fear and Trembling,* the apostles were able to say, "We must obey God rather than any human authority" (Acts 5:29).

Our Marxist observer may still not be satisfied. After all, he might reply, the apostles were flogged for preaching, and while preaching can be construed (by Christians, if not by atheists) as a form of love of one's neighbor, it is focused on the neighbors' eternal happiness, once again to the neglect of their earthly happiness.

It is primarily left to Anti-Climacus to make it clear that Religiousness C is not just a matter of preaching and private charity, that the works of love to which the Christian is called are indeed a threat to the powers that be. In Religiousness B the specifically Christian inwardness derives from Christ as the paradox who is to be believed. In Religiousness C the specifically Christian outwardness derives from Christ as the prototype (PC 195, 197–98, 202, 225, 238–40; JFY 145–209) or the paradigm (PC 107–9) to be imitated. He does not cease to be the paradox (PC 23–31), but this aspect of Christian faith is *aufgehoben* in the call to a discipleship that imitates the life of Christ on earth.

But Christ's life on earth was a continuous and ultimately fatal confrontation with the established order.[5] And no wonder. Everyone, at least everyone important, knew that the authentic expected one, the Messiah, "will come as the most glorious flowering and the highest unfolding of the established order . . . he will recognize the established order as the authority" (PC 47). But Jesus became offensive by his conspicuous failure to flatter the power structure in this way. To make matters worse, "his company is the lowest class of people . . . sinners and tax-collectors—whom anyone who is anybody at all shuns for the sake of his good name and reputation . . . his company is lepers, whom everyone avoids, lunatics, who only arouse horror, the sick and the wretched, poverty and misery" (PC 54).

In other words, while refusing to kowtow to the best and the brightest, his compassion lacked the decency to respect class boundaries. He forgot "that with regard to differences in life everyone wants to cling to his own. . . . Sausage peddlers will consider that in being compassionate it is descending too far down to go to paupers in the poorhouse and express equality with them; the compassion of sausage peddlers is trapped in one consideration, consideration for other sausage peddlers and then for saloon keepers. Thus their compassion is not totally reckless." Indeed, even the journalists "who live on the pennies of the poor class under the guise of asserting and defending their rights would be the first to render it ludicrous if this reckless compassion made even a merely moderate appearance." But Jesus was bent on making himself *"literally one with the most wretched"* (PC 59).[6]

The reckless compassion that violated class boundaries and did not merely preach but enacted equality with "the poor class" presented itself as the coming of the Kingdom of God. But merely to preach that God is on the side of the poor and oppressed is to engage in ideology critique, to challenge the theological, political, and economic metanarratives that make it possible to identify a class-structured society with the Kingdom of God. What is more, to practice what one preaches along these lines is to engage in behavior that cannot be perceived as anything but a threat by those in power, even if it is not a direct attempt to seize power. And according to Religiousness C, Christians are called to just such a dangerous practice, dangerous to the established order and therefore dangerous to them.

If the Climacus writings seem to call for restaging the debate between Christianity and Nietzsche, the subsequent writings from the pen of Kierkegaard seem to call for restaging the debate between Christianity and Marxism. As in the previous case, this latter opportunity does not seem to be exactly what the age demands. But Kierkegaard's writings have the nasty habit of insisting that we distinguish what the age demands from what it needs.

| N O T E S

1. For example, CUP is described as "Kierkegaard's most thorough and most systematic effort to explain his views on religion," in the introduction to *Existentialism: Basic Writings,* ed. Charles Guignon and Derk Pereboom (Indianapolis, Ind.: Hackett, 1995), 9. See note 6 below.

2. See chapter 9, note 13.

3. For a fuller treatment of the theory of the stages as culminating in Religiousness C, see Westphal, "Kierkegaard's Teleological Suspension of Religiousness B," chap. 7 of *Foundations of Kierkegaard's Vision of Community.* I am told that someone else has used the notion of Religiousness C, but I have not been able to confirm this and thus do not know what meaning has been given to the term, if indeed it has been used before.

4. Following Christ is the theme of the discourse that opens this series. See UDVS 217.

5. The theme of Christ as pattern (Lowrie's rendering; the Hongs use "Prototype") is introduced in *Christian Discourses,* but without this element of confrontation. Instead, Christ's lowliness is a consolation to believers of lowly station (CD 45–46; cf. 57, 78). The tension of Christ as pattern and the established order is hinted at on pp. 127–28.

6. Kierkegaard's commitment to hidden inwardness begins as early as his dissertation, where he speaks of the religious life as the true "transubstantiation" of actuality (CI 297). Walsh points out that this term signifies "an inward change that takes place in the substance of an actuality that outwardly remains the same" (*Living Poetically*, 58). It is only here in *Practice in Christianity* that we get a fully explicit teleological suspension of the religion of hidden inwardness. Lowrie had reason to quote Georg Brandes's claim that in this book the reader "will find Kierkegaard's whole train of thought and his most profound feeling." Lowrie himself finds the works in which Religiousness C comes to fruition "to define the tendency and purpose of the earlier, the strictly pseudonymous works" (*Training in Christianity* [Princeton, N.J.: Princeton University Press, 1941], vi–vii).

PART
THREE

Text

Part 2, Section 2, Chapter 2
Subjective Truth, Inwardness;
Truth Is Subjectivity

[189] Whether truth is defined more empirically as the agreement of thinking with being or more idealistically as the agreement of being with thinking, the point in each case is to pay scrupulous attention to what is understood by being and also to pay attention to whether the knowing human spirit might not be lured out into the indefinite and fantastically become something such as no *existing* human being has ever been or can be, a phantom with which the individual busies himself on occasion, yet without ever making it explicit to himself by means of dialectical middle terms how he gets out into this fantastical realm, what meaning it has for him to be there, whether the entire endeavor out there might not dissolve into a tautology within a rash, fantastical venture.

If, in the two definitions given, being [*Væren*] is understood as empirical being, then truth itself is transformed into a *desideratum* [something wanted] and everything is placed in the process of becoming [*Vorden*], because the empirical object is not finished, and the existing knowing spirit is itself in the process of becoming. Thus truth is an approximating whose beginning cannot be established absolutely, because there is no conclusion that has retroactive power. On the other hand, every beginning, when it is *made* (if it is not arbitrariness by not being conscious of this), does not occur by virtue of immanental thinking but *is made* by virtue of a resolution, essentially by virtue of faith. That the knowing spirit is an existing spirit, and that every human being is such a spirit existing for himself, I cannot repeat often enough, because the fantastical disregard of this has been the cause of much confusion. May no one misunderstand me. I am indeed a poor existing [190] spirit like all other human beings, but if in a legitimate and honest way I could be assisted in becoming something extraordinary, the pure *I-I,* I would always be willing to give thanks for the gift and the good deed. If, however, it can occur only in the way mentioned earlier, by saying *eins, zwei, drei, kokolorum* or by tying a ribbon around the little finger and throwing it away in some remote place when the moon is full—then I would rather remain what I am, a poor existing individual human being.

The term "being" in those definitions must, then, be understood much more abstractly as the abstract rendition or the abstract prototype of what being *in concreto* is as empirical being. If it is understood in this way, nothing stands in the way of abstractly defining truth as something finished, because, viewed abstractly, the agreement between thinking and being is always finished, inasmuch as the beginning of the process of becoming lies precisely in the concretion that abstraction abstractly disregards.

But if being is understood in this way, the formula is a tautology; that is, thinking and being signify one and the same, and the agreement spoken of is only an abstract identity with itself. Therefore, none of the formulas says more than that truth is, if this is understood in such a way that the copula is accentuated truth *is*—that is, truth is a redoubling [*Fordoblelse*]. Truth is the first, but truth's other, that it *is,* is the same as the first; this, its being, is the abstract form of truth. In this way it is expressed that truth is not something simple but in an entirely abstract sense a redoubling, which is nevertheless canceled at the very same moment.

Abstraction may go on by paraphrasing this as much as it pleases—it will never come any further. As soon as the being of truth becomes empirically concrete, truth itself is in the process of becoming and is indeed in turn, by intimation, the agreement between thinking and being, and is indeed actually that way for God, but it is not that way for any existing spirit, because this spirit, itself existing, is in the process of becoming.

For the existing spirit *qua* existing spirit, the question about [191] truth persists, because the abstract answer is only for that *abstractum* which an existing spirit becomes by abstracting from himself *qua* existing, which he can do only momentarily, although at such moments he still pays his debt to existence by existing nevertheless. Consequently, it is an existing spirit who asks about truth, presumably because he wants to exist in it, but in any case the questioner is conscious of being an existing individual human being. In this way I believe I am able to make myself understandable to every Greek and to every rational human being. If a German philosopher follows his inclination to put on an act [*skabe sig*] and first transforms himself [*skabe sig om*] into a super-rational something, just as alchemists and sorcerers bedizen themselves fantastically, in order to answer the question about truth in an extremely satisfying way, this is of no more concern to me than his satisfying answer, which no doubt is extremely satisfying—if one is fantastically dressed up. But whether a German philosopher is or is not doing this can easily be ascertained by anyone who with enthusiasm concentrates his soul on willing to allow himself to be guided by a sage of that kind, and uncritically just uses his guidance compliantly by willing to form his existence according to it. When a person as a learner enthusiastically relates in this way to such a German professor, he accomplishes the most superb epigram upon him, because a speculator of that sort is anything but served by a learner's honest and enthusiastic zeal for expressing and accomplishing, for existentially appropriating his wisdom, since this wisdom is something that the Herr Professor himself has imagined and has written books about but has never attempted himself. It has not even occurred to him that it should be done. Like the customs clerk who, in the belief that his business was merely to write, wrote what he himself could not read, so there are speculative thinkers who merely write, and write that which, if it is to be read with the aid of action, if I may put it that way, proves to be nonsense, unless it is perhaps intended only for fantastical beings.

When for the existing spirit *qua* existing there is a question about truth, that abstract reduplication [*Reduplikation*] of truth [192] recurs; but existence itself, existence itself in the questioner, who does indeed exist, holds the two factors apart, one from the other, and reflection shows two relations. To objective reflection, truth becomes something objective, an object, and the point is to disregard the subject. To subjective reflection, truth becomes appropriation, inwardness, subjectivity, and the point is to immerse oneself, existing, in subjectivity.

But what then? Are we to remain in this disjunction, or does mediation offer its kind assistance here, so that truth becomes subject-object? Why not? But can mediation then help the existing person so that he himself, as long as he is existing, becomes mediation, which is, after all, *sub specie aeterni,* whereas the poor existing one is existing? It certainly does not help to make a fool of a person, to entice him with the subject-object when he himself is prevented from entering into the state in which he can relate himself to it, prevented because he himself, by virtue of existing, is in the process of becoming. Of what help is it to explain how the eternal truth is to be understood eternally when the one to use the explanation is prevented from understanding it in this way because he is existing and is merely a fantast if he fancies himself to be *sub specie aeterni,* consequently when he must avail himself precisely of the explanation of how the eternal truth is to be understood in the category of time by someone who by existing is himself in time, something the honored professor himself admits, if not always, then every three months when he draws his salary.

With the subject-object of mediation, we have merely reverted to abstraction, inasmuch as the definition of truth as subject-object is exactly the same as: the truth *is,* that is, the truth is a redoubling [*Fordoblelse*]. Consequently, the exalted wisdom has again been absentminded enough to forget that it was an existing spirit who asked about truth. Or is perhaps the existing spirit himself the subject-object? In that case, I am obliged to ask: Where is such an existing human being who is also a subject-object? Or shall we perhaps here again first transmute the existing spirit into a something in general and then explain everything except what was asked about: How [193] an existing subject *in concreto* relates himself to the truth, or what then must be asked about: How the individual existing subject then relates himself to this something that seems to have not a little in common with a paper kite or with the lump of sugar that the Dutch used to hang from the ceiling and everyone would lick.

We return, then, to the two ways of reflection and have not forgotten that it is an existing spirit who is asking, simply an individual human being, and are not able to forget, either, that his existing is precisely what will prevent him from going both ways at once, and his concerned questions will prevent him from lightmindedly and fantastically becoming a subject-object. Now, then, which of the ways is the way of truth for the existing spirit? Only the fantastical *I-I* is simultaneously finished with both ways or advances methodically along both ways simultaneously, which for an existing human being is such an inhuman way of walking that I dare not recommend it.

Since the questioner specifically emphasizes that he is an existing person, the way to be commended is naturally the one that especially accentuates what it means to exist.

The way of objective reflection turns the subjective individual into something accidental and thereby turns existence into an indifferent, vanishing something. The way to the objective truth goes away from the subject, and while the subject and subjectivity become indifferent [*ligegyldig*], the truth also becomes indifferent, and that is precisely its objective validity [*Gyldighed*], because the interest, just like the decision, is subjectivity. The way of objective reflection now leads to abstract thinking, to mathematics, to historical knowledge of various kinds, and always leads away from the subjective individual, whose existence or nonexistence becomes, from an objective point of view, altogether properly, infinitely indifferent, altogether properly, because, as Hamlet says, existence and nonexistence have only subjective significance. At its maximum, this way will lead to a contradiction, and to the extent [194] that the subject does not become totally indifferent to himself, this is merely an indication that his objective striving is not objective enough. At its maximum, it will lead to the contradiction that only objectivity has come about, whereas subjectivity has gone out, that is, the existing subjectivity that has made an attempt to become what in the abstract sense is called subjectivity, the abstract form of an abstract objectivity. And yet, viewed subjectively, the objectivity that has come about is at its maximum either a hypothesis or an approximation, because all eternal decision is rooted specifically in subjectivity.

But the objective way is of the opinion that it has a security that the subjective way does not have (of course, existence, what it means to exist, and objective security cannot be thought together). It is of the opinion that it avoids a danger that lies in wait for the subjective way, and at its maximum this danger is madness. In a solely subjective definition of truth, lunacy and truth are ultimately indistinguishable, because they may both have inwardness.* But one does not become lunatic by becoming objective. At this point I might perhaps add a little comment that does not seem superfluous in an objective age. Is the absence of inwardness also lunacy? The objective truth as such does not at all decide that the one stating it is sensible; on the contrary, it can even betray that the man is lunatic, although what he says is entirely true and especially objectively true.

I shall here allow myself to relate an incident that, without any modification whatever by me, comes directly from a madhouse. A patient in such an institution wants to run away and actually carries out his plan by jumping through a window. He now finds himself in the garden of the institution and wishes to take to the road of freedom. Then it occurs to him [195] (shall I say that he was sagacious enough or lunatic enough to have this whimsical idea?): When you arrive in the city, you will be recognized and will

---

* Even this is not true, however, because madness never has the inwardness of infinity. Its fixed idea is a kind of objective something, and the contradiction of madness lies in wanting to embrace it with passion. The decisive factor in madness is thus not the subjective, but the little finitude that becomes fixed, something the infinite can never become.

very likely be taken back right away. What you need to do, then, is to convince everyone completely, by the objective truth of what you say, that all is well as far as your sanity is concerned. As he is walking along and pondering this, he sees a skittle ball lying on the ground. He picks it up and puts it in the tail of his coat. At every step he takes, this ball bumps him, if you please, on his r——, and every time it bumps him he says, "Boom! The earth is round." He arrives in the capital city and immediately visits one of his friends. He wants to convince him that he is not lunatic and therefore paces up and down the floor and continually says, "Boom! The earth is round!" But is the earth not round? Does the madhouse demand yet another sacrifice on account of this assumption, as in those days when everyone assumed it to be as flat as a pancake? Or is he lunatic, the man who hopes to prove that he is not lunatic by stating a truth universally accepted and universally regarded as objective? And yet, precisely by this it became clear to the physician that the patient was not yet cured, although the cure certainly could not revolve around getting him to assume that the earth is flat. But not everyone is a physician, and the demand of the times has considerable influence on the question of lunacy. Now and then, one would indeed almost be tempted to assume that the modern age, which has modernized Christianity, has also modernized Pilate's question, and that the need of the age to find something in which to repose declares itself in the question: What is lunacy? When an assistant professor, every time his coattail reminds him to say something, says *de omnibus dubitandum est* [everything must be doubted] and briskly writes away on a system in which there is sufficient internal evidence in every other sentence that the man has never doubted anything— he is not considered lunatic.

Don Quixote is the prototype of the subjective lunacy in which the passion of inwardness grasps a particular fixed finite idea. But when inwardness is absent, parroting lunacy sets in, which is just as comic, and it would be desirable for an imag- [196] inatively constructing psychologist to depict it by taking a handful of such philosophers and putting them together. When the insanity is a delirium of inwardness, the tragic and the comic are that the something that infinitely pertains to the unfortunate person is a fixed detail that pertains to no one else. But when the insanity is the absence of inwardness, the comic is that the something known by the blissful person is the truth, truth that pertains to the whole human race but does not in the least pertain to the highly honored parroter. This kind of insanity is more inhuman than the other. One shrinks from looking the first one in the eye, lest one discover the depth of his frantic state, but one does not dare to look at the other at all for fear of discovering that he does not have proper eyes but glass eyes and hair made from a floor mat, in short, that he is an artificial product. If one happens to meet a mentally deranged person of that sort, whose illness is simply that he has no mind, one listens to him in cold horror. One does not know whether one dares to believe that it is a human being with whom one is speaking, or perhaps a "walking stick," an artificial contrivance of Døbler that conceals in itself a barrel organ [*Positiv*]. To drink *Dus* with the executioner can indeed be unpleasant for a self-respecting man, but to get into a rational and speculative conversation with a walking stick—now that is almost enough to drive one crazy.

Subjective reflection turns inward toward subjectivity and in this inward deepening will be of the truth, and in such a way that, just as in the preceding, when objectivity was advanced, subjectivity vanished, here subjectivity as such becomes the final factor and objectivity the vanishing. Here it is not forgotten, even for a single moment, that the subject is existing, and that existing is a becoming, and that truth as the identity of thought and being is therefore a chimera of abstraction and truly only a longing of creation, not because truth is not an identity, but because the knower is an existing person, and thus truth cannot be an identity for him as long as he exists. If this is not held fast, then with the aid of speculative thought we promptly enter into the fantastical *I-I* that recent speculative thought certainly has used but without explaining [197] how a particular individual relates himself to it, and, good Lord, of course no human being is more than a particular individual.

If the existing person could actually be outside himself, the truth would be something concluded for him. But where is this point? The *I-I* is a mathematical point that does not exist at all; accordingly anyone can readily take up this standpoint—no one stands in the way of anyone else. Only momentarily can a particular individual, existing, be in a unity of the infinite and the finite that transcends existing. This instant is the moment of passion. Modern speculative thought has mustered everything to enable the individual to transcend himself objectively, but this just cannot be done. Existence exercises its constraint, and if philosophers nowadays had not become pencil-pushers serving the trifling busyness of fantastical thinking, it would have discerned that suicide is the only somewhat practical interpretation of its attempt. But pencil-pushing modern speculative thought takes a dim view of passion, and yet, for the existing person, passion is existence at its very highest—and we are, after all, existing persons. In passion, the existing subject is infinitized in the eternity of imagination and yet is also most definitely himself. The fantastical *I-I* is not infinitude and finitude in identity, since neither the one nor the other is actual; it is a fantastical union with a cloud, an unfruitful embrace, and the relation of the individual *I* to this mirage is never stated.

All essential knowing pertains to existence, or only the knowing whose relation to existence is essential is essential knowing. Essentially viewed, the knowing that does not inwardly in the reflection of inwardness pertain to existence is accidental knowing, and its degree and scope, essentially viewed, are a matter of indifference. That essential knowing is essentially related to existence does not, however, signify the above-mentioned abstract identity between thinking and being, nor does it signify that the knowledge is objectively related to something existent [*Tilvæ-rende*] as its object, but it means that the knowledge is related to the knower, who is essentially an existing person [*Existerende*], and that all essen- [198] tial knowing is therefore essentially related to existence and to existing. Therefore, only ethical and ethical-religious knowing is essential knowing. But all ethical and all ethical-religious knowing is essentially a relating to the existing of the knower.

Mediation is a mirage, just as the *I-I* is. Viewed abstractly, everything is and nothing becomes. Mediation cannot possibly find its place in abstraction, since it has *movement* as its presupposition. Objective knowledge can certainly have the existent [*Tilværende*] as its object, but since the knowing subject is existing [*existe-rende*] and himself in the process of becoming by existing, speculative thought must first explain how a particular existing subject relates himself to the knowledge of mediation, what he is at the moment, whether, for example, he is not at that very moment rather absentminded, and where he is, whether he is not on the moon. There is this continual talk about mediation and mediation. Is mediation, then, a human being, just as Per Degn assumes *Imprimatur* to be a human being? How does a human being go about becoming something of that sort? Is this dignity, this great *philosophicum*, attained by studying? Or does the magistrate give it away as he gives away sexton and gravedigger positions? Just try to become involved with these and other similar simple questions raised by a simple human being, who would so very much like to be mediation if he could become that in a legitimate and honorable manner, and not either by saying *eins, zwei, drei, kokolorum* or by forgetting that he himself is an existing human being, for whom existing is consequently something essential, and for whom existing ethically-religiously is a suitable *quantum satis* [sufficient amount]. To a speculative thinker it may seem *abgeschmackt* [in bad taste] to ask questions in this way, but it is especially important not to polemicize in the wrong place and hence not to begin fantastically-objectively a *pro* and *contra* as to whether or not there is mediation, but firmly to maintain what it means to be a human being.

In order to clarify the divergence of objective and subjective reflection, I shall now describe subjective reflection in its [199] search back and inward into inwardness. At its highest, inwardness in an existing subject is passion; truth as a paradox corresponds to passion, and that truth becomes a paradox is grounded precisely in its relation to an existing subject. In this way the one corresponds to the other. In forgetting that one is an existing subject, one loses passion, and in return, truth does not become a paradox; but the knowing subject shifts from being human to being a fantastical something, and truth becomes a fantastical object for its knowing.

When the question about truth is asked objectively, truth is reflected upon objectively as an object to which the knower relates himself: What is reflected upon is not the relation but that what he relates himself to is the truth, the true. If only that to which he relates himself is the truth, the true, then the subject is in the truth. When the question about truth is asked subjectively, the individual's relation is reflected upon subjectively. If only the how of this relation is in truth, the individual is in truth, even if he in this way were to relate himself to untruth.*

Let us take the knowledge of God as an example. Objectively, what is reflected upon is that this is the true God; subjectively, that the individual relates himself to a something *in such a way* that his relation is in truth a God-relation. Now, on which side is the truth? Alas, must we not at this point resort to mediation and say: It is on neither side; it is in the mediation? Superbly stated, if only someone could say how an existing person goes about being in mediation, because to be in mediation is to be finished; to exist is to become. An existing person cannot be in two places at the same time, cannot be subject-object. When he is closest to being in two places at the same time, he is in passion; but passion is only momentary, and passion is the highest pitch of subjectivity.

The existing person who chooses the objective way now enters upon all approximating deliberation intended to bring forth God objectively, which is not achieved in all eternity, [200] because

---

* The reader will note that what is being discussed here is essential truth, or the truth that is related essentially to existence, and that it is specifically in order to clarify it as inwardness or as subjectivity that the contrast is pointed out.

God is a subject and hence only for subjectivity in inwardness. The existing person who chooses the subjective way instantly comprehends the whole dialectical difficulty because he must use some time, perhaps a long time, to find God objectively. He comprehends this dialectical difficulty in all its pain, because he must resort to God at that very moment, because every moment in which he does not have God is wasted.* At that very moment he has God, not by virtue of any objective deliberation but by virtue of the infinite passion of inwardness. The objective person is not bothered by dialectical difficulties such as what it means to put a whole research period into finding God, since it is indeed possible that the researcher would die tomorrow, and if he goes on living, he cannot very well regard God as something to be taken along at his convenience, since God is something one takes along à tout prix [at any price], which, in passion's understanding, is the true relationship of inwardness with God.

It is at this point, dialectically so very difficult, that the road swings off for the person who knows what it means to think dialectically and, existing, to think dialectically, which is quite different from sitting as a fantastical being at a desk and writing about something one has never done oneself, quite different from writing de omnibus dubitandum and then as an existing person being just as credulous as the most sensate human being. It is here that the road swings off, and the change is this: whereas objective knowledge goes along leisurely on the long road of approximation, itself not actuated by passion, to subjective knowledge every delay is a deadly peril and the decision so infinitely important that it is immediately urgent, as if the opportunity had already passed by unused.

[201] Now, if the problem is to calculate where there is more truth (and, as stated, simultaneously to be on both sides equally is not granted to an existing person but is only a beatifying delusion for a deluded *I-I*), whether on the side of the person who only objectively seeks the true God and the approximating truth of the God-idea or on the side of the person who is infinitely concerned that he in truth relate himself to God with the infinite passion of

---

* In this way God is indeed a postulate, but not in the loose sense in which it is ordinarily taken. Instead, it becomes clear that this is the only way an existing person enters into a relationship with God: when the dialectical contradiction brings passion to despair and assists him in grasping God with "the category of despair" (faith), so that the postulate, far from being the arbitrary, is in fact *necessary* defense [N ø d- værge], self-defense; in this way God is not a postulate, but the existing person's postulating of God is — a necessity [Nødvendighed].

need—then there can be no doubt about the answer for anyone who is not totally botched by scholarship and science. If someone who lives in the midst of Christianity enters, with knowledge of the true idea of God, the house of God, the house of the true God, and prays, but prays in untruth, and if someone lives in an idolatrous land but prays with all the passion of infinity, although his eyes are resting upon the image of an idol—where, then, is there more truth? The one prays in truth to God although he is worshiping an idol; the other prays in untruth to the true God and is therefore in truth worshiping an idol.

If someone objectively inquires into immortality, and someone else stakes the passion of the infinite on the uncertainty—where, then, is there more truth, and who has more certainty? The one has once and for all entered upon an approximation that never ends, because the certainty of immortality is rooted in subjectivity; the other is immortal and therefore struggles by contending with the uncertainty.

Let us consider Socrates. These days everyone is dabbling in a few proofs or demonstrations—one has many, another fewer. But Socrates! He poses the question objectively, problematically: if there is an immortality. So, compared with one of the modern thinkers with the three demonstrations, was he a doubter? Not at all. He stakes his whole life on this "if"; he dares to die, and with the passion of the infinite he has so ordered his whole life that it might be acceptable—*if* there is an immortality. Is there any better demonstration for the immortality of the soul? But those who have the three demonstrations do not order their lives accordingly. If there is an immortality, it must be nauseated by their way of living—is there any better counterdemonstration to the three demon- [202] strations? The "fragment" of uncertainty helped Socrates, because he himself helped with the passion of infinity. The three demonstrations are of no benefit whatever to those others, because they are and remain slugs and, failing to demonstrate anything else, have demonstrated it by their three demonstrations.

In the same way a girl has perhaps possessed all the sweetness of being in love through a weak hope of being loved by the beloved, because she herself staked everything on this weak hope; on the other hand, many a wedded matron, who more than once has submitted to the strongest expression of erotic love, has certainly had demonstrations and yet, strangely enough, has not possessed *quod erat demonstrandum* [that which was to be demonstrated]. The Socratic ignorance was thus the expression, firmly maintained with all the passion of inwardness, of the relation of the

eternal truth to an existing person, and therefore it must remain
for him a paradox as long as he exists. Yet it is possible that in
the Socratic ignorance there was more truth in Socrates than in
the objective truth of the entire system that flirts with the demands of the times and adapts itself to assistant professors.

*Objectively the emphasis is on **what** is said; subjectively the
emphasis is on **how** it is said.* This distinction applies even esthetically and is specifically expressed when we say that in the
mouth of this or that person something that is truth can become
untruth. Particular attention should be paid to this distinction in
our day, for if one were to express in a single sentence the difference between ancient times and our time, one would no doubt
have to say: In ancient times there were only a few individuals
who knew the truth; now everyone knows it, but inwardness has
an inverse relation to it.* Viewed esthetically, the contradiction
that emerges when truth becomes untruth in this and that
person's mouth is best interpreted comically. Ethically-religiously, the emphasis is again on: *how*. But this is not to be understood as manner, modulation of voice, oral delivery, etc., but it
is to be understood as the [203] relation of the existing person, in
his very existence, to what is said. Objectively, the question is
only about categories of thought; subjectively, about inwardness.
At its maximum, this "how" is the passion of the infinite, and the
passion of the infinite is the very truth. But the passion of the
infinite is precisely subjectivity, and thus subjectivity is truth.
From the objective point of view, there is no infinite decision, and
thus it is objectively correct that the distinction between good
and evil is canceled, along with the principle of contradiction, and
thereby also the infinite distinction between truth and falsehood.
Only in subjectivity is there decision, whereas wanting to become
objective is untruth. The passion of the infinite, not its content, is
the deciding factor, for its content is precisely itself. In this way
the subjective "how" and subjectivity are the truth.

But precisely because the subject is existing, the "how" that is
subjectively emphasized is dialectical also with regard to time. In
the moment of the decision of passion, where the road swings off
from objective knowledge, it looks as if the infinite decision were
thereby finished. But at the same moment, the existing person is
in the temporal realm, and the subjective "how" is transformed
into a striving that is motivated and repeatedly refreshed by the
decisive passion of the infinite, but it is nevertheless a striving.

---

*See *Stages on Life's Way,* p. 366 fn.

When subjectivity is truth, the definition of truth must also contain in itself an expression of the antithesis to objectivity, a memento of that fork in the road, and this expression will at the same time indicate the resilience of the inwardness. Here is such a definition of truth: *An objective uncertainty, held fast through appropriation with the most passionate inwardness, is the truth,* the highest truth there is for an *existing* person. At the point where the road swings off (and where that is cannot be stated objectively, since it is precisely subjectivity), objective knowledge is suspended. Objectively he then has only uncertainty, but this is precisely what intensifies the infinite passion of inwardness, and truth is precisely the daring venture of choosing the objective uncertainty with the passion of the infinite. I observe nature in order to find God, and I do indeed [204] see omnipotence and wisdom, but I also see much that troubles and disturbs. The *summa summarum* [sum total] of this is an objective uncertainty, but the inwardness is so very great, precisely because it grasps this objective uncertainty with all the passion of the infinite. In a mathematical proposition, for example, the objectivity is given, but therefore its truth is also an indifferent truth.

But the definition of truth stated above is a paraphrasing of faith. Without risk, no faith. Faith is the contradiction between the infinite passion of inwardness and the objective uncertainty. If I am able to apprehend God objectively, I do not have faith; but because I cannot do this, I must have faith. If I want to keep myself in faith, I must continually see to it that I hold fast the objective uncertainty, see to it that in the objective uncertainty I am "out on 70,000 fathoms of water" and still have faith.

The thesis that subjectivity, inwardness, is truth contains the Socratic wisdom, the undying merit of which is to have paid attention to the essential meaning of existing, of the knower's being an existing person. That is why, in his ignorance, Socrates was in the truth in the highest sense within paganism. To comprehend this, that the misfortune of speculative thought is simply that it forgets again and again that the knower is an existing person, can already be rather difficult in our objective age. "But to go beyond Socrates when one has not even comprehended the Socratic— that, at least, is not Socratic." See "The Moral" in *Fragments.*

Just as in *Fragments,* let us from this point try a category of thought that actually does go beyond. Whether it is true or false is of no concern to me, since I am only imaginatively constructing, but this much is required, that it be clear that the Socratic is presupposed in it, so that I at least do not end up behind Socrates again.

When subjectivity, inwardness, is truth, then truth, objectively defined, is a paradox; and that truth is objectively a paradox shows precisely that subjectivity is truth, since the objectivity does indeed thrust away, and the objectivity's repulsion, or the expression for the objectivity's repulsion, is [205] the resilience and dynamometer of inwardness. The paradox is the objective uncertainty that is the expression for the passion of inwardness that is truth. So much for the Socratic. The eternal, essential truth, that is, the truth that is related essentially to the existing person by pertaining essentially to what it means to exist (viewed Socratically, all other knowledge is accidental, its degree and scope indifferent), is a paradox. Nevertheless the eternal, essential truth is itself not at all a paradox, but it is a paradox by being related to an existing person. Socratic ignorance is an expression of the objective uncertainty; the inwardness of the existing person is truth. In anticipation of what will be discussed later, the following comment is made here: Socratic ignorance is an analogue to the category of the absurd, except that there is even less objective certainty in the repulsion exerted by the absurd, since there is only the certainty that it is absurd, and for that very reason there is infinitely greater resilience in the inwardness. The Socratic inwardness in existing is an analogue to faith, except that the inwardness of faith, corresponding not to the repulsion exerted by ignorance but to the repulsion exerted by the absurd, is infinitely deeper.

Viewed Socratically, the eternal essential truth is not at all paradoxical in itself, but only by being related to an existing person. This is expressed in another Socratic thesis: that all knowing is a recollecting. This thesis is an intimation of the beginning of speculative thought, but for that very reason Socrates did not pursue it; essentially it became Platonic. This is where the road swings off, and Socrates essentially emphasizes existing, whereas Plato, forgetting this, loses himself in speculative thought. Socrates' infinite merit is precisely that of being an *existing* thinker, not a speculative thinker who forgets what it means to exist. To Socrates, therefore, the thesis that all knowing is a recollecting has, at the moment of parting and as a continually annulled possibility of speculating, a double significance: (1) that the knower is essentially *integer* [uncorrupted] and that for him there is no other dubiousness with regard to knowledge of the eternal truth than this, that he exists, a dubiousness so essential and decisive to him that it sig- [206] nifies that existing, the inward deepening in and through existing, is truth; (2) that existence in temporality has no decisive significance, because there is continually the possibility of taking oneself back into eternity by recollecting, even though this possibility is continually annulled because the inward deepening in existing fills up time.*

---

*This may be the proper place to elucidate a dubiousness in the design of *Fragments,* a dubiousness that was due to my not wanting immediately to make the matter as dialectically difficult as it is, because in our day terminologies and the like are so muddled that it is almost impossible to safeguard oneself against confusion. In order, if possible, to elucidate properly the difference between the Socratic (which was supposed to be the philosophical, the pagan philosophical position) and the category of imaginatively constructed thought, which actually goes beyond the Socratic, I carried the Socratic back to the thesis that all knowing is a recollecting. It is commonly accepted as such, and only for the person who with a very special interest devotes himself to the Socratic, always returning to the sources, only for him will it be important to distinguish between Socrates and Plato on this point. The thesis certainly belongs to both of them, but Socrates continually parts with it because he wants to exist. By holding Socrates to the thesis that all knowing is recollecting, one turns him into a speculative philosopher instead of what he was, an existing thinker who understood existing as the essential. The thesis that all knowing is recollecting belongs to speculative thought, and recollecting is immanence, and from the point of view of speculation and the eternal there is no paradox. The difficulty, however, is that no human being is speculation, but the speculating person is an existing human being, subject to the claims of existence. To forget this is no merit, but to hold this fast is indeed a merit, and that is precisely what Socrates did. To emphasize existence, which contains within it the qualification of inwardness, is the Socratic, whereas the Platonic is to pursue recollection and immanence. Basically Socrates is thereby beyond all speculation, because he does not have a fantastical beginning where the speculating person changes clothes and then goes on and on and speculates, forgetting the most important thing, to exist. But precisely because Socrates is in this way beyond speculative thought, he acquires, when rightly depicted, a certain analogous likeness to what the imaginary construction set forth as that which truly goes beyond the Socratic: the truth as paradox is an analog to the paradox *sensu eminentiori* [in the more eminent sense]; the passion of inwardness in existing is then an analog to faith *sensu eminentiori.* That the difference is infinite nevertheless, that the designations in *Fragments* of that which truly goes beyond the Socratic are unchanged, I can easily show, but I was afraid to make complications by promptly using what seem to be the same designations, at least the same words, about the different things when the imaginary construction was to be presented as different from these. [207] Now, I think there would be no objection to speaking of the paradox in connection with Socrates and faith, since it is quite correct to do so, provided that it is understood correctly. Besides, the ancient Greeks also use the word πίστις [faith], although by no means in the sense of the imaginary construction, and use it so as to make possible some very illuminating observations bearing upon its dissimilarity to faith *sensu eminentiori,* especially with reference to one of Aristotle's works where the term is employed.

[207] The great merit of the Socratic was precisely to emphasize that the knower is an existing person and that to exist is the essential. To go beyond Socrates by failing to understand this is nothing but a mediocre merit. This we must keep *in mente* [in mind] and then see whether the formula cannot be changed in such a way that one actually does go beyond the Socratic.

So, then, subjectivity, inwardness, is truth. Is there a *more inward* expression for it? Yes, if the discussion about "Subjectivity, inwardness, is truth" begins in this way: "Subjectivity is untruth." But let us not be in a hurry. Speculative thought also says that subjectivity is untruth but says it in the very opposite direction, namely, that objectivity is truth. Speculative thought defines subjectivity negatively in the direction of objectivity. The other definition, however, puts barriers in its own way at the very moment it wants to begin, which makes the inwardness so much more inward. Viewed Socratically, subjectivity is untruth if it refuses to comprehend that subjectivity is truth but wants, for example, to be objective. Here, on the other hand, in wanting to begin to become truth by becoming subjective, subjectivity is in the predicament of being untruth. Thus the work goes backward, that is, backward in inwardness. The way is so far from being in the direction of the objective that the beginning only lies even deeper in subjectivity.

But the subject cannot be untruth eternally or be presupposed to have been untruth eternally; he must have become that in time or he becomes that in time. The Socratic paradox consisted in this, that the eternal truth was related to an existing person. But now existence has accentuated the existing person a second time; a change so essential has taken place in him that he in no way can take himself back into eternity by [208] Socratically recollecting. To do this is to speculate; to be able to do this but, by grasping the inward deepening in existence, to annul the possibility of doing it is the Socratic. But *now* the difficulty is that what accompanied Socrates as an annulled possibility has become an impossibility. If speculating was already of dubious merit in connection with the Socratic, it is now only confusion.

The paradox emerges when the eternal truth and existing are placed together, but each time existing is accentuated, the paradox becomes clearer and clearer. Viewed Socratically, the knower was an existing person, but now the existing person is accentuated in such a way that existence has made an essential change in him.

Let us now call the individual's untruth *sin*. Viewed eternally, he cannot be in sin or be presupposed to have been eternally in sin. Therefore, by coming into existence (for the beginning was that subjectivity is untruth), he becomes a sinner. He is not born as a sinner in the sense that he is presupposed to be a sinner before he is born, but he is born in sin and as a sinner. Indeed, we could call this *hereditary sin*. But if existence has in this way obtained power over him, he is prevented from taking himself back into eternity through recollection. If it is already paradoxical that the eternal truth is related to an existing person, now it is absolutely paradoxical that it is related to such an existing person. But the more difficult it is made for him, recollecting, to take himself out of existence, the more inward his existing can become in existence; and when it is made impossible for him, when he is lodged in existence in such a way that the back door of recollection is forever closed, then the inwardness becomes the deepest. But let us never forget that the Socratic merit was precisely to emphasize that the knower is existing, because the more difficult the matter becomes, the more one is tempted to rush along the easy road of speculative thought, away from terrors and decisions, to fame, honor, a life of ease, etc. If even Socrates comprehended the dubiousness of taking himself speculatively out of existence back into eternity, when there was no dubiousness for the existing person except that he existed and, [209] of course, that existing was the essential—now it is impossible. He must go forward; to go backward is impossible.

Subjectivity is truth. The paradox came into existence through the relating of the eternal, essential truth to the existing person. Let us now go further; let us assume that the eternal, essential truth is itself the paradox. How does the paradox emerge? By placing the eternal, essential truth together with existing. Consequently, if we place it together in the truth itself, the truth becomes a paradox. The eternal truth has come into existence in time. That is the paradox. If the subject just mentioned was prevented by sin from taking himself back into eternity, now he is not to concern himself with this, because now the eternal, essential truth is not behind him but has come in front of him by existing itself or by having existed, so that if the individual, existing, does not lay hold of the truth in existence, he will never have it.

Existence can never be accentuated more sharply than it has been here. The fraud of speculative thought in wanting to recollect itself out of existence has been made impossible. This is the only point to be comprehended here, and every speculation that insists on being speculation shows *eo ipso* [precisely thereby] that it has not comprehended this. The individual can thrust all this away and resort to speculation, but to accept it and then want to cancel it through speculation is impossible, because it is specifically designed to prevent speculation.

When the eternal truth relates itself to an existing person, it becomes the paradox. Through the objective uncertainty and ignorance, the paradox thrusts away in the inwardness of the existing person. But since the paradox is not in itself the paradox, it does not thrust away intensely enough, for without risk, no faith; the more risk, the more faith; the more objective reliability, the less inwardness (since inwardness is subjectivity); the less objective reliability, the deeper is the possible inwardness. When the paradox itself is the paradox, it thrusts away by virtue of the absurd, and the corresponding passion of inwardness is faith.

But subjectivity, inwardness, is truth; if not, we have forgotten the Socratic merit. But when the retreat out of exis- [210] tence into eternity by way of recollection has been made impossible, then, with the truth facing one as the paradox, in the anxiety of sin and its pain, with the tremendous risk of objectivity, there is no stronger expression for inwardness than—to have faith. But without risk, no faith, not even the Socratic faith, to say nothing of the kind we are discussing here.

When Socrates believed that God is, he held fast the objective uncertainty with the entire passion of inwardness, and faith is precisely in this contradiction, in this risk. Now it is otherwise. Instead of the objective uncertainty, there is here the certainty that, viewed objectively, it is the absurd, and this absurdity, held fast in the passion of inwardness, is faith. Compared with the earnestness of the absurd, the Socratic ignorance is like a witty jest, and compared with the strenuousness of faith, the Socratic existential inwardness resembles Greek nonchalance.

What, then, is the absurd? The absurd is that the eternal truth has come into existence in time, that God has come into existence, has been born, has grown up, etc., has come into existence exactly as an individual human being, indistinguishable from any other human being, inasmuch as all immediate recognizability is pre-Socratic paganism and from the Jewish point of view is idolatry. Every qualification of that which actually goes beyond the Socratic must essentially have a mark of standing in relation to the god's having come into existence, because faith, *sensu strictissimo* [in the strictest sense], as explicated in *Fragments,* refers to coming into existence. When Socrates believed that God is [*er til*], he no doubt perceived that where the road swings off there is a road of objective approximation, for example, the observation of nature, world history, etc. His merit was precisely to shun this road, where the quantifying siren song spellbinds and tricks the existing person. In relation to the absurd, the objective approximation resembles the comedy *Misforstaaelse paa Misforstaaelse* [Misunderstanding upon Misunderstanding], which ordinarily is played by assistant professors and speculative thinkers.

It is by way of the objective repulsion that the absurd is the [211] dynamometer of faith in inwardness. So, then, there is a man who wants to have faith; well, let the comedy begin. He wants to have faith, but he wants to assure himself with the aid of objective deliberation and approximation. What happens? With the aid of approximation, the absurd becomes something else; it becomes probable, it becomes more probable, it may become to a high degree and exceedingly probable. Now he is all set to believe it, and he dares to say of himself that he does not believe as shoemakers and tailors and simple folk do, but only after long deliberation. Now he is all set to believe it, but, lo and behold, now it has indeed become impossible to believe it. The almost probable, the probable, the to-a-high-degree and exceedingly probable — that he can almost know, or as good as know, to a higher degree and exceedingly almost *know* — but *believe* it, that cannot be done, for the absurd is precisely the object of faith and only that can be believed.

Or there is a man who says he has faith, but now he wants to make his faith clear to himself; he wants to understand himself in his faith. Now the comedy begins again. The object of faith becomes almost probable, it becomes as good as probable, it becomes probable, it becomes to a high degree and exceedingly probable. He has finished; he dares to say of himself that he does not believe as shoemakers and tailors or other simple folk do but that he has also understood himself in his believing. What wondrous understanding! On the contrary, he has learned to know something different about faith than he believed and has learned to know that he no longer has faith, since he almost knows, as good as knows, to a high degree and exceedingly almost knows.

Inasmuch as the absurd contains the element of coming into existence, the road of approximation will also be that which confuses the absurd fact of coming into existence, which is the object of faith, with a simple historical fact, and then seeks historical certainty for that which is absurd precisely because it contains the contradiction that something that can become historical only in direct opposition to all human understanding has become historical. This contradiction is the absurd, which can only be believed. If a historical certainty is ob- [212] tained, one obtains merely the certainty that what is certain is not what is the point in question. A witness can testify that he has believed it and then testify that, far from being a historical certainty, it is in direct opposition to his understanding, but such a witness repels in the same sense as the absurd repels, and a witness who does not repel in this way is *eo ipso* a deceiver or a man who is talking about something altogether different; and such a witness can be of no help except in obtaining certainty about something altogether different. One hundred thousand individual witnesses, who by the special nature of their testimony (that they have believed the absurd) remain individual witnesses, do not become something else *en masse* so that the absurd becomes less absurd. Why? Because one hundred thousand people individually have believed that it was absurd? Quite the contrary, those one hundred thousand witnesses repel exactly as the absurd does.

But I do not need to develop this further here. In *Fragments* (especially where the difference between the follower at first hand and the follower at second hand is annulled) and in Part One of this book, I have with sufficient care shown that all approximation is futile, since the point is rather to do away with introductory observations, reliabilities, demonstrations from effects, and the whole mob of pawnbrokers and guarantors, in order to get the absurd clear—so that one can believe if one will—I merely say that this must be extremely strenuous.

If speculative thought wants to become involved in this and, as always, say: From the point of view of the eternal, the divine, the theocentric, there is no paradox—I shall not be able to decide whether the speculative thinker is right, because I am only a poor existing human being who neither eternally nor divinely nor theocentrically is able to observe the eternal but must be content with existing. This much, however, is certain, that with speculative thought everything goes backward, back past the Socratic, which at least comprehended that for an existing person existing is the essential; and much less has speculative thought taken the time to comprehend [213] what it means to be *situated* in existence the way the existing person is in the imaginary construction.

The difference between the Socratic position and the position that goes beyond the Socratic is clear enough and is essentially the same as in *Fragments,* for in the latter nothing has changed, and in the former the matter has only been made somewhat more difficult, but nevertheless not more difficult than it is. It has also become somewhat more difficult because, whereas in *Fragments* I set forth the thought-category of the paradox only in an imaginary construction, here I have also latently made an attempt to make clear the necessity of the paradox, and even though the attempt is somewhat weak, it is still something different from speculatively canceling the paradox.

Christianity has itself proclaimed itself to be the eternal, essential truth that has come into existence in time; it has proclaimed itself as *the paradox* and has required the inwardness of faith with regard to what is an offense to the Jews, foolishness to the Greeks—and an absurdity to the understanding. It cannot be expressed more strongly that subjectivity is truth and that objectivity only thrusts away, precisely by virtue of the absurd, and it seems strange that Christianity should have come into the world in order to be explained, alas, as if it were itself puzzled about itself and therefore came into the world to seek out the wise man, the speculative thinker, who can aid with the explanation. It cannot be expressed more inwardly that subjectivity is truth than when subjectivity is at first untruth, and yet subjectivity is truth.

Suppose that Christianity was and wants to be a mystery, an utter mystery, not a theatrical mystery that is revealed in the fifth act, although the clever spectator [*Tilskuer*] already sees through [*gennemskue*] it in the course of the exposition. Suppose that a revelation *sensu strictissimo* [in the strictest sense] must be a mystery and be recognizable just by its being a mystery, whereas a revelation *sensu laxiori* [in the broader sense], the withdrawing into the eternal through recollection, is a revelation in the direct sense. Suppose that the difference in intellectual endowment is the difference in being able to [214] state more and more clearly that it is and remains a mystery for existing human beings. Suppose that the intellectual endowment in relation to misunderstanding differs according to the individual's ability more and more deceptively to give the appearance of having understood the mystery. Suppose that it is nevertheless a blessing that, situated at the extremity of existence, one relates oneself to this mystery without understanding it, only having faith. Suppose that Christianity does not at all want to be understood; suppose that, in order to express this and to prevent anyone, misguided, from taking the road of objectivity, it has proclaimed itself to be the paradox. Suppose that it wants to be only for existing persons and essentially for persons existing in inwardness, in the inwardness of faith, which cannot be expressed more definitely than this: it is the absurd, adhered to firmly with the passion of the infinite. Suppose that it does not want to be understood and that the maximum of any eventual understanding is to understand that it cannot be understood. Suppose that it so decisively accentuates existing that the single individual becomes a sinner, Christianity the paradox, and existence the time of decision.

Suppose that speculating is a temptation, the most precarious of all. Suppose that the speculator is not the prodigal son, for this is what the concerned God presumably would call the offended one whom he continues to love nevertheless, but the naughty child who refuses to stay where existing human beings belong, in the children's nursery and the education room of existence where one becomes adult only through inwardness in existing, but who instead wants to enter God's council, continually screaming that, from the point of view of the eternal, the divine, the theocentric, there is no paradox. Suppose that the speculative thinker is the restless resident who, although it is obvious that he is a renter, yet in view of the abstract truth that, eternally and divinely perceived, all property is in common, wants to be the owner, so that there is nothing to do except to send for a police officer, who would presumably say, just as the subpoena servers say to Gert Westphaler: We are sorry to have to come on this errand.

Has being human now become something different from [215] what it was in the old days, is the condition not the same: to be an individual *existing* being, and is not existing the essential as long as one is in existence? "But people know so much more now." "Quite right, but suppose that Christianity is not a matter of knowing; then much knowledge is of no benefit, except to ease a person more readily into the confusion of regarding Christianity as a matter of knowledge." And if people do know more now— and we are not speaking of the knowledge of railroads, machines, and kaleidoscopes, but of knowing more of the religious—how have they come to know more? Presumably, through Christianity. So this is how Christianity is rewarded. One learns something from Christianity, misunderstands it, and in new misunderstanding uses it against Christianity.

If the terror in the old days was that one could be offended, the terror these days is that there is no terror, that one, two, three, before looking around, one becomes a speculative thinker who speculates about faith. About what faith? Is it about the faith that he has and especially about whether he does or does not have it? Alas, no, that is too little for an objective speculator. Consequently, he speculates about objective faith. What does that mean—objective faith? It means a sum of tenets. But suppose Christianity is nothing of the kind; suppose that, on the contrary, it is inwardness, and therefore the paradox, in order to thrust away objectively, so that it can be for the existing person in the inwardness of existence by placing him decisively, more decisively than any judge can place the accused, between time and eternity in time, between heaven and hell in the time of salvation. Objective faith—it is indeed as if Christianity had also been proclaimed as a little system of sorts, although presumably not as good as the Hegelian system. It is as if Christ—it is not my fault that I say it—as if Christ had been a professor and as if the apostles had formed a little professional society of scholars. Truly, if at one time it was difficult to become a Christian, I believe now it becomes more difficult year by year, because it has now become so easy to become one; there is a bit of competition only in becoming a speculative thinker. And yet the speculator is [216] perhaps furthest removed from Christianity, and perhaps it is preferable by far to be someone who takes offense but still continually relates himself to Christianity, whereas the speculator has understood it. To that extent there is hope that there still remains a similarity between a Christian now and in those early days and that wanting to become a Christian will once again become foolishness. In those early days, a Christian was a fool in the eyes of the world. To the pagans and Jews it was foolishness for him to want to become one. Now one is a Christian as a matter of course. If someone wants to be a Christian with infinite passion, he is a fool, just as it is always foolishness to will to exert oneself with infinite passion in order to become what one is as a matter of course, as if someone would give all his fortune to purchase a precious gem—which he owned. Formerly a Christian was a fool in the eyes of the world; now all people are Christians, but he nevertheless becomes a fool—in the eyes of Christians.

Suppose that it is this way. I say merely "suppose," and more I do not say. But since we are now admittedly growing weary of speculative thinkers who examine one another in print in the systematic rigmarole, it may at least be a change to go through the question in another way.

"But from the eternal, divine, and especially theocentric point of view, there is no paradox. True speculative thought, therefore, does not stop with the paradox but goes further and explains it." "May I now ask for a little peace and request that he not begin again? After all, I did say that I cannot become involved with the supraterrestrial and the subterranean." "The beginning and the consummation of the explanation are with me, and it is for this explanation that the eternal truth has been waiting; it is quite correct that it entered into time, but the first edition was only an imperfect attempt. Because the eternal truth required an explanation, it entered into the world and anticipated this by occasioning a discussion. Similarly, a professor publishes the outline of a system, assuming that the work, by being reviewed and debated, will come out sooner or later in a new and totally revised form. Only this second edition, when it has waited for the advice and judgment of [217] experts, is the truth, and thus speculative thought is the true and only satisfactory edition of the provisional truth of Christianity."

By means of a few examples, we shall now illustrate how speculative thought, for the very reason that it refuses to comprehend that subjectivity is truth, has earned the gratitude of Christianity, which once and for all is the paradox and is paradoxical at every point, whereas speculative thought, remaining in immanence, which is recollection's removal of itself from existence, at every point produces a volatilization. By means of the tour de force of not thinking anything decisive about what is most decisive (which, through the decision, is specifically designed to forestall immanence) but utilizing the expression of decision as a locution, the volatilization becomes a pagan reminiscence, to which there is nothing to object if it breaks directly with Christianity but much to object if it is supposed to be Christianity.

The thesis that God has existed in human form, was born, grew up, etc. is certainly the paradox *sensu strictissimo,* the absolute paradox. But as the absolute paradox it cannot be related to a relative difference. A relative paradox is related to a relative difference between more or less sagacious people. But the absolute paradox, precisely because it is absolute, can be related only to the absolute difference by which a human being differs from God; it cannot be related to relative bickering between one human being and another about whether one is a little smarter than the other. But the absolute difference between God and a human being is simply this, that a human being is an individual existing being (and this holds for the best brain just as fully as for the most obtuse), whose essential task therefore cannot be to think *sub specie aeterni,* because as long as he exists, he himself, although eternal, is essentially an existing person and the essential for him must therefore be inwardness in existence; God, however, is the infinite one, who is eternal. As soon as I make the understanding of the paradox commensurate with the difference between being more or less intellectually endowed (a difference that still does not ever transcend being human, unless someone [218] were to become so brilliant that he became not only a human being but also God), my discussion of understanding *eo ipso* demonstrates that what I have understood is not the absolute paradox but a relative paradox, because the only possible understanding of the absolute paradox is that it cannot be understood. "But then speculative thought cannot ever grasp it." "Entirely correct, this is just what is said by the paradox, which thrusts away only in the direction of inwardness in existence." Perhaps this is so because objectively there is no truth for existing beings, but only approximations, whereas subjectively truth for them is in inwardness, because the decision of truth is in subjectivity.

The modern mythical allegorizing trend summarily declares Christianity to be a myth. Such a procedure is at least forthright behavior, and everyone can easily form a judgment about it. The friendship of speculative thought is of another kind. To be on the safe side, speculative thought opposes the ungodly mythical allegorizing trend and then goes on to say, "Speculative thought, on the other hand, accepts the paradox, but it does not stop with it." "Nor is there any need for that, because when a person in faith continues to adhere firmly to it, in his existence deepening himself in the inwardness of faith, he does not stop either." Speculative thought does not stop—what does that mean? Does it mean that Messrs. Speculators cease to be human beings, individual existing human beings, and *en famille* [as a family] become all sorts of things? If not, one is certainly obliged to stop with the paradox, since it is grounded in and is the expression for precisely this, that the eternal, essential truth relates itself to existing individuals with the summons that they go further and further in the inwardness of faith.

What on the whole does it mean to *explain* something? Does explaining mean to show that the obscure something in question is not this but something else? That would be a strange explanation. I should think that by the explanation it would become clear that the something in question is this definite something, so that the explanation would remove not the thing in question but the obscurity. Otherwise the explanation [219] is something other than an explanation; it is a correction. An explanation of the paradox makes clear what the paradox is and removes the obscurity; a correction removes the paradox and makes clear that there is no paradox. But the latter is certainly no explanation of the paradox but rather an explanation that there is no paradox. But if the paradox emerges from the placing together of the eternal and an existing individual human being, does the explanation, in removing the paradox, then also remove existing from the existing person? And if on his own, or with the assistance of another, an existing person has arrived at or has been brought almost to the point where it seems to him as if he did not exist, what is he then? Then he is absentminded. Consequently, the explanation of the absolute paradox that declares there is no paradox except to a certain degree, in other words, that there are only relative paradoxes, is an explanation not for existing individuals but for the absentminded. Well, then everything is in order. The explanation is that the paradox is the paradox only to a certain degree, and it is quite in order that it, namely, the explanation, is for an existing person who is an existing person only to a certain degree, since he forgets it every other moment, and an existing person of that kind is simply absentminded.

Then when someone speaks of the absolute paradox, which is an offense to the Jews, foolishness to the Greeks, and the absurd to the understanding, and addresses his words to speculative thought, it is not so impolite as to tell him bluntly that he is a fool but rather gives an explanation that contains a correction and thus indirectly gives him to understand that he was in error. This is the way a humane, superior intellect always behaves toward the more limited. The procedure is altogether Socratic; there would be an un-Socratic element only if the one speaking is indeed closer to the truth than the speculative explanation, for then there remains the dissimilarity that Socrates politely and indirectly took the untruth away from the learner and gave him the truth, whereas speculative thought politely and indirectly takes the truth away from the learner and gives him the untruth. But politeness still remains the common denominator. And when Christianity declares it- [220] self to be the paradox, the speculative explanation is not an explanation but a correction, a polite and indirect correction, such as befits a superior intellect in relation to the more limited.

Does *explaining* the paradox mean to turn the expression "paradox" into a *rhetorical* expression, into something the honorable speculative thinker indeed says has its validity—but then in turn does not have its validity? In that case, the *summa summarum* [sum total] is indeed that there is no paradox. Honor be to the Herr Professor! I say this not to take his honor away from him, as if I, too, could cancel [hæve] the paradox. Not at all. But if the professor has canceled it, then it is of course canceled; in that case I daresay that it is canceled—unless the annulment [Ophævelse] pertains to the professor more than to the paradox, so that he, instead of canceling the paradox, himself becomes an alarming, fantastical swelling [Hævelse]. In other cases, one assumes that explaining something means to have it become clear in its significance, that it is this and not something else. To explain the paradox would then be to comprehend ever more deeply what a paradox is and that the paradox is the paradox.

Thus God is a supreme conception that cannot be explained by anything else but is explainable only by immersing oneself in the conception itself. The highest principles for all thinking can be demonstrated only indirectly (negatively). Suppose that the paradox is the boundary for an *existing person's* relation to an eternal, essential truth—in that case the paradox will not be explainable by anything else if the explanation is supposed to be for existing persons. But understood speculatively, even the absolute paradox (because speculative thought is not afraid of using decisive terms; the only thing it fears is thinking something decisive with them) expresses only a relative difference between more and less gifted and educated people. In this way the shape of the world will gradually be changed. When Christianity entered into the world, there were no professors or assistant professors whatever—then it was a paradox for all. It can be assumed that in the present generation every tenth person is an assistant professor; conse-[221] quently it is a paradox for only nine out of ten. And when the fullness of time finally comes, that matchless future, when a generation of assistant professors, male and female, will live on the earth—then Christianity will have ceased to be a paradox.

On the other hand, the person who takes it upon himself to explain the paradox, on the assumption that he knows what he wants, will focus directly upon showing that it must be a paradox. To explain the unutterable joy—what does that mean? Does it mean to explain that it is this and that? In that case, the predicate "unutterable" becomes just a rhetorical predicate, a strong expression, and the like. The explaining jack-of-all-trades has everything in readiness before the beginning of the performance, and now it begins. He dupes the listener; he calls the joy unutterable, and then a new surprise, a truly surprising surprise—he utters it. Suppose that the unutterable joy is based upon the contradiction that an existing human being is composed of the infinite and the finite, is situated in time, so that the joy of the eternal in him becomes unutterable because he is existing; it becomes a supreme drawing of breath that cannot take shape, because the existing person is existing. In that case, the explanation would be that it is unutterable; it cannot be anything else—no nonsense. If, however, a profound person first condemns someone or other who denies that there is an unutterable joy and then says: No, I assume that there is an unutterable joy, but I go further and utter it, then he is only making a fool of himself, and the only difference between him and the other whom he condemns is that the other is more honest and direct and says what the profound person is also saying, since they both are saying essentially the same thing.

Does explaining what is decisive mean to transform the expression into a rhetorical locution, so that one does not, like the light-minded person, deny all decision, but assumes it, yet assumes it only to a certain degree? What does it mean to assert that a decision is to a certain degree? It means to deny decision. Decision is designed specifically to put an end to that perpetual prattle about "to a certain degree." So the decision [222] is assumed—but, lo and behold, assumed only to a certain degree. Speculative thought is not afraid to use expressions of decision; the only thing it fears is thinking something decisive with them. And when Christianity wants to be the eternal decision for the existing subject and speculative thought explains that the decision is relative, it is not explaining Christianity but correcting it. Whether speculative thought is in the right is an entirely different question; here the question is only how its explanation of Christianity is related to the Christianity that it explains.

Does explaining something mean to *annul* it? I do know that the word *aufheben* has various, indeed opposite, meanings in the German language. It has often been noted that the word can mean both *tollere* [annul, annihilate] and *conservare* [preserve]. I am not aware that the Danish word *ophæve* [annul] allows any such equivocation, but I do know that our German-Danish philosophers use it like the German word. Whether it is a good quality in a word to have opposite meanings, I do not know, but anyone who wants to express himself with precision usually avoids the use of such a word in decisive places. There is a simple folk saying that humorously denotes the impossible: to have one's mouth full of crackers and to whistle at the same time. Speculative thought accomplishes a tour de force somewhat like that by using a word that also denotes the very opposite. In order to denote very clearly that speculation knows nothing of any decision, it itself uses an ambiguous word in order to denote the kind of understanding that is speculative understanding. Upon closer inspection, the confusion becomes more evident. *Aufheben* in the sense of *tollere* means to annihilate; in the sense of *conservare,* it means to preserve [*bevare*] in altogether unaltered condition, to do nothing at all to what is being preserved. If the government dissolves [*ophæve*] a political society, it abolishes it; if a man keeps or preserves something for me, it is of particular importance to me that he make no change whatever in it. Neither of these meanings is the philosophical *aufheben.* So speculation annuls all difficulty and then leaves me with the difficulty of understanding just what it is doing with this *aufheben.* But now let [223] this *aufheben* mean reducing something to a relative factor, which it does mean when what is decisive, the paradox, is reduced to a relative factor, which means that there is no paradox, no decision, since the paradox and the decisive are what they are just because of their unyielding resistance. Whether speculative thought is in the right is a different question, but here what is asked is only how its explanation of Christianity is related to the Christianity that it explains.

By no means does speculative thought say that Christianity is untruth; on the contrary, it specifically says that speculation comprehends the truth of Christianity. More could certainly not be asked for. Has Christianity ever asked to be more than the truth? And when speculation comprehends it, everything is as it should be. And yet, no, that is not how it is. In relation to Christianity, systematic speculation is only a bit cunning in the use of all kinds of diplomatic locutions that bedazzle the credulous. Christianity as it is understood by the speculative thinker is something different from what is presented to the simple. To them it is the paradox, but the speculative thinker knows how to cancel the paradox. Then it is not Christianity that is and was and remains the truth, and the speculative thinker's understanding is not the understanding that Christianity is the truth—no, it is the speculative thinker's understanding of Christianity that is the truth of Christianity. The understanding is thus something other than the truth. It is not the case that the truth is understood only when the understanding has understood everything implied in the truth, but it is rather the case that only when that κατὰ δύναμιν [potential] truth is understood in the way a speculative thinker understands it, only then—well, then it is not speculation that has become true, but it is the truth that has come into existence. Consequently, the truth is not a given and the understanding is not what is awaited, but what is awaited is that speculation's understanding will be finished, because only then has truth come into existence. Thus speculative knowledge is not as knowledge usually is, something indifferent in relation to what is known, so that this is not changed by being known but remains the same. No, speculative knowledge is [224] itself the object of knowing, so that the latter is no longer the same as it was but has come into existence simultaneously with speculation as the truth.

Whether speculative thought is in the right is a different question. What is asked here is only how its explanation of Christianity is related to the Christianity that it explains. And how should they be related? Speculative thought is objective, and objectively there is no truth for an existing individual but only an approximation, since by existing he is prevented from becoming entirely objective. Christianity, on the other hand, is subjective; the inwardness of faith in the believer is the truth's eternal decision.

Objectively there is no truth; an objective knowledge about the truth or the truths of Christianity is precisely untruth. To know a creed by rote is paganism, because Christianity is inwardness.

Let us take the paradox of the forgiveness of sins. Socratically, the forgiveness of sins is a paradox, inasmuch as the eternal truth relates itself to an existing person, *sensu strictiori* [in the stricter sense], because the existing person is a sinner, a qualification by which existence is accentuated a second time, because it wants to be an eternal decision in time with retroactive power to annul the past, and because it is bound up with God's having existed in time. The individual existing human being has to feel himself a sinner (not objectively, which is nonsense, but subjectively, and this is the deepest pain). With all his understanding to the very last turn (if one person has a little more understanding than the other, it makes no essential difference, and to appeal to one's great understanding is merely to betray one's deficient inwardness, or else it runs out very soon), he must want to understand the forgiveness of sins—and then despair of understanding. With the understanding in direct opposition, the inwardness of faith must grasp the paradox, and that faith battles in just this way, as the Romans once did, blinded by the light of the sun, is the resilience of inwardness.* If any other understanding ever forces [225] itself upon him, he sees that he is about to lose his faith, just as a girl, when she has become the beloved's wife, upon discover-

---

*That one can battle in this way, blinded by the sun, and yet see to battle, the Romans demonstrated at Zama. That one can battle in this way, blinded, [225] and yet see to conquer, the Romans demonstrated at Zama. And now the battle of faith, is that supposed to be tomfoolery, a staged swordplay of gallantry, this battle that is longer than a Thirty Years' War, because one does not fight merely to acquire but fights even more vehemently to preserve, this battle in which every day is just as hot as the day of battle at Zama! While the understanding despairs, faith presses forward victoriously in the passion of inwardness. But when the believer uses all his understanding, every last turn of despair, just to discover the difficulty of the paradox, then truly no part is left with which to explain the paradox—but for all that, there can indeed be the ample firmness of faith in the passion of inwardness. Sitting calmly on a ship in fair weather is not a metaphor for having faith; but when the ship has sprung a leak, then enthusiastically to keep the ship afloat by pumping and not to seek the harbor—that is the metaphor for having faith. Even if the image ultimately contains an impossibility, this is merely the imperfection of the image, but faith holds out. While the understanding, like a desperate passenger, stretches its arms toward land, but in vain, faith works vigorously in the depths—joyful and victorious, against the understanding it rescues the soul. To exist in faith is that kind of contradiction; to an existing person, compromise is a mirage, since it is a contradiction that

ing that it is easy to understand that she became this man's chosen one, ought to see that this explanation is easily understood as an indication that she is no longer in love.

But a speculative thinker goes about it in a different way. He appears before an esteemed public and says, "Ladies and gentlemen, for that is how I must address you. To a congregation of believers, the paradox can be proclaimed only by a believer, but to an esteemed public the truth can be proclaimed by a speculative thinker. Therefore the forgiveness of sins is a paradox (general excitement). The pantheistic line is a fallacy that speculative thought opposes, but speculative thought does not stop with the paradox; it explains and annuls it." The highly esteemed speculative thinker did not, then, stake all his understanding when he despaired; his despair was [226] only to a certain degree, a simulated movement; he reserved part of his understanding—for the explanation. This can be called: deriving benefit from one's understanding. The believer derives no benefit whatever from his; he uses up all of it in despair. But the speculator knows how to stretch it out sufficiently; he takes one-half of it for despairing (as if it were not nonsense to despair by halves) and the other half for perceiving that there is no reason for the understanding to despair. Well, of course, then the matter becomes something different; so where is the error? In the deceitfulness of the first movement, of course, and therefore not actually in his not stopping with faith but in his never reaching it.

Now, suppose that the basis of the paradox of the forgiveness of sins is that the poor existing human being is existing, that he is half-godforsaken even when in the inwardness of faith he is victorious against the understanding. Suppose that only eternity can give an eternal certainty, whereas existence has to be satisfied with a struggling certainty, which is gained not as the battle becomes easier or more illusory but only as it becomes harder. In that case, the explanation is indeed that it is and remains a paradox, and all is lost only when one thinks that there is no paradox or only to a certain degree. But, the esteemed public may say, if the forgiveness of sins is anything like that, how, then, can one

---

an eternal spirit exists. Whether anyone has done this, whether anyone is doing it—of what concern is that to me, if this is indeed what it is to have faith? Although I am still far from having fully understood the difficulty of Christianity (and an explanation that makes the difficulty easy must be regarded as a temptation), I nevertheless perceive that the battle of faith is not a topic for vaudeville poets and its strenuousness is not a divertissement for assistant professors.

believe it? Answer: If it is not anything like that, how, then, can one believe it?

Whether Christianity is in the right is another question. Here the question is only how the speculative explanation is related to the Christianity that it explains. But if Christianity is perhaps in the wrong, this much is certain: speculative thought is definitely in the wrong, because the only consistency outside Christianity is that of pantheism, the taking of oneself out of existence back into the eternal through recollection, whereby all existence-decisions become only shadow play compared with what is eternally decided from behind. Like all *simulated* decision, the simulated decision of speculative thought is nonsense, because decision is the eternal protest against fictions. The pantheist is eternally reassured backward; the moment that is the moment of existence in time, [227] the seventy years, is something vanishing. The speculative thinker, on the other hand, wants to be an existing person, but an existing person who is not subjective, not in passion, indeed, is existing *sub specie aeterni*—in short, he is absentminded. But what is explained in absentmindedness must not be trusted absolutely—such an explanation, and here I agree with speculative thought, is an explanation only to a certain degree.

If the speculative thinker explains the paradox in such a way that he cancels it and now consciously knows that it is canceled, that consequently the paradox is not the essential relation of eternal essential truth to an existing person in the extremities of existence, but only an accidental relative relation to limited minds—then there is an essential difference between the speculative thinker and the simple person, whereby all existence is fundamentally confused. God is insulted by obtaining a group of hangers-on, a support staff of good minds, and humankind is vexed because there is not an equal relationship with God for all human beings. The religious formula set forth above for the difference between the simple person's knowledge and the simple wise person's knowledge of the simple, that the difference is a meaningless trifle, that the wise person knows that he knows or knows that he does not know what the simple person knows—speculative thought does not respect this formula at all. Nor does it respect the equality implicit in the difference between the wise person and the simple person—that they know the same thing. That is, the speculator and the simple person in no way know the same thing when the simple person believes the paradox and the speculator knows that it is annulled. According, however, to the formula just cited, which honors God and loves human beings, the difference will be that the wise person also knows that it must be a paradox, the paradox he himself believes. Consequently, they do indeed know essentially the same thing; the wise person does not know anything else about the paradox, but he knows that he knows this about the paradox. The simple wise person will then immerse himself in comprehending [228] the paradox as paradox and will not become involved in explaining the paradox by understanding that it is not a paradox.

If, for example, the simple wise person spoke with a simple person about the forgiveness of sins, the simple person would most likely say, "But I still cannot comprehend the divine mercy that can forgive sins; the more intensely I believe it, the less I am able to understand it." (Thus probability does not seem to increase as the inwardness of faith is augmented, rather the opposite.) But the simple wise person will most likely say, "It is the same with me. You know I have had the opportunity to be able to devote much time to research and reflection, and yet the *summa summarum* of all this is at most that I comprehend that it cannot be otherwise, that it must be incomprehensible. Look, this difference certainly cannot distress you or make you think wistfully about your own more laborious circumstances in life or about your perhaps more modest capabilities, as if I had some advantage over you. My advantage, when regarded as the fruit of study, is something both to laugh at and to weep over. Yet you are never to scorn this study, just as I myself do not regret it, since on the contrary it pleases me most when I smile at it, and just then enthusiastically resume the effort of thinking."

Such a confession is made in all sincerity, and it is not present in the wise person merely once in a while but is essentially present in him whenever he is occupied in thinking. Once a year to consider that one ought always to thank God would hardly be a proper understanding of these words. Similarly, once in a while, on a great occasion, to consider, deeply moved, that before God all human beings are essentially equal is not truly to understand this equality, particularly if one's daily work and striving in more than one way consign it to oblivion. But to comprehend equality most earnestly just when one is most earnestly aware of what differentiates—that is the noble piety of the simple wise person.

Much that is strange has been said about Christianity, much that is lamentable, much that is outrageous, but the most obtuse thing ever said is that it is true to a certain degree. Much that is strange has been said about enthusiasm, much that is [229] lamentable, much that is outrageous, but the most obtuse thing said about it is that it is to a certain degree. Much that is strange has been said about erotic love, much that is lamentable, much that is outrageous, but the most obtuse thing said about it is that it is to a certain degree. When a person has prostituted himself by speaking in this way about enthusiasm and love, has betrayed his obtuseness, which is not, however, a matter of the understanding, since the cause of it is just that the understanding has become too large, in the same sense as the cause of liver disease is that the liver has become too large, and therefore, as another author has remarked, "It is the dumbness the salt takes on when it loses its strength"—then one phenomenon still remains, and that is Christianity. If enthusiasm's vision has been incapable of helping him break with the understanding, if love has been incapable of snatching him from bondage, let him look at Christianity. Let him be offended; even so, he is a human being. Let him despair of ever becoming a Christian himself; even so, he may be closer than he thinks. Let him to his very last drop of blood work to root out Christianity; even so, he is a human being—but if here he also has it in him to say, "It is true to a certain degree," then he is obtuse.

Perhaps someone thinks that I shudder in saying this, that I must be prepared for a terrible chastisement from the speculative thinker. Not at all. The speculator will here again be consistent and say, "What the man is saying is true to a certain degree, except that one must not stop there." It would indeed also be strange if an insignificant person like me were to succeed in what not even Christianity has succeeded—bringing the speculative thinker into passion. And if that should happen, well, then my fragment of philosophy would suddenly take on a significance of which I had scarcely ever dreamed. But the person who is neither cold nor hot is an abomination, and God is no more served by dud individualities than a rifleman is served by a rifle that in the moment of decision clicks instead of firing. If Pilate had not asked objectively what truth is, he would never have let Christ be crucified. If he had asked the question subjectively, then the passion of in- [230] wardness regarding *what he in truth had to do* about the decision facing him would have prevented him from doing an injustice. In that case, not only his wife would have been troubled by her frightening dream, but Pilate himself would have become sleepless. But when a person has before his eyes something as immensely big as the objective truth, he can easily cross out his fragment of subjectivity and what he as a subjective individual has to do. Then the approximation-process of the objective truth is symbolically expressed by washing one's hands, because objectively there is no decision, whereas the subjective decision demonstrates that one was nevertheless in untruth by not comprehending that the decision is indeed rooted in subjectivity.

If, however, subjectivity is truth and subjectivity is the existing subjectivity, then, if I may put it this way, Christianity is a perfect fit. Subjectivity culminates in passion, Christianity is paradox; paradox and passion fit each other perfectly, and paradox perfectly fits a person situated in the extremity of existence. Indeed, in the whole wide world there are not to be found two lovers who fit each other as do paradox and passion, and their quarrel is only like the lovers' quarrel when the quarrel is about whether it was he who awakened her passion or it was she who awakened his—and similarly here, the existing person has been situated in the extremity of existence by the paradox itself. And what is more glorious for lovers than to be granted a long time together without the occurrence of any change in the relationship except that it becomes more inward? And this is indeed granted to that very unspeculative understanding between passion and paradox, for they have been granted all of time, and not until eternity is there a change.

The speculative thinker, however, behaves differently; he believes only to a certain degree—he puts his hand to the plow and looks around in order to find something to know. In a Christian sense, what he finds to know is hardly anything good. Even if it were not the case that it cannot be otherwise, something a simple wise person seeking to understand the paradox will endeavor to show, even if there were a little rem- [231] nant of divine willfulness in the paradox, God, I daresay, is certainly one who is allowed to attach importance to his person, and therefore he is not constrained to reduce the price of the God-relationship because of a religious slackness (and this term is much more suitable here than when we speak of a slack grain market). And even if God were willing, the passionate one would never want it. It never occurs to a girl truly in love that she has purchased her happiness at too high a price, but rather that she has not purchased it at a price high enough. And just as the passion of the infinite is itself the truth, so it is also the case with the highest that you get what you pay for, and that a low price merely signifies poor business acumen, whereas in relation to God the highest price is no merit, since the highest price is precisely to will to do everything and yet know that this is nothing (for if it is something, the price is lower) and yet to will it.

Since I am not totally unfamiliar with what has been said and written about Christianity, I could presumably say a thing or two about it. I shall, however, not do so here but merely repeat that there is one thing I shall beware of saying about it: that it is true to a certain degree. It is indeed just possible that Christianity is

the truth; it is indeed just possible that someday there will be a
judgment in which the separation will hinge on the relation of inwardness to Christianity. Suppose that someone stepped forward
who had to say, "Admittedly I have not believed, but I have so
honored Christianity that I have spent every hour of my life pondering it." Or suppose that someone came forward of whom the
accuser had to say, "He has persecuted the Christians," and the accused one responded, "Yes, I acknowledge it; Christianity has so
inflamed my soul that, simply because I realized its terrible
power, I have wanted nothing else than to root it out of the world."
Or suppose that someone came forward of whom the accuser had
to say, "He has renounced Christianity," and the accused one responded, "Yes, it is true, for I perceived that Christianity was
such a power that if I gave it one finger it would take all of me,
and I could not belong to it completely." But suppose, now, that
eventually an active assistant professor came along [232] at a
hurried and bustling pace and said something like this, "I am not
like those three; I have not only believed but have even explained
Christianity and have shown that what was proclaimed by the
apostles and appropriated in the first centuries is true only to a
certain degree. On the other hand, through speculative understanding I have shown how it is the true truth, and for that reason I must request suitable remuneration for my meritorious
services to Christianity."

Of these four, which position would be the most terrible? It is
indeed just possible that Christianity is the truth. Suppose that
its ungrateful children want to have it declared incapable of managing its own affairs and placed under the guardianship of speculative thought. Suppose, then, that Christianity, like that Greek
poet whose children also insisted that their aged father be declared incompetent but who amazed the judges and the people by
writing one of his most beautiful tragedies to show that he was
still competent—suppose that Christianity in like manner rose
rejuvenated to its feet—there would still be no one whose position
would become as awkward as that of the assistant professors.

I do not deny that it is prestigious to stand so high above
Christianity. I do not deny that it is comfortable to be a Christian
and yet to be exempted from the martyrdom that always remains
even if no external persecution is inflicted, and even if a Christian remains unnoticed as if he had never lived at all—the martyrdom of believing against the understanding, the mortal
danger of lying out on 70,000 fathoms of water, and only there
finding God. See, the wader feels his way with his foot, lest he go
out so far that he cannot touch bottom. In the same way, with his

understanding, the sensible person feels his way in probability and finds God where probability suffices and thanks him on the great festival days of probability when he has obtained a really good job and there is the probability of quick advancement to boot. And he thanks him when for a wife he finds a girl both beautiful and congenial, and even Councilor of War Marcussen says that it will be a happy marriage, that the girl has the kind of beauty that in all probability will last a long time, and that she is built in such a [233] way that in all probability she will bear healthy and strong children. To believe against the understanding is something else, and to believe with the understanding cannot be done at all, because the person who believes with the understanding talks only about job and wife and fields and oxen and the like, which are in no way the object of faith, since faith *always* thanks God, is *always* in mortal danger in that collision of the infinite and the finite that is precisely a mortal danger for one who is composed of both. The believer cares so little for probability that he fears it most of all, since he knows very well that with it he is beginning to lose his faith.

Faith has, namely, two tasks: to watch for and at every moment to make the discovery of improbability, the paradox, in order then to hold it fast with the passion of inwardness. The improbable, the paradox, is ordinarily conceived of as something to which faith is related only passively; one will have to be satisfied temporarily with this situation, but little by little things will improve—indeed, this is probable. What wondrous confusion-compounding in speaking about faith! One is supposed to begin to believe on the basis of a confidence that there is the probability that things will surely improve. When that is done, one still manages to smuggle in probability and to keep oneself from believing. When that is done, it is easy to understand that the fruit of having had faith for a long time is that one ceases to have faith rather than, as one might think, that the fruit would be to have faith ever more inwardly. No, faith, self-active, relates itself to the improbable and the paradox, is self-active in discovering it and in holding it fast at every moment—in order to be able to believe. It already takes all the passion of the infinite and its concentration to stop with the improbable, inasmuch as the improbable and the paradox are not to be reached by the understanding's quantifying of the more and more difficult. Where understanding despairs, faith is already present in order to make the despair properly decisive, lest the movement of faith become a transaction within the haggling territory of the understanding. But to believe against the understanding is a martyrdom; to begin to enlist the understanding a little is a temptation and retrogres- [234] sion. The speculative thinker is exempted from this martyrdom. That he must pursue his studies and especially that he must read many of the modern books, I am willing to admit, is onerous, but the martyrdom of faith is indeed something else.

What I recoil from, then, even more than from dying or from losing my dearest treasure, is to say of Christianity that it is true to a certain degree. Even if I live to be seventy years old, even if I from year to year shorten the night's sleep and lengthen the day's work, pondering over Christianity—what is such little study but a trifle if it is supposed to justify me in judging so superiorly of Christianity! It would be much more pardonable, much more human, for me to become so embittered toward Christianity on the basis of a superficial acquaintance with it that I would declare it to be untruth. But superiority seems to me to be the real perdition that makes every saving relationship impossible—and it is indeed just possible that Christianity is the truth.

This almost seems to be earnestness. If I now dared to proclaim stridently that I had come into the world and was called to counteract speculative thought, that this was my judging mission, whereas my prophetic mission was to herald a matchless future, and that therefore, on the basis of my being strident and called, people could safely depend on what I said—there would presumably be many who, failing to regard the whole thing as a fantastical reminiscence in the head of a silly person, would regard it as earnestness. But I can say nothing like that about myself. The resolution with which I began may rather be considered a whim. In any case, it is so far from being a call to me, even remotely so, that on the contrary the call that I did follow came not to me, if you please, but to someone else; and even for him it was very far from being anything like a call in the stricter sense. But even if a call did come to him, I am still uncalled when I follow it.

The event is quite simple. It was four years ago, on a Sunday—well, perhaps no one will believe me, because once again it is a Sunday, but it is nevertheless quite certain that it was a Sunday, about two months after the Sunday mentioned pre- [235] viously. It was rather late, toward evening. Evening's taking leave of day and of the person who has experienced the day is enigmatic speech; its warning is like the caring mother's instruction to the child to come home in good time. But its invitation, even though the leave-taking is without fault in thus being misunderstood, is an inexplicable beckoning, as if rest were to be found only if one remained out for a nocturnal rendezvous, not with a woman but, womanlike, with the infinite, persuaded by the night wind as it monotonously repeats itself, as it searches forest and field and sighs as if looking for something, persuaded by the distant echo of stillness within oneself, as if it had a presentiment of something, persuaded by the sublime tranquillity of heaven, as if it had been found, persuaded by the audible soundlessness of the dew, as if this were the explanation and the refreshment of infinitude, like the fruitfulness of the quiet night, only half-understood like the semitransparency of the nocturnal mist.

Contrary to my usual practice, I had come out to that garden called the garden of the dead, where the visitor's leave-taking is again doubly difficult, since it is meaningless to say "once more," because the last time is already past, and since there is no reason to cease taking leave when the beginning is made after the last time is past. Most of the visitors had already gone home. Just one person disappeared among the trees. Not caring to meet anyone, he avoided me, since he was seeking the dead, not the living. In this garden there is always the beautiful agreement among the visitors that one does not go out there in order to see and to be seen, but each visitor avoids the other. One does not need company either, least of all a talkative friend, here where everything is eloquence, where the dead person calls out the brief word placed upon his grave, not as a pastor does, who preaches widely and broadly on the word, but as a silent man does, who says only this word, but says it with a passion as if the dead might burst the grave—or is it not odd to place upon his grave "We shall meet again" and then to remain down there? And yet what inwardness there is in the words just because of the contradiction. That someone who is coming tomorrow says, "We shall meet [236] again," is not startling. But for someone to have everything against him, to have no direct expression for his inwardness, none, and yet to stand by his word—that is true inwardness. Inwardness is untrue in direct proportion to the ready availability of external expressions in countenance and bearing, in words and assuring protestations—not just because the expression itself is untrue, but because the untruth is that the inwardness was merely an element. The dead person remains completely quiet while time passes. The famous warrior's sword has been laid upon his grave, and shamelessness has torn down the picket fence surrounding it, but the dead one did not rise up and draw his sword to defend himself and his resting place. He does not gesticulate, he does not protest, he does not flare up in a moment of inwardness, but, silent as the grave and quiet as a dead person, he maintains his inwardness and stands by his word. Praised be the living person who externally relates himself as a dead person to his inwardness and thereby maintains it, not as the excitement of a moment and as a woman's infatuation, but as the eternal, which has been gained through death. Such a person is a man. It is not unlovely for a woman to bubble over in momentary inwardness, nor is it unlovely for her to forget it again very soon—the one corresponds to the other, and both correspond to the feminine nature and to what is ordinarily understood by inwardness.

Tired from walking, I sat down on a bench, a marveling witness of how that proud ruler who now for thousands of years has been the hero of the day and will continue to be that until the last day, of how the sun in its brilliant departure cast a transfiguring glow over the entire surroundings, while my eyes gazed beyond the wall enclosing the garden into that eternal symbol of eternity—the infinite horizon. What sleep is for the body, rest such as this is for the soul, so that it can exhale properly. At that very moment, I discovered to my surprise that the trees that hid me from the eyes of others had hidden others from mine, for I heard a voice just beside me. It has always wounded my modesty to witness the expression of the kind of feeling that another person surrenders himself to only when he thinks he is not being observed, because there is an [237] inwardness of feeling that out of decency is hidden and is manifest only to God, just as a woman's beauty will be concealed from everyone and disclosed only to the beloved—therefore I decided to move away. But the first words I heard held me captive, and since I feared that the noise of my leaving might disturb more than my staying there quietly, I chose the latter and then became a witness of a situation that, however solemn it was, suffered no infringement because of my presence.

Through the leaves I saw that there were two: an old man with chalk-white hair and a child, a boy of about ten years. Both were in mourning clothes and sat beside a freshly covered grave, from which it was easy to conclude that it was a recent loss that occupied them. The old man's august form became even more solemn in the transfiguring glow of twilight, and his voice, calm and yet fervent, rendered the words clearly and distinctly with the inwardness they had in the speaker, who paused now and then when his voice choked with weeping or his mood ended in a sigh. Mood is like the Niger River in Africa; no one knows its source, no one knows its outlet—only its reach is known! From the conversation I learned that the little boy was the old man's grandson and the person whose grave they were visiting was the boy's father. Presumably all the others in the family were dead, since no one was mentioned. On a later visit I verified this by reading the name on the gravestone and the names of the many dead. As they talked, the old man told the child that he no longer had a father, had no one to cling to except an old man, who was too old for him and who himself longed to leave the world, but that there was a God in heaven after whom all fatherliness in heaven and on earth is called, that there was one name in which there was salvation, the name of Jesus Christ. He paused for a moment and then said half-aloud to himself: That this consolation should become for me a terror, that he, my son, who now lies buried in the grave, could abandon it! For what purpose all my hope, for what purpose all my concern, for what purpose all his wisdom, now that his death in the midst of his error makes a believer's soul uncertain about his salvation, brings my gray hair in sorrow to the [238] grave, makes a believer leave the world in apprehensiveness, makes an old man hurry like a doubter after a certainty and look back dejected for the surviving one.

Then he spoke again with the child and told him that there was a wisdom that wanted to fly past faith, that on the other side of faith there was a wide range like the blue mountains, a specious continent, which to the mortal eye looked like a certainty greater than that of faith, but the believer feared this mirage as the skipper fears a similar mirage at sea, feared that it was a sham eternity in which a mortal cannot live, but in which, if he steadily stares into it, he will lose his faith. He became silent again, and then said to himself half-aloud: That he, my unhappy son, should have allowed himself to be deceived! For what purpose, then, all his learning, so that he could not even make himself intelligible to me, so that I could not speak with him about his error because it was too elevated for me! Then he rose and led the child to the grave, and in a voice the impression of which I shall never forget he said, "Poor boy, you are just a child, and yet you will soon be alone in the world. Do you promise me by the memory of your dead father, who, if he could speak to you now, would speak in this way and now speaks with my voice; do you promise by the sight of my old age and my gray hair; do you promise by the solemnity of this hallowed place, by the God whose name I trust you have learned to call upon, by the name of Jesus Christ, in whom alone there is salvation—do you promise me that you will hold fast to this faith in life and in death, that you will not let yourself be deceived by any phantom, no matter how the shape of the world is changed—do you promise me that?" Overcome by the impression, the little one dropped to his knees, but the old man raised him up and pressed him to his breast.

I owe it to the truth to confess that this was the most heartrending scene I have ever witnessed. What may momentarily make someone or other inclined to consider the whole thing a fiction—that an old man speaks this way with a child—was precisely what shook me most: the unhappy old man who had become solitary in the world with a child and had no one with [239] whom to speak about his concern except a child, and had only one person to save, a child, and yet could not presuppose the maturity to understand, and yet did not dare to wait for the advent of maturity, because he himself was an old man. It is beautiful to be an old person, gratifying for the old man to see the generation growing up around him, a joyous arithmetical task to add to the sum every time the number is increased. But if it becomes his lot to have to recalculate, if the arithmetical task becomes that of having to subtract every time death takes away and takes away, until quits [qvit] is called and the old man is left behind to give the receipt [qvittere]—what then is as hard as being an old person! Just as need can bring a person to extremities, so it seems to me that the old man's suffering found its strongest expression in what poetically might be called an improbability—that an old person has his one and only confidant in a child, and that a sacred promise, an oath, is required of a child.

Although only a spectator and a witness, I was deeply affected. At one moment it seemed to me as if I myself were the young man whom the father had buried in terror. At the next moment it seemed to me as if I were the child who was bound by the sacred promise. But I felt no urge to rush forward and emotionally express my sympathy to the old man, assuring him with tears and quivering voice that I would never forget this scene, or perhaps even beseeching him to put me under oath. Only for rash [overilede] people, barren clouds, and bursts of passing showers [Ilinger] is nothing more precipitous [ilsom] than to take an oath, because, being unable to keep it, they must keep on taking it. In my opinion, "to want never to forget this impression" is different from saying once in a solemn moment, "I will never forget this." The former is inwardness, the latter perhaps only momentary inwardness. And if one never forgets it, the solemnity with which it was said does not seem so important, since the sustained solemnity with which one day by day keeps oneself from forgetting it is a truer solemnity. The feminine approach is always dangerous. A tender handshake, a passionate embrace, a tear in the eye are still not exactly the same as the quiet dedication of [240] resolution. Inwardness of spirit is indeed always like a stranger and foreigner in a body—why, then, gesticulations? What Shakespeare's Brutus says when the conspirators want to bind themselves by an oath to the enterprise is so true: "No, not an oath . . . . . let priests and cowards and rogues, marrowless oldsters and crushed souls swear . . . . . but do not weaken the quiet strength of our purpose, our inner invincible fire, by thinking that our cause, our performance, needs an oath [*Eed*]." The momentary outpouring of inwardness frequently leaves behind a lethargy [*Mathed*] that is dangerous. Furthermore, in yet another way a simple observation has taught me circumspection with regard to making oaths and promises, so that true inwardness is even constrained to express itself with the opposite. There is nothing that hasty and easily excited people are more inclined to do than to require sacred promises, because the inner weakness needs the powerful stimulation of the moment. Having to make a sacred promise to such a person is very dubious, and therefore it is much better to forestall this solemn scene and at the same time to bind oneself with a little *reservatio mentalis* [mental reservation], that is, if the requirement of a promise is justified at all. One thereby benefits the other person, prevents profanation of the sacred, prevents him from becoming bound by an oath—it would all end with his breaking the oath anyway. For example, if Brutus, in view of the fact that the conspirators, with hardly a single exception, were no doubt excitable fellows and therefore precipitous in making oaths and sacred promises and requesting sacred promises, had pushed them aside and had for that reason prevented the making of a promise, and if at the same time he quietly dedicated himself, since he regarded it as a just cause and their turning to him as also somewhat justified—then it appears to me that his inwardness would have been even greater. Now he is a bit bombastic, and although there is truth in what he says, there is still a little untruth in his saying it to the conspirators without really making clear to himself to whom he is speaking.

Then I, too, went home. I basically understood the old man right away, because in many ways my studies had led me to [241] notice a dubious relation between modern Christian speculative thought and Christianity, but it had not occupied me in any decisive way. Now the matter had its significance. The august old man with his faith seemed to me a totally justified individuality whom existence had wronged, inasmuch as modern speculative thought, like a monetary reform, made doubtful the property title of faith. The august old man's pain over losing his son, not only through death but, as he understood it, even more terribly through speculative thought, moved me deeply, and at the same time the contradiction in his situation, that he could not even explain how the enemy force was operating, became for me a decisive summons to find a definite clue. The whole thing appealed to me like a complicated criminal case in which the very convoluted circumstances have made it difficult to track down the truth. This was something for me. I thought as follows: You are quite bored with life's diversions, bored with girls, whom you love only in passing; you must have something that can totally occupy your time. Here it is: find out where the misunderstanding between speculative thought and Christianity lies. This, then, was my resolution. I have not spoken about it to anyone at all, and I am sure that my landlady has detected no change in me, neither the same evening nor the next day.

"But," I said to myself, "since you are not a genius and by no means have the mission of making all humankind blissfully happy at any cost, and since you have not promised anyone anything either, you can undertake the matter entirely *con amore* [with love] and proceed altogether *methodice* [methodically], as if a poet and a dialectician kept your every step under surveillance, now that you have gained a more definite understanding of your own whimsical idea that you must try to make something difficult." My studies, which had already in a sense led me to my goal, now became more definitely organized, but the old gentleman's august figure always hovered before my thoughts every time I wanted to transform my deliberations into learned knowledge. But primarily I sought through my own reflection to pick up a clue to the ultimate misunderstanding. I need not report my many mistakes, but [242] it finally became clear to me that the deviation of speculative thought and, based thereupon, its presumed right to reduce faith to a factor might not be something accidental, might be located far deeper in the orientation of the whole age— most likely in this, that because of much knowledge people have entirely forgotten what it means to *exist* and what *inwardness* is.

When I had comprehended this, it also became clear to me that if I wanted to communicate anything about this, the main point must be that my presentation would be made in an *indirect* form. That is, if inwardness is truth, results are nothing but junk with which we should not bother one another, and wanting to communicate results is an unnatural association of one person with another, inasmuch as every human being is spirit and truth is the self-activity of appropriation, which a result hinders. Suppose that the teacher, in regard to essential truth (for otherwise the direct relation between teacher and learner is entirely in order), has much inwardness and would like, as people say, to proclaim his teaching day in and day out. If he assumes that there is a direct relation between him and the learner, then his inwardness is not inwardness but a spontaneous outpouring, because respect for the learner, that he in himself is his own inwardness, is the teacher's inwardness. Suppose that a learner is enthusiastic and in the strongest terms proclaims his praise of the teacher and thus, as we say, lays bare his inwardness; his inwardness is not inwardness but a spontaneous devotedness, because the pious, silent agreement, according to which the learner personally appropriates what is taught, distancing himself from the teacher because he turns inward into himself—precisely that is inwardness. Pathos is certainly inwardness, but it is spontaneous inwardness and therefore can be expressed. But pathos in the form of contrast is inwardness; it remains with the communicator even when expressed, and it cannot be appropriated directly except through the other's *self*-activity, and the contrastive form is the dynamometer of inwardness. The more consummate the contrastive form, the greater the inwardness; and the less it is present, to the point of being direct communication, the less [243] the inwardness. For an enthusiastic genius who would like to make all humankind blissfully happy and lead them to the truth, it can be difficult enough to learn to constrain himself in this way and to grasp the *N.B.* [*nota bene,* note well] of reduplication, because truth is not like a circular letter on which signatures are collected, but is in the *valore intrinseco* [intrinsic worth] of inwardness. Understanding this comes more naturally to a vagabond and frivolous person. As soon as truth, the essential truth, can be assumed to be known by everyone, appropriation and inwardness must be worked for, and here can be worked for only in an indirect form. The position of the apostle is something else, because he must proclaim an unknown truth, and therefore direct communication can always have its validity temporarily.

Oddly enough, although there is so much clamoring for the positive and for the direct communication of results, it does not occur to anyone to complain about God, who as the eternal spirit, as the source of derived spirits, would seem to be able in the communication of truth to relate himself directly to the derived spirit in a quite different sense than when the relation is between derived spirits who, viewed *essentially,* are equals within a common derivation from God. No anonymous author can more slyly hide himself, and no maieutic can more carefully recede from a direct relation than God can. He is in the creation, everywhere in the creation, but he is not there directly, and only when the single individual turns inward into himself (consequently only in the inwardness of self-activity) does he become aware and capable of seeing God.

The direct relationship with God is simply paganism, and only when the break has taken place, only then can there be a true God-relationship. But this break is indeed the first act of inwardness oriented to the definition that truth is inwardness. Nature is certainly the work of God, but only the work is directly present, not God. With regard to the individual human being, is this not acting like an illusive author, who nowhere sets forth his result in block letters or provides it beforehand in a preface? And why is God illusive? Precisely because he is [244] truth and in being illusive seeks to keep a person from untruth. The observer does not glide directly to the result but on his own must concern himself with finding it and thereby break the direct relation. But this break is the actual breakthrough of inwardness, an act of self-activity, the first designation of truth as inwardness.

Or is it not the case that God is so unnoticeable, so hidden yet present in his work, that a person might very well live on, marry, be respected and esteemed as husband, father, and captain of the popinjay shooting club, without discovering God in his work, without ever receiving any impression of the infinitude of the ethical, because he managed with an analogy to the speculative confusion of the ethical and the world-historical by managing with custom and tradition in the city where he lived? Just as a mother admonishes her child who is about to attend a party, "Now, mind your manners and watch the other polite children and behave as they do," so he, too, could live on and behave as he saw others behave. He would never do anything first and would never have any opinion unless he first knew that others had it, because "the others" would be his very first. On special occasions he would act like someone who does not know how to eat a course that is served at a banquet; he would reconnoiter until he saw how the others did it etc. Such a person could perhaps know ever so much, perhaps even know the system by rote; he could perhaps live in a Christian country, know how to bow his head every time God's name was mentioned, perhaps also see God in nature if he was in the company of others who saw God; in short, well, he could be a congenial partygoer—and yet he would be deceived by the direct relation to truth, to the ethical, to God.

If one were to portray such a person in an imaginary construction, he would be a satire on what it is to be a human being. It is really the God-relationship that makes a human being a human being, but this is what he would lack. Yet no one would hesitate to consider him an actual human being (for the absence of inwardness is not seen directly), although he would be more like a puppet character that very deceptively imitates all the human externalities—would even have chil- [245] dren with his wife. At the end of his life, one would have to say that one thing had escaped him: he had not become aware of God. If God could have permitted a direct relationship, he would certainly have become aware. If God had taken the form, for example, of a rare, enormously large green bird, with a red beak, that perched in a tree on the embankment and perhaps even whistled in an unprecedented manner—then our partygoing man would surely have had his eyes opened; for the first time in his life he would have been able to be the first.

All paganism consists in this, that God is related directly to a human being, as the remarkably striking to the amazed. But the spiritual relationship with God in truth, that is, inwardness, is first conditioned by the actual breakthrough of inward deepening that corresponds to the divine cunning that God has nothing remarkable, nothing at all remarkable, about him—indeed, he is so far from being remarkable that he is invisible, and thus one does not suspect that he is there [er til], although his invisibility is in turn his omnipresence. But an omnipresent being is the very one who is seen everywhere, for example, as a police officer is—how illusive, then, that an omnipresent being is cognizable precisely by his being invisible,* simply and solely by this, because his very visibility would annul his omnipresence. This relation between omnipresence and invisibility is like the relation between mystery and revelation, that the mystery expresses that the revelation is revelation in the stricter sense, that the mystery is the one and only mark by which it can be known, since otherwise a [246] revelation becomes something like a police officer's omnipresence.

If God [Gud] wants to reveal himself in human form and provide a direct relation by taking, for example, the form of a man who is twelve feet tall, then that imaginatively constructed partygoer and captain of the popinjay shooting club will surely become aware. But since God is unwilling to deceive, the spiritual relation in truth specifically requires that there be nothing at all remarkable about his form; then the partygoer must say:

---

*In order to indicate how illusive the rhetorical can be, I shall show here how one could perhaps produce an effect upon a listener rhetorically, even though what was said would be a dialectical retrogression. Suppose a pagan religious orator says that here on earth the god's temple is actually empty, but (and here the rhetorical begins) in heaven, where everything is more perfect, where water is air, and air is ether, there are also temples and shrines for the gods, but the difference is that the gods actually dwell in these temples—that the god actually dwells in the temple is dialectical retrogression, because his not dwelling in the temple is an expression for the spiritual relation to the invisible. But rhetorically it produces the effect.— Incidentally, I had in mind a specific passage by a Greek author, but I shall not quote him.

There is nothing to see, not the slightest. If the god [*Guden*] has nothing whatever that is remarkable about him, the partygoer is perhaps deceived in not becoming aware at all. But the god is without blame in this, and the actuality of this deception is continually also the possibility of the truth. But if the god has something remarkable about him, he deceives, inasmuch as a human being thus becomes aware of the untruth, and this awareness is also the impossibility of the truth.

In paganism, the direct relation is idolatry; in Christianity, everyone indeed knows that God cannot manifest himself in this way. But this knowledge is not inwardness at all, and in Christianity it can certainly happen with a rote knower that he becomes utterly "without God in the world," which was not the case in paganism, where there was still the untrue relation of idolatry. Idolatry is certainly a dismal substitute, but that the rubric "God" disappears completely is even more mistaken.

Accordingly, not even God relates himself directly to a derived spirit (and this is the wondrousness of creation: not to produce something that is nothing in relation to the Creator, but to produce something that is something and that in the true worship of God can use this something to become by itself nothing before God); even less can one human being relate himself in this way to another *in truth*. Nature, the totality of creation, is God's work, and yet God is not there, but within the individual human being there is a possibility (he is spirit according to his possibility) that in inwardness is awakened to a God-relationship, and then it is possible to see God every- [247] where. Compared with the spiritual relationship in inwardness, the sensate distinctions of the great, the amazing, the most crying-to-heaven superlatives of a southern nation are a retrogression to idolatry. Is it not as if an author wrote 166 folio volumes and the reader read and read, just as when someone observes and observes nature but does not discover that the meaning of this enormous work lies in the reader himself, because amazement at the many volumes and the five hundred lines to the page, which is similar to amazement at how immense nature is and how innumerable the animal species are, is not understanding.

With regard to the essential truth, a direct relation between spirit and spirit is unthinkable. If such a relation is assumed, it actually means that one party has ceased to be spirit, something that is not borne in mind by many a genius who both assists people *en masse* into the truth and is good-natured enough to think that applause, willingness to listen, signatures, etc. mean accepting the truth. Just as important as the truth, and of the two the even more important one, is the mode in which the truth is accepted, and it is of slight help if one gets millions to accept the truth if by the very mode of their acceptance they are transposed into untruth. And therefore all good-naturedness, all persuasion, all bargaining, all direct attraction with the aid of one's own person in consideration of one's suffering so much for the cause, of one's weeping over humankind, of one's being so enthusiastic, etc.—all such things are a misunderstanding, in relation to the truth a forgery by which, according to one's ability, one helps any number of people to acquire a semblance of truth.

Socrates was a teacher of the ethical, but he was aware that there is no direct relation between the teacher and the learner, because inwardness is truth, and inwardness in the two is precisely the path away from each other. Probably because he perceived this he was so very pleased with his advantageous appearance. What was it? Well, guess again! In our day, we say of a clergyman that he has a very advantageous appearance; we are pleased about this and understand that he is a handsome man, that the clerical gown is very becoming to [248] him, that he has a sonorous voice and a figure that every tailor—but what am I saying—that every listener must be pleased with. Ah, yes, when one is so equipped by nature and so dressed by the tailor, one can easily be a teacher of religion, even with success, because the conditions of teachers of religion vary greatly—indeed, more than one thinks when one hears complaints that some pastoral appointments are so opulent and others so meager. The difference is much greater—some teachers of religion are crucified—and yet the religion is fully the same! No one cares much about the reduplicated repetition of the substance of the teaching in the conception of how the teacher ought to be. Orthodoxy is set forth, and the teacher is prinked up in pagan-esthetic categories. Christ is presented in biblical expressions. That he bore the sin of the whole world will not really move the congregation; yet the speaker proclaims it, and in order to make the contrast strong, he describes Christ's beauty (because the contrast between guiltlessness and sin is not strong enough), and the believing congregation is stirred by this totally pagan qualification of the god in human form: beauty.

But back to Socrates. He did not have an appearance as advantageous as the one described. He was very ugly, had clumsy feet, and more than that, a number of bumps on his forehead and other places, which were bound to convince everyone that he was a depraved character. This, you see, was what Socrates understood by his advantageous appearance, and he was so pleased as Punch about it that he would have considered it chicanery on the part of the god if, in order to keep him from being a teacher of

morals, he had been given the pleasing appearance of a senti-
mental zither player, the languishing look of a *Schäfer* [amorous
swain], the small feet of a dance director in the Friendship Society, and *in toto* as advantageous an appearance as a job seeker in
Adresseavisen or a theological graduate who had set his hopes on
a patronage appointment could possibly wish for himself. Now,
then, why was that old teacher so pleased with his advantageous
appearance, unless it was because he perceived that it might help
to place the learner at a distance so that he would not be caught
[249] in a direct relation to the teacher, perhaps would admire
him, perhaps would have his clothes made in the same way, but
might understand through the repulsion of opposition, which in
turn was his irony in a higher sphere, that the learner essentially
has himself to deal with and that the inwardness of truth is not
the chummy inwardness with which two bosom friends walk arm
in arm with each other but is the separation in which each person
for himself is existing in what is true.

Thus I had fully realized that every direct communication
with regard to truth as inwardness is a misunderstanding, even
though it can vary according to the variety of that which is responsible for it, be it a lovable predilection, a nebulous sympathy,
cryptic vanity, obtuseness, brashness, and other things. But just
because I had become clear about the form of communication, it
did not mean that I had something to communicate, although it
was nevertheless entirely in order that the form first became
clear to me, because the form is indeed the inwardness.

My main thought was that, because of the copiousness of
knowledge, people in our day have forgotten what it means *to exist,* and what *inwardness* is, and that the misunderstanding between speculative thought and Christianity could be explained
by that. I now resolved to go back as far as possible in order not to
arrive too soon at what it means to exist religiously, not to mention existing Christianly-religiously, and in that way leave dubi-
eties behind me. If people had forgotten what it means to exist
religiously, they had probably also forgotten what it means to
exist humanly; therefore this would have to be brought out. But
this must not on any account be done didactically, because then
the misunderstanding would in a new misunderstanding instantly make capital of the explanatory attempt, as if existing
consisted in coming to know something about a particular point.
If this is communicated as knowledge, the recipient is mistakenly
induced to understand that he is gaining something to know, and
then we are back in knowledge again. Only the person who has
an idea of a misunderstanding's tenacity in assimilating even the

most rigorous attempt at explanation and yet remaining a misun- [250] derstanding, only he will be aware of the difficulty of an authorship in which care must be taken with every word, and every word must go through the process of double-reflection. Direct communication about what it means to exist and about inwardness will only have the result that the speculative thinker will benevolently take it in hand and let one slip in along with it. The system is hospitable! Just as a bourgeois-philistine, without regard to compatibility, takes along every Tom, Dick, and Harry when he goes on an excursion to the woods, inasmuch as there is room enough in the four-seated Holstein carriage, so also is the system hospitable—there is indeed plenty of room.

I will not conceal the fact that I admire Hamann, although I readily admit that, if he is supposed to have worked coherently, the elasticity of his thoughts lacks evenness and his preternatural resilience lacks self-control. But the originality of genius is there in his brief statements, and the pithiness of form corresponds completely to the desultory hurling forth of a thought. With heart and soul, down to his last drop of blood, he is concentrated in a single word, a highly gifted genius's passionate protest against a system of existence. But the system is hospitable. Poor Hamann, you have been reduced to a subsection by Michelet. Whether your grave has ever been marked, I do not know; whether it is now trampled upon, I do not know; but I do know that by hook or by crook you have been stuck into the subsection uniform and thrust into the ranks. I do not deny that Jacobi has often inspired me, although I am well aware that his dialectical skill is not in proportion to his noble enthusiasm, but he is the eloquent protest of a noble, unadulterated, lovable, highly gifted mind against the systematic crimping of existence, a triumphant consciousness of and an inspired battling for the significance of existence as something longer and deeper than the few years during which one forgets oneself in studying the system. Poor Jacobi! Whether anyone visits your grave, I do not know; but I do know that the subsection-plow plows under all your eloquence, all your inwardness, while a few paltry words are being registered about your importance in the sys- [251] tem. It is said of Jacobi that he represented feeling enthusiasm; such a report ridicules both feeling and enthusiasm, which have precisely the secret that neither can be reported secondhand and therefore cannot in the form of a result conveniently make a rote parroter blissfully happy through a *satisfactio vicaria* [vicarious satisfaction].

So, then, I resolved to begin, and the first thing I wanted to do in order to start from the bottom was *to have the existence-relation*

between the esthetic and the ethical come into existence in an exist-
ing individuality. The task was set, and I foresaw that the work
would be copious enough, and above all that I would have to be
prepared to remain still at times when the spirit would not support me with pathos. But what happened then I shall tell in an
appendix to this chapter.

Collins, James. *The Mind of Kierkegaard*. Princeton, N.J.: Princeton University Press, 1983.

Connell, George B., and C. Stephen Evans, eds. *Foundations of Kierkegaard's Vision of Community*. Atlantic Highlands, N.J.: Humanities, 1992.

Dunning, Stephen N. *Kierkegaard's Dialectic of Inwardness*. Princeton, N.J.: Princeton University Press, 1985.

Elrod, John. *Being and Existence in Kierkegaard's Pseudonymous Works*. Princeton, N.J.: Princeton University Press, 1975.

———. *Kierkegaard and Christendom*. Princeton, N.J.: Princeton University Press, 1981.

Evans, C. Stephen. *Kierkegaard's "Fragments" and "Postscript": The Religious Philosophy of Johannes Climacus*. Atlantic Highlands, N.J.: Humanities, 1983.

———. *Passionate Reason: Making Sense of Kierkegaard's "Philosophical Fragments."* Bloomington: Indiana University Press, 1992.

Ferreira, M. Jamie. *Transforming Vision: Imagination and Will in Kierkegaardian Faith*. Oxford: Clarendon Press, 1991.

Hall, Ronald L. *Word and Spirit: A Kierkegaardian Critique of the Modern Age*. Bloomington: Indiana University Press, 1993.

Hannay, Alastair. *Kierkegaard*. London: Routledge, 1982.

Kirmmse, Bruce H. *Kierkegaard in Golden Age Denmark*. Bloomington: Indiana University Press, 1990.

Lowrie, Walter. *Kierkegaard*. 2. vols. New York: Harper & Row, 1962.

Mackey, Louis. *Kierkegaard: A Kind of Poet*. Philadelphia: University of Pennsylvania Press, 1971.

Malantschuk, Gregor. *Kierkegaard's Thought*. Trans. Howard V. and Edna H. Hong. Princeton, N.J.: Princeton University Press, 1971.

Matuštík, Martin J., and Merold Westphal, eds. *Kierkegaard in Post / Modernity*. Bloomington: Indiana University Press, 1995.

Nordentoft, Kresten. *Kierkegaard's Psychology*. Trans. Bruce H. Kirmmse. Pittsburgh, Pa.: Duquesne University Press, 1978.

Pattison, George. *Kierkegaard: The Aesthetic and the Religious*. London: Macmillan, 1992.

Perkins, Robert L., ed. *International Kierkegaard Commentary: The Concept of Anxiety*. Macon, Ga.: Mercer University Press, 1985.
————, ed. *International Kierkegaard Commentary: The Corsair Affair*. Macon, Ga.: Mercer University Press, 1990.
————, ed. *International Kierkegaard Commentary: Either/Or. Part I*. Macon, Ga.: Mercer University Press, 1995.
————, ed. *International Kierkegaard Commentary: Either/Or. Part II*. Macon, Ga.: Mercer University Press, 1995.
————, ed. *International Kierkegaard Commentary: Fear and Trembling and Repetition*. Macon, Ga.: Mercer University Press, 1993.
————, ed. *International Kierkegaard Commentary: Philosophical Fragments*. Macon, Ga.: Mercer University Press, 1994.
————, ed. *International Kierkegaard Commentary: The Sickness unto Death*. Macon, Ga.: Mercer University Press, 1987.
————, ed. *International Kierkegaard Commentary: Two Ages: The Present Age and the Age of Revolution: A Literary Review*. Macon, Ga.: Mercer University Press, 1984.
————, ed. *Kierkegaard's Fear and Trembling: Critical Appraisals*. University: University of Alabama Press, 1981.
Roberts, Robert C. *Rethinking Kierkegaard's "Philosophical Fragments."* Macon, Ga.: Mercer University Press, 1986.
Taylor, Mark C. *Kierkegaard's Pseudonymous Authorship*. Princeton, N.J.: Princeton University Press, 1975.
Thompson, Josiah, ed. *Kierkegaard: A Collection of Critical Essays*. Garden City, N.Y.: Doubleday, 1972.
Walsh, Sylvia. *Living Poetically: Kierkegaard's Existential Aesthetics*. University Park: Pennsylvania State University Press, 1994.
Weston, Michael. *Kierkegaard and Modern Continental Philosophy*. New York: Routledge, 1994.
Westphal, Merold. *Kierkegaard's Critique of Reason and Society*. University Park: Pennsylvania State University Press, 1991.

INDEX

Abraham, 26–30, 44, 62, 74, 151, 153, 155
abstract thinking, 134–39, 172
absurd, the, 29, 122, 124–26, 175
Adorno, T., 9, 17, 46–47, 57
aesthetic, the (*also* esthetic), 20–25, 31, 39, 102, 104, 129, 138, 144, 155, 165, 185
Alston, W., 96
apostle, 12–13
appropriation, 49, 52, 61, 64, 66, 101, 119, 146, 168, 170, 191
approximation, 49–50, 101, 107, 112, 115–16
Aquinas, T., 95
Aristotle, 24, 31, 56, 75, 84, 94, 101–2, 111, 135, 137–38, 142
attack upon Christendom, 5–7, 27, 158, 177. *See also* Christendom
Aufhebung, 25–26, 28, 32, 39, 67, 146, 148, 163
Augustine, 40–41, 44, 52–53
authority, 12–14, 19, 36, 192
Avineri, S., 97

Barrett, L., 168, 178
Barthes, R., 9–10, 17–18
becoming, 115, 136, 145–46
before God, 16–17
Begriff, 43, 131, 142, 144, 146
Beiser, F., 97–98, 141
Berry, W., 188
Best, S., 57

Betti, E., 18
Bloom, H., 18
Brandes, G., 200
Buber, M., 57, 189
Butler, B., 37

Camus, A., 57
Caputo, J., 18, 50, 57, 94, 132
Christendom, 21, 27, 29, 39, 55, 62–63, 83, 135, 141, 145, 154, 159, 167. *See also* attack upon Christendom
Cochrane, C., 31
Collins, J., 7
comfort, 163
comic, 66, 69, 83–84
contradiction, 67–69, 124–25, 135–36, 154, 161, 164–66, 175, 180–83
Corsair affair, the, 5–6
crowd, the, 6, 13, 16, 141
cynicism, 68, 114, 168

death of the author, 9–17
decision, 52, 71, 90, 101–2, 146
Derrida, J., 10–12, 17–19, 46–47, 57, 69, 90, 93, 96, 115, 130–31, 141, 177, 189
Descartes, R., 37, 41–42, 67, 74, 79, 95, 117
despair, 174
Dewey, J., 68
dialectic, 36–39, 50–51, 154, 157, 177

dialectical, the, 46, 67, 71, 80, 82, 88, 93, 150, 152, 175–76, 180–88
Don Giovanni, 23–24
Don Quixote, 117–18, 120, 131
Dostoyevski, F., 23
double reflection, 61, 63–65
Dunning, S., 132

Elrod, J., 58
Empedocles, 145
epistemological Stoicism, 119
equality, 13, 107, 112, 128, 133, 147, 176, 184, 188, 191, 199
essential knowing, 116
esthetic, the. See aesthetic
eternal, the, 30
eternal happiness, 101, 109, 120– 22, 139, 152–53, 156–57, 170, 174–75, 177, 183, 193, 195
eternal validity, 24
ethical, the, 20–23, 25–29, 39, 100, 102–6, 129, 136, 151, 154, 165, 186
Evans, D., 131
Evans, S., 76–77, 94–95, 132, 166, 178
existentialism, 3, 31, 66, 84, 86, 91, 140, 170

faith, 36, 39–45, 51, 56, 73, 77–78, 95–96, 119, 121–22, 126–27, 133, 157, 176, 182, 185, 192
Ferreira, M., 94–96
Feuerbach, L., 182, 188
Fichte, J., 85, 97
Findlay, J. N., 94
Flay, J., 96
forgiveness, 174
Foucault, M., 9–12, 17–19, 47, 69
foundationalism, 79, 85 86, 96, 98
Frank, M., 19
Freud, S., 63
Friedlander, P., 32
Fukuyama, F., 97

Gadamer, H.-G., 9–11, 13–14, 17– 18, 93, 131–32, 141
Garcia, L., 95
genius, the, 12–13
governance, 13, 19
Green, R., 97

Grundtvig, N. F. S., 50, 57, 112
guilt, 169–75, 186
Guthrie, W. K. C., 32

Habermas, J., 13
Harvey, I., 19
Hegel, G., vii–viii, 3, 20–21, 24, 26–27, 29, 42–43, 46, 55, 127– 28, 130, 140, 153
    The Difference between Fichte's and Schelling's System of Philosophy, 98
    The Encyclopedia Logic, 36– 38, 46–47, 80, 96–98, 131–32, 141–42, 177
    Faith and Knowledge, 47
    Lectures on the History of Philosophy, 47, 97, 112, 141, 177
    Lectures on the Philosophy of Religion, 47, 141, 177
    Lectures on the Philosophy of World History, 47, 86, 111, 142
    Natural Law, 112
    Phenomenology of Spirit, 20–21, 31, 43, 47–48, 79, 81–82, 85–86, 88–90, 94, 96–98, 100, 103, 112, 131–32, 137, 141, 148– 49, 151, 163–64, 176
    Philosophy of Mind, 31, 57, 100, 103, 112
    Philosophy of Right, 31–32, 100, 112, 136, 141
    Science of Logic, 88–90, 97– 98, 111, 141, 177
Heidegger, M., viii, ix, 12, 18, 31, 46, 57, 66, 68, 72, 112, 141, 176–77, 189
Henze, D., 93
herd, the, 142
holism, 79, 85–86, 97–98, 107
Holmer, P., 93
Horkheimer, M., 46
Hume, D., 73, 76, 79, 88, 134, 141, 171, 183
humor, 35, 69, 165–70, 178, 194
Huntington, P., 132
Husserl, E., 18, 44, 64–65, 93, 98, 141

ideology, 27, 30, 55, 57, 146, 194, 199
idolatry, 118
immanence, 175, 183–88
immediacy, 21, 23–24, 43, 63, 73, 78, 88–89, 92, 94, 98, 107, 115, 152–53, 156, 161, 185–86
incarnation, 16, 81–82, 122, 124–26, 147, 175, 181, 192
indirect communication, 16, 60–65, 93, 129
individualism, ix, 139–41, 178
infant baptism, 145, 191
interest, 51–52, 138
interesting, the, 22–23
inwardness, 52, 61, 64, 112, 119, 122, 129, 133, 136, 159, 164, 167, 170, 174, 178, 191, 194, 195
irony, 31, 35, 37, 123, 160, 165–70, 178, 185, 194
irrationalism, ix, 181

Jacobi, F., 42, 72
James, W., 48
Jaspers, K., 66
Judge William, 24–26, 29, 39, 102, 105, 111

Kant, I., viii, 24, 31, 46–47, 68, 81–82, 85, 88, 90, 93, 96, 112, 114–15, 130
Kaufmann, W., 47
Kellner, D., 57
kenosis, 16
Kierkegaard's writings
    Christian Discourses, 95, 112, 199
    The Concept of Anxiety, 5, 26, 36, 93, 117
    The Concept of Irony, 4, 31, 48, 121, 144, 178, 199
    The Corsair Affair, 5, 15, 46, 57
    Eighteen Upbuilding Discourses, 7, 12, 60, 132
    Either/Or, 5, 6, 8, 15, 21–22, 25–26, 31, 38–39, 54, 111, 129, 141, 167, 176–77, 188–89
    Fear and Trembling, 5–6, 26–27, 29, 32, 38–40, 46–

47, 54–55, 75, 77, 79, 94, 102, 112, 122, 146, 151, 176–79, 197
    For Self-examination, 6
    Johannes Climacus, 47, 94, 131, 142
    Judge for Yourselves, 6, 198
    On Authority and Revelation, 13
    Philosophical Fragments, 5, 15, 20, 28–30, 32, 36, 40, 53, 56, 60–62, 68, 72, 74–75, 94–95, 109, 121–22, 126, 129, 144, 146, 150, 158, 175, 180, 183, 187, 189, 196
    The Point of View for My Work as an Author, 7, 13–15, 129
    Practice in Christianity, 5–6, 20, 28, 159, 189, 198, 200
    Prefaces: Light Reading for Certain Classes as the Occasion May Require, 5
    Repetition, 5, 20
    The Sickness unto Death, 5, 20, 31, 57, 77, 93, 122, 132, 135, 143, 171, 175
    Stages on Life's Way, 5, 15, 20–21, 26, 130, 179
    Søren Kierkegaard's Journals and Papers, 4, 13, 87, 95–96, 114, 141, 197
    Three Discourses on Imagined Occasions, 7
    Two Ages, 46, 63, 113, 133, 142
    Upbuilding Discourses in Various Spirits, 60, 112, 197, 199
    Works of Love, 5, 60, 112, 143, 195–97
Kirmmse, B., 46, 57, 143

leap, the, 39, 70–74, 77–80, 86, 90, 115
Lessing, G., 49, 59–92, 96, 119, 128
Levinas, E., 111–12, 130, 142, 170–71, 178, 189, 196
Lévi-Strauss, C., 11

Locke, J., 31, 55, 57
Lowrie, W., 4, 7
Luther, M., 71
Lyotard, J., 47, 178

Mackey, L., 17, 19, 93
madness, 117, 120, 135
maieutic, the, 61–63, 192
Malantschuk, G., 19, 70
Marcel, G., 98, 113, 189
Marion, J.-L., 131–32
marriage, 24–25
Marx, K., 3, 27, 30, 55, 194–99
mediation, 115–16, 146–47, 152–
    55, 170
mens auctoris, 9, 13–14, 93
Merleau-Ponty, M., 64–65, 93, 176
monasticism, 152, 154–55, 159
Moore, G. E., 37
Mozart, W., 8

Nagel, T., 127, 132
Nietzsche, F., viii, ix, 12, 26, 30,
    67, 102, 111, 130, 141–42, 172,
    188, 190, 194, 199
nihilism, 68, 114
Nouwen, H., 111

objectivity, 49–56, 104, 114–16,
    126, 129, 135, 138, 144, 148–
    49, 171
offense, 133, 189
Olsen, R. See Regina
omnipotence, 16
Orphics, the, 145
Otto, R., 163, 177
Outka, G., 112, 133

pantheism, 83, 140, 171
paradox, 29, 68, 122, 124 26, 128,
    133, 135, 175, 180–81
Pascal, B., 69
passion, 77, 95, 150, 154, 159
pathos, 66, 69, 71, 150–51, 175
Peirce, C., 13, 119
Penelhum, T., 94–95
Perkins, R., 7, 32
phenomenology, 44–45
Plantinga, A., 96
Plato, 24, 28–30, 37, 40–41, 43, 56,
    121, 123, 127, 130, 135, 141, 158

Pojman, L., 72–74, 94–95
postmodernism, vii–ix, 3, 9–13,
    68, 91–92, 94
present age, the, 16, 29, 35, 110,
    140–41
presuppositions, 42, 87–90
pseudonymity, 8–17, 60
public, the, 16, 55, 141
punishment, 172
Pythagoras, 135, 145

Quine, W., 90, 97

reader, the, 11–17, 193
realized eschatology, 29
reason, 29–30, 46, 70, 80, 82, 131,
    180
recollection, 28, 30, 62, 123, 126,
    128, 144, 173, 183–85
reflection, 23, 77, 89–90, 101
Regina, 4–5
Reinhold, K., 88–89
relativism, 114
religious, the, 20–21, 26–27, 30,
    104, 129, 136, 159, 165
Religiousness A, 175–76, 180,
    185–87
Religiousness B, 175–76, 180,
    186–87, 195
Religiousness C, 197–99
repentance, 21, 26
resignation, 151–59, 178
revelation, 30, 62, 144, 183
Ricoeur, P. 176
risk, 53, 71, 78–80, 119, 121
Rockmore, T., 98
Rorty, R., 94
Rousseau, J., 11
Russell, B., 86

Sartre, J.-P., 31, 66, 69, 72, 93–94,
    110, 113, 130, 142, 176, 189
satire, 54, 75, 103, 116–17, 149,
    158
Saunders, J., 93
Schelling, F., 85, 94, 107
Schiller, F., 105
self, viii–ix
self-choice, 24
Simonides, 135
sin, 26, 122–24, 135

Sittlichkeit, 24, 26, 31, 62, 68, 102–3, 105, 107, 120, 154, 160, 167, 194

skepticism, 37, 68, 75–77, 79–80, 96, 141

Smith, H., 131

Socrates, 28, 30, 32, 37, 45, 60–62, 65–66, 68–69, 120–28, 135–36, 150, 158, 167, 182, 184

speculation, 36, 42, 53, 55–56, 67, 80, 82–84, 90, 93, 102, 104, 124, 126–29, 138, 144, 146–47, 151, 154, 157, 170, 182

spheres of existence. *See* stages on life's way; the aesthetic; the ethical; the religious

Spiegelberg, H., 48

Spinoza, 83, 108

spirit, 20, 44, 81–82, 89, 115, 139

stages on life's way, 20–31

striving, 66, 69, 81, 91–92, 154

subjectivity, 51–53, chaps. 6–13, 159

sub specie aeterni, ix, 67, 90, 115, 130, 134, 136, 145–46, 181–82

suffering, 158–65

system, 42, 44, 82–84, 86–88, 90–92, 97, 100, 103, 114–15, 134, 136, 170, 188

task, 75–76, 103, 105, 108, 120, 129, 135–38, 145, 148, 169–70

Taylor, C., 31, 57–58, 143

teleological suspension, 26, 28–29, 39, 112, 146, 158, 167, 170, 194

temporality, 11, 18, 51, 68, 80, 83–84, 91–92, 96, 115, 123, 134, 136, 144, 156–57, 177

Tillich, P., 51, 131

Tolstoy, L., 112

transcendence, 175, 183

transcendental ego, 85, 90, 97, 113, 115

truth, 92, 114–30, 135

understanding, 37, 46, 82, 131, 135, 181, 183

unhappy consciousness, 148, 151, 158, 163

volitionalism, 71–77, 95

Vorstellung, 43, 131, 142, 144, 146

Walsh, S., 178, 199

Westphal, M., 32, 96–97, 112, 142, 149, 176, 199
  God, Guilt, and Death, 149–77
  Hegel, Freedom, and Modernity, 32, 132, 142, 176–77
  History and Truth in Hegel's Phenomenology, 96–97, 131
  Kierkegaard's Critique of Reason and Society, 32, 46, 57, 93

Whitehead, A., 86

Wittgenstein, L., 68

Wolterstorff, N., 96

Wood, A., 32

world historical, the, 69, 100–108, 114–15, 136–37, 139, 170, 188

Ziolkowski, E., 131